Amazon SageMaker Best Practices

Proven tips and tricks to build successful machine learning solutions on Amazon SageMaker

Sireesha Muppala, PhD

Randy DeFauw

Shelbee Eigenbrode

BIRMINGHAM—MUMBAI

Amazon SageMaker Best Practices

Copyright © 2021 Packt Publishing

Group Product Manager: Kunal Parikh
Publishing Product Manager: Devika Battike
Senior Editor: Roshan Kumar
Content Development Editor: Tazeen Shaikh
Technical Editor: Arjun Varma
Copy Editor: Safis Editing
Project Coordinator: Aparna Ravikumar Nair
Proofreader: Safis Editing
Indexer: Tejal Daruwale Soni
Production Designer: Joshua Misquitta

First published: September 2021
Production reference: 1190821

Published by Packt Publishing Ltd.
Livery Place
35 Livery Street
Birmingham
B3 2PB, UK.
ISBN 978-1-80107-052-2
www.packt.com

To my dad, for showing me the value of hard work and perseverance.

– Sireesha Muppala, PhD

To my wife and boys, who tolerate my curiosity for all things data; and to my AWS colleagues, who provide a great home for builders.

– Randy DeFauw

To my husband, Steve, and daughter, Emily, for their continuous support and understanding when I take on a new challenge – more importantly, for always being "my why." To my colleagues and friends, for always raising the bar and making me a better builder.

– Shelbee Eigenbrode

Contributors

About the authors

Sireesha Muppala, PhD is a Principal Enterprise Solutions Architect, AI/ML at **Amazon Web Services (AWS)**. Sireesha holds a PhD in computer science and post-doctorate from the University of Colorado. She is a prolific content creator in the ML space with multiple journal articles, blogs, and public speaking engagements. Sireesha is a co-creator and instructor of the Practical Data Science specialization on Coursera. Sireesha is a co-creator and instructor of the Practical Data Science specialization on Coursera. She is a co-director of **Women In Big Data** (**WiBD**), Denver chapter. Sireesha enjoys helping organizations design, architect, and implement ML solutions at scale.

I would like to thank my advisor, Dr Xiaobo Zhou, Professor and Associate Dean at UCCS, for getting me started on statistical learning.

Randy DeFauw is a Principal Solutions Architect at AWS. He holds an MSEE from the University of Michigan, where his graduate thesis focused on computer vision for autonomous vehicles. He also holds an MBA from Colorado State University. Randy has held a variety of positions in the technology space, ranging from software engineering to product management. He entered the big data space in 2013 and continues to explore that area. He is actively working on projects in the ML space, including reinforcement learning. He has presented at numerous conferences, including GlueCon and Strata, published several blogs and white papers, and contributed many open source projects to GitHub.

I'd like to thank Professor Sridhar Lakshmanan, who started my journey in computer vision and ML at the University of Michigan.

Shelbee Eigenbrode is a Principal AI and ML Specialist Solutions Architect at AWS. She holds six AWS certifications and has been in technology for 23 years, spanning multiple industries, technologies, and roles. She is currently focusing on combining her DevOps and ML background to deliver and manage ML workloads at scale. With over 35 patents granted across various technology domains, she has a passion for continuous innovation and using data to drive business outcomes. Shelbee co-founded the Denver chapter of Women in Big Data.

About the reviewers

Brent Rabowsky is a data science consultant with over 10 years' experience in the field of ML. At AWS, he uses his expertise to help AWS customers with their data science projects. He joined Amazon.com on a ML and algorithms team and previously worked on conversational AI agents for government contractors and a research institute. He also served as a technical reviewer of the book *Data Science on AWS* by Chris Fregly and Antje Barth, published by O'Reilly.

Antje Barth is a senior developer advocate for AI and ML at AWS, based in Düsseldorf, Germany. Antje is co-author of the O'Reilly book *Data Science on AWS*, co-founder of the Düsseldorf chapter of Women in Big Data, and frequently speaks at AI and ML conferences and meetups around the world. She also chairs and curates content for O'Reilly AI Superstream events. Previously, Antje was an engineer at Cisco and MapR, focused on data center technologies, cloud computing, big data, and AI applications.

Table of Contents

3

Data Labeling with Amazon SageMaker Ground Truth

4

Data Preparation at Scale Using Amazon SageMaker Data Wrangler and Processing

Section 2: Model Training Challenges

6

Training and Tuning at Scale

7

Profile Training Jobs with Amazon SageMaker Debugger

Section 3: Manage and Monitor Models

8

Managing Models at Scale Using a Model Registry

9

Updating Production Models Using Amazon SageMaker Endpoint Production Variants

10

Optimizing Model Hosting and Inference Costs

11

Monitoring Production Models with Amazon SageMaker Model Monitor and Clarify

Section 4: Automate and Operationalize Machine Learning

12
Machine Learning Automated Workflows

13
Well-Architected Machine Learning with Amazon SageMaker

14
Managing SageMaker Features across Accounts

Other Books You May Enjoy
Index

Preface

Amazon SageMaker is a fully managed AWS service that provides the ability to build, train, deploy, and monitor machine learning models. The book begins with a high-level overview of Amazon SageMaker capabilities that map to the various phases of the machine learning process to help set the right foundation. You'll learn efficient tactics to address data science challenges such as processing data at scale, data preparation, connecting to big data pipelines, identifying data bias, running A/B tests, and model explainability using Amazon SageMaker.

As you advance, you'll understand how you can tackle the challenge of training at scale, including how to use large datasets while saving costs, monitoring training resources to identify bottlenecks, speeding up long training jobs, and tracking multiple models trained for a common goal. Moving ahead, you'll find out how you can integrate Amazon SageMaker with other AWS services to build reliable, cost-optimized, and automated machine learning applications. In addition to this, you'll build ML pipelines integrated with MLOps principles and apply best practices to build secure and performant solutions.

By the end of the book, you'll confidently be able to apply Amazon SageMaker's wide range of capabilities to the full spectrum of machine learning workflows.

Who this book is for

This book is for expert data scientists responsible for building machine learning applications using Amazon SageMaker. Working knowledge of Amazon SageMaker, machine learning, deep learning, and experience using Jupyter Notebooks and Python is expected. Basic knowledge of AWS services related to data, security, and monitoring will help you make the most out of the book.

What this book covers

Chapter 1, Amazon SageMaker Overview, provides a high-level overview of the Amazon SageMaker capabilities that map to the various phases of the machine learning process. This sets a foundation for a best practice discussion of using SageMaker capabilities to handle data science challenges.

Chapter 2, Data Science Environments, provides a brief overview of technical requirements along with a discussion on setting up the necessary data science environments using Amazon SageMaker. This sets the foundation for building and automating ML solutions throughout the rest of the book.

Chapter 3, Data Labeling with Amazon SageMaker Ground Truth, kicks off with a review of challenges involved in labeling data at scale – costs, time, unique labeling needs, inaccuracies, and bias. Best practices to use Amazon SageMaker Ground Truth to address the challenges identified are discussed.

Chapter 4, Data Preparation at Scale Using Amazon SageMaker Data Wrangler and Processing, kicks off with a review of challenges involved in data preparation at scale – compute/memory resource constraints, long processing times, along with the challenges of the duplication of feature engineering efforts, bias detection, and understanding feature importance. A discussion on Amazon SageMaker capabilities to address these challenges along with best practices to apply follows.

Chapter 5, Centralized Feature Repository with Amazon SageMaker Feature Store, provides best practices for using a centralized repository for features built with Amazon SageMaker Feature Store. Techniques to ingest features and provide access to features to satisfy access time requirements are discussed.

Chapter 6, Training and Tuning at Scale, provides best practices for training and tuning machine learning models with large datasets using Amazon SageMaker. Techniques such as distributed training with data and model parallelism, automated model tuning, and grouping multiple training jobs to identify the best performing job are discussed.

Chapter 7, Profile Training Jobs with Amazon SageMaker Debugger, discusses best practices to debug, monitor, and profile training jobs to detect long-running non-converging jobs and eliminate resource bottlenecks. The monitoring and profiling capabilities offered by Amazon SageMaker Debugger help improve training time and reduce training costs.

Chapter 8, Managing Models at Scale Using a Model Registry, introduces SageMaker Model Registry as a centralized catalog of trained models. Models can be deployed from the registry and the metadata maintained in the registry is useful to understand the deployment history of an individual model. Model Registry is an important component of addressing the challenge of model deployment automation with CI/CD.

Chapter 9, Updating Production Models Using Amazon SageMaker Endpoint Production Variants, addresses the challenge of updating models in production with minimal disruption to the model consumers using Amazon SageMaker Endpoint production variants. The same production variants will be used to showcase advanced strategies such as canary deployments, A/B testing, blue/green deployments that balance cost with downtime, and ease of rollbacks.

Chapter 10, Optimizing Model Hosting and Inference Costs, introduces best practices to optimize hosting and inference costs on Amazon SageMaker. Multiple deployment strategies are discussed to meet the computation needs and response time requirements under varying inference traffic demands.

Chapter 11, Monitoring Production Models with Amazon SageMaker Model Monitor and Clarify, introduces best practices to monitor the quality of production models and receive proactive alerts on model quality degradation. You will learn how to monitor for data bias, model bias, bias drift, and feature attribution drift using Amazon SageMaker Model Monitor and SageMaker Clarify.

Chapter 12, Machine Learning Automated Workflows, brings together data processing, training, deployment, and model management into automated workflows that can be orchestrated and integrated into end-to-end solutions.

Chapter 13, Well-Architected Machine Learning with Amazon SageMaker, applies best practices provided by the AWS Well-Architected Framework to building ML solutions on Amazon SageMaker.

Chapter 14, Managing SageMaker Features across Accounts, discusses best practices for using Amazon SageMaker capabilities in a cross-account setup involving multiple AWS accounts, which allows you to better govern and manage machine learning activities across the machine learning development lifecycle.

To get the most out of this book

You should have an AWS account and working knowledge of AWS and Amazon SageMaker. You should also be familiar with basic machine learning concepts. The code samples are written in Python and normally executed in a Jupyter notebook. You will not need Python or other software installed on your computer.

To set up your data science environment, you should also have familiarity with the concepts of Infrastructure-as-Code and Configuration-as-Code. It's helpful if you are also familiar with AWS CloudFormation but it is not required.

Software/hardware covered in the book	Operating system requirements
AWS Account	Windows, macOS, or Linux
Amazon SageMaker	Windows, macOS, or Linux
Amazon SageMaker Studio	Windows, macOS or Linux
Amazon Athena	Windows, macOS or Linux

If you are using the digital version of this book, we advise you to type the code yourself or access the code from the book's GitHub repository (a link is available in the next section). Doing so will help you avoid any potential errors related to the copying and pasting of code.

Download the example code files

You can download the example code files for this book from GitHub at `https://github.com/PacktPublishing/Amazon-SageMaker-Best-Practices`. If there's an update to the code, it will be updated in the GitHub repository.

We also have other code bundles from our rich catalog of books and videos available at `https://github.com/PacktPublishing/`. Check them out!

Download the color images

We also provide a PDF file that has color images of the screenshots and diagrams used in this book. You can download it here:

`https://static.packt-cdn.com/downloads/9781801070522_ColorImages.pdf`

Conventions used

There are a number of text conventions used throughout this book.

`Code in text`: Indicates code words in text, database table names, folder names, filenames, file extensions, pathnames, dummy URLs, user input, and Twitter handles. Here is an example: "To use Amazon SageMaker Debugger, you must enhance `Estimator` with three additional configuration parameters: `DebuggerHookConfig`, `Rules`, and `ProfilerConfig`."

A block of code is set as follows:

```
#Feature group name
weather_feature_group_name_offline = 'weather-feature-group-
offline' + strftime('%d-%H-%M-%S', gmtime())
```

When we wish to draw your attention to a particular part of a code block, the relevant lines or items are set in bold:

```
@smp.step
def train_step(model, data, target):

    output = model(data)
    long_target = target.long()
    loss = F.nll_loss(output, long_target, reduction="mean")
    model.backward(loss)
    return output, loss
return output, loss
```

Any command-line input or output is written as follows:

```
$ mkdir css
$ cd css
```

Bold: Indicates a new term, an important word, or words that you see onscreen. For instance, words in menus or dialog boxes appear in **bold**. Here is an example: "Keep in mind that when you use multiple instances in the training cluster, all instances should be in the same **Availability Zone**."

> **Tips or important notes**
> Appear like this.

Get in touch

Feedback from our readers is always welcome.

General feedback: If you have questions about any aspect of this book, email us at customercare@packtpub.com and mention the book title in the subject of your message.

Errata: Although we have taken every care to ensure the accuracy of our content, mistakes do happen. If you have found a mistake in this book, we would be grateful if you would report this to us. Please visit www.packtpub.com/support/errata and fill in the form.

Piracy: If you come across any illegal copies of our works in any form on the internet, we would be grateful if you would provide us with the location address or website name. Please contact us at copyright@packt.com with a link to the material.

If you are interested in becoming an author: If there is a topic that you have expertise in and you are interested in either writing or contributing to a book, please visit authors.packtpub.com.

Share your thoughts

Once you've read *Amazon SageMaker Best Practices*, we'd love to hear your thoughts! Scan the QR code below to go straight to the Amazon review page for this book and share your feedback.

https://packt.link/r/1-801-07052-0

Your review is important to us and the tech community and will help us make sure we're delivering excellent quality content.

Section 1: Processing Data at Scale

This section sets the foundation for the rest of the book with an overview of Amazon SageMaker capabilities, a review of technical requirements, and insights on setting up the data science environment on AWS. This section then addresses the challenges involved in labeling and preparing large volumes of data. You will learn how to apply appropriate Amazon SageMaker capabilities and related services to derive features from raw data and persist features for reuse. Further, you will also learn how to persist features in a centralized repository to share across multiple ML projects.

This section comprises the following chapters:

- *Chapter 1, Amazon SageMaker Overview*
- *Chapter 2, Data Science Environments*
- *Chapter 3, Data Labeling with Amazon SageMaker Ground Truth*
- *Chapter 4, Data Preparation at Scale Using Amazon SageMaker Data Wrangler and Processing*
- *Chapter 5, Centralized Feature Repository with Amazon SageMaker Feature Store*

1

Amazon SageMaker Overview

This chapter will provide a high-level overview of the Amazon SageMaker capabilities that map to the various phases of the **machine learning** (**ML**) process. This will set a foundation for the best practices discussion of using SageMaker capabilities in order to handle various data science challenges.

In this chapter, we're going to cover the following main topics:

- Preparing, building, training and tuning, deploying, and managing ML models
- Discussion of data preparation capabilities
- Feature tour of model-building capabilities
- Feature tour of training and tuning capabilities
- Feature tour of model management and deployment capabilities

Technical requirements

All notebooks with coding exercises will be available at the following GitHub link:

```
https://github.com/PacktPublishing/Amazon-SageMaker-Best-
Practices
```

Preparing, building, training and tuning, deploying, and managing ML models

First, let's review the ML life cycle. By the end of this section, you should understand how SageMaker's capabilities map to the key phases of the ML life cycle. The following diagram shows you what the ML life cycle looks like:

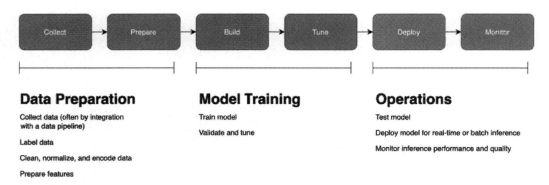

Figure 1.1 – Machine learning life cycle

As you can see, there are three phases of the ML life cycle at a high level:

- In the **Data Preparation** phase, you collect and explore data, label a ground truth dataset, and prepare your features. Feature engineering, in turn, has several steps, including data normalization, encoding, and calculating embeddings, depending on the ML algorithm you choose.

- In the **Model Training** phase, you build your model and tune it until you achieve a reasonable validation score that aligns with your business objective.

- In the **Operations** phase, you test how well your model performs against real-world data, deploy it, and monitor how well it performs. We will cover model monitoring in more detail in *Chapter 11, Monitoring Production Models with Amazon SageMaker Model Monitor and Clarify*.

This diagram is purposely simplified; in reality, each phase may have multiple smaller steps, and the whole life cycle is iterative. You're never really *done* with ML; as you gather data on how your model performs in production, you'll likely try to improve it by collecting more data, changing your features, or tuning the model.

So how do SageMaker capabilities map to the ML life cycle? Before we answer that question, let's take a look at the SageMaker console (*Figure 1.2*):

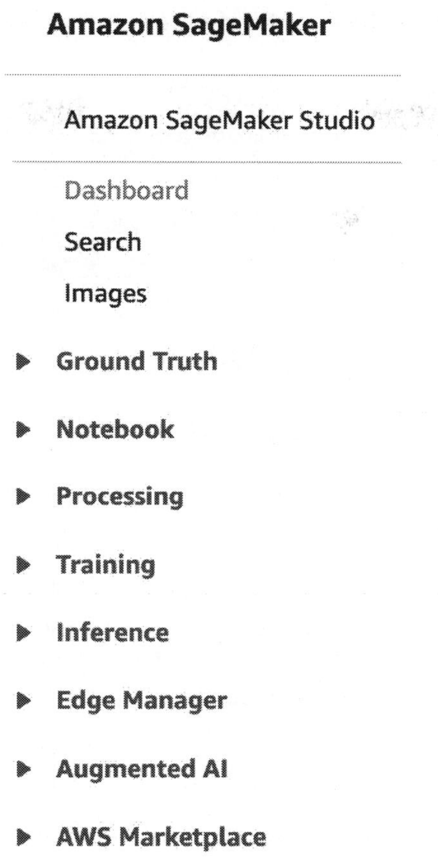

Amazon SageMaker

Amazon SageMaker Studio

Dashboard

Search

Images

▶ **Ground Truth**

▶ **Notebook**

▶ **Processing**

▶ **Training**

▶ **Inference**

▶ **Edge Manager**

▶ **Augmented AI**

▶ **AWS Marketplace**

Figure 1.2 – Navigation pane in the SageMaker console

The appearance of the console changes frequently and the preceding screenshot shows the current appearance of the console at the time of writing.

These capability groups align to the ML life cycle, shown as follows:

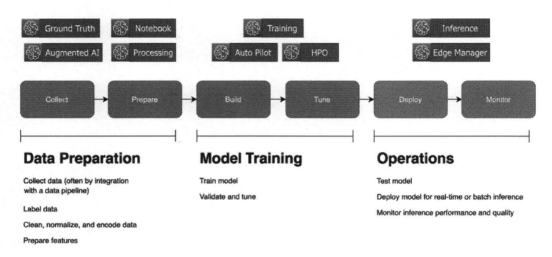

Figure 1.3 – Mapping of SageMaker capabilities to the ML life cycle

SageMaker Studio is not shown here, as it is an integrated workbench that provides a user interface for many SageMaker capabilities. The marketplace provides both data and algorithms that can be used across the life cycle.

Now that we have had a look at the console, let's dive deeper into the individual capabilities of SageMaker in each life cycle phase.

Discussion of data preparation capabilities

In this section, we'll dive into SageMaker's data preparation and feature engineering capabilities. By the end of this section, you should understand when to use SageMaker Ground Truth, Data Wrangler, Processing, Feature Store, and Clarify.

SageMaker Ground Truth

Obtaining labeled data for classification, regression, and other tasks is often the biggest barrier to ML projects, as many companies have a lot of data but have not explicitly labeled it according to business properties such as *anomalous* and *high lifetime value*. **SageMaker Ground Truth** helps you systematically label data by defining a labeling workflow and assigning labeling tasks to a human workforce.

Over time, Ground Truth can learn how to label data automatically, while still sending low-confidence results to humans for review. For advanced datasets such as 3D point clouds, which represent data points like shape coordinates, Ground Truth offers assistive labeling features, such as adding bounding boxes to the middle frames of a sequence once you label the start and end frames. The following diagram shows an example of labels applied to a dataset:

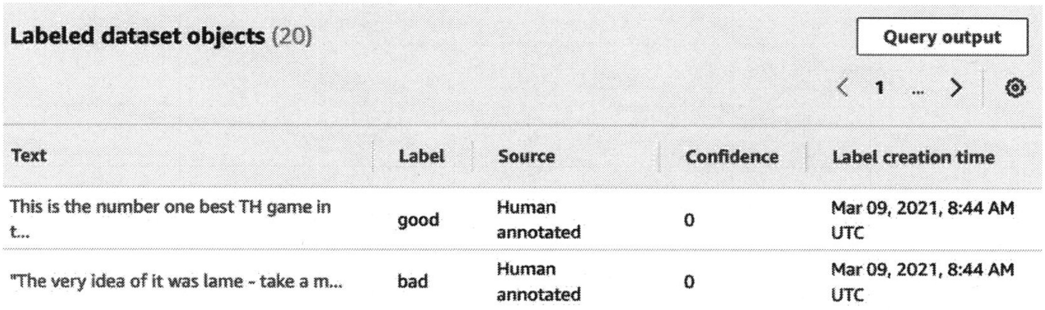

Labeled dataset objects (20)				Query output
				‹ 1 … › ⚙
Text	**Label**	**Source**	**Confidence**	**Label creation time**
This is the number one best TH game in t...	good	Human annotated	0	Mar 09, 2021, 8:44 AM UTC
"The very idea of it was lame - take a m...	bad	Human annotated	0	Mar 09, 2021, 8:44 AM UTC

Figure 1.4 – SageMaker Ground Truth showing the labels applied to sentiment reviews

The data is sourced from the *UCI Machine Learning Repository* (https://archive. ics.uci.edu/ml/datasets/Sentiment+Labelled+Sentences). To counteract individual worker bias or error, a data object can be sent to multiple workers. In this example, we only have one worker, so the confidence score is not used.

Note that you can also use Ground Truth in other phases of the ML life cycle; for example, you may use it to check the labels generated by a production model.

SageMaker Data Wrangler

Data Wrangler helps you understand your data and perform feature engineering. Data Wrangler works with data stored in S3 (optionally accessed via Athena) and Redshift and performs typical visualization and transformations, such as *correlation plots* and *categorical encoding*. You can combine a series of transformations into a data flow and export that flow into an MLOps pipeline. The following screenshot shows an example of Data Wrangler information for a dataset:

Table Summary: Summary				
summary	UDI	Product ID	Type	Air temperature [K]
count	10000	10000	10000	10000
mean	5000.5	None	None	300.004929999998...
stddev	2886.8956799071675	None	None	2.0002586829161944
min	1	H29424	H	295.3
max	10000	M24859	M	304.5

Figure 1.5 – Data Wrangler displaying summary table information regarding a dataset

You may also use Data Wrangler in the operations phase of the ML life cycle if you want to analyze the data coming into an ML model for production inference.

SageMaker Processing

SageMaker Processing jobs help you run data processing and feature engineering tasks on your datasets. By providing your own Docker image containing your code, or using a pre-built Spark or sklearn container, you can normalize and transform data to prepare your features. The following diagram shows the logical flow of a SageMaker Processing job:

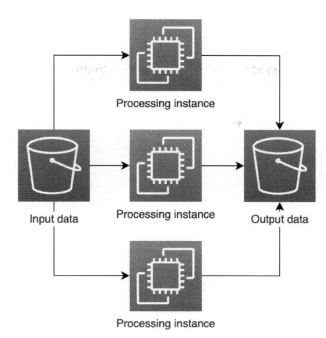

Figure 1.6 – Conceptual overview of a Spark processing job. Spark jobs are particularly handy for processing larger datasets

You may also use processing jobs to evaluate the performance of ML models during the **Model Training** phase and to check data and model quality in the **Model Operations** phase.

SageMaker Feature Store

SageMaker Feature Store helps you organize and share your prepared features. Using a feature store improves quality and saves time by letting you reuse features rather than duplicate complex feature engineering code and computations that have already been done. Feature Store supports both batch and stream storage and retrieval. The following screenshot shows an example of feature group information:

FEATURE GROUP: reviews-feature-group-1612804563

Feature group summary	Feature definitions	Feature group tags	Sample query

Q *Search by feature name*

Feature Name	Feature Type
input_ids	String
input_mask	String
segment_ids	String
label_id	segment_ids
review_id	String
date	String
label	Integral
split_type	String

Figure 1.7 – Feature Store showing a feature group with a set of related features

Feature Store also helps during the Model Operations phase, as you can quickly look up complex feature vectors to help obtain real-time predictions.

SageMaker Clarify

SageMaker Clarify helps you understand model behavior and calculate bias metrics from your model. It checks for imbalance in the dataset, models that give different results based on certain attributes, and bias that appears due to data drift. It can also use leading explainability algorithms such as SHAP to help you explain individual predictions to get a sense of which features drive model behavior. The following figure shows an example of class imbalance scores for a dataset, where we have many more samples from the *Gift Card* category than the other categories:

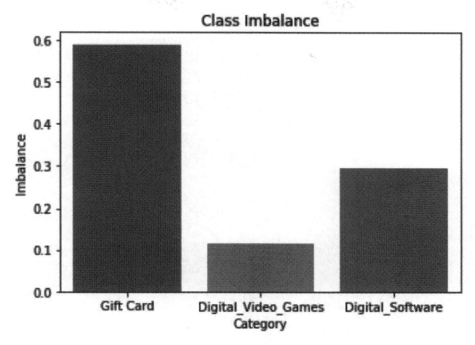

Figure 1.8 – Clarify showing class imbalance scores in a dataset. Class imbalance can lead to biased results in an ML model

Clarify can be used throughout the entire ML life cycle, but consider using it early in the life cycle to detect imbalanced data (datasets that have many examples of one class but few of another).

Now that we've introduced several SageMaker capabilities for data preparation, let's move on to model-building capabilities.

Feature tour of model-building capabilities

In this section, we'll dive into SageMaker's model-building capabilities. By the end of this section, you should understand when to use SageMaker Studio or SageMaker notebook instances, and how to choose between SageMaker's built-in algorithms, frameworks, and libraries, versus a **bring your own** (**BYO**) approach.

SageMaker Studio

SageMaker Studio is an **integrated development environment (IDE)** for ML. It brings together Jupyter notebooks, experiment management, and other tools into a unified user interface. You can easily share notebooks and notebook snapshots with other team members using Git or a shared filesystem. The following screenshot shows an example of one of SageMaker Studio's built-in visualizations:

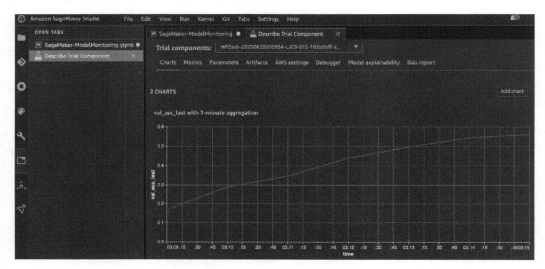

Figure 1.9 – SageMaker Studio showing an experiment graph

SageMaker Studio can be used in all phases of the ML life cycle.

SageMaker notebook instances

If you prefer a more traditional Jupyter or JupyterLab experience, and you don't need the additional integrations and collaboration tools that Studio provides, you can use a regular SageMaker notebook instance. You choose the notebook instance compute capacity (that is, whether you want GPUs and how much storage you need), and SageMaker provisions the environment with the Jupyter Notebook and JupyterLab and several of the common ML frameworks and libraries installed.

The notebook instance also supports Docker in case you want to build and test containers with ML code locally. Best of all, the notebook instances come bundled with over 100 example notebooks. The following figure shows an example of the JupyterLab interface in a notebook:

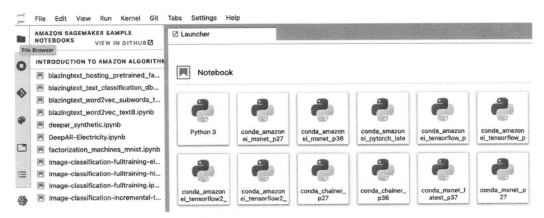

Figure 1.10 – JupyterLab interface in a SageMaker notebook, showing a list of example notebooks

Similar to SageMaker Studio, you can perform almost any part of the ML life cycle in a notebook instance.

SageMaker algorithms

SageMaker bundles open source and proprietary algorithms for many common ML use cases. These algorithms are a good starting point as they are tuned for performance, often supporting distributed training. The following table lists the SageMaker algorithms provided for different types of ML problems:

ML domain	Data type	Problem	Algorithms
Supervised learning	Tabular	Classification	Factorization Machines, K-Nearest Neighbors (k-NN), Linear Learner, XGBoost
		Regression	Factorization Machines, K-Nearest Neighbors (k-NN), Linear Learner, XGBoost
		Forecasting	DeepAR
Unsupervised learning	Tabular	Dimensionality reduction	Principal component analysis
		Anomaly detection	Random cut forest
		IP anomaly detection	IP Insights
		Embeddings	Object2Vec
		Clustering	K-Means
	Text	Topic modeling	Latent Dirichlet Allocation (LDA), Neural Topic Model (NTM)
Text analysis	Text	Text classification	BlazingText
		Translation, Speech to text	Sequence to Sequence
Image analysis	Image	Image classification	Image classification
		Object detection and classification	Object detection
		Computer vision	Semantic segmentation

Figure 1.11 – SageMaker algorithms for various ML scenarios

BYO algorithms and scripts

If you prefer to write your own training and inference code, you can work with a supported ML, graph, or RL framework, or bundle your own code into a Docker image. The BYO approach works well if you already have a library of model code, or if you need to build a model for a use case where a pre-built algorithm doesn't work well. Data scientists who use R like to use this approach. SageMaker supports the following frameworks:

- Supported machine learning frameworks: XGBoost, sklearn

- Supported deep learning frameworks: TensorFlow, PyTorch, MXNet, Chainer

- Supported reinforcement learning frameworks: Ray RLLib, Coach

- Supporting graph frameworks: Deep Graph Library

Now that we've introduced several SageMaker capabilities for model building, let's move on to training and tuning capabilities.

Feature tour of training and tuning capabilities

In this section, we'll dive into SageMaker's model training capabilities. By the end of this section, you should understand the basics of SageMaker training jobs, Autopilot and Hyperparameter Optimization (HPO), SageMaker Debugger, and SageMaker Experiments.

SageMaker training jobs

When you launch a model training job, SageMaker manages a series of steps for you. It launches one or more training instances, transfers training data from S3 or other supported storage systems to the instances, gets your training code from a Docker image repository, and starts the job. It monitors job progress and collects model artifacts and metrics from the job. The following screenshot shows an example of the hyperparameters tracked in a training job:

Hyperparameters

Key	Value
eta	0.2
gamma	4
max_depth	5
min_child_weight	6
num_round	800
objective	binary:logistic
subsample	0.8

Figure 1.12 – SageMaker training jobs capture data such as input hyperparameter values

For larger training datasets, SageMaker manages distributed training. It will distribute subsets of data from storage to different training instances and manage the inter-node communication during the training job. The specifics vary based on the ML framework you're using, but note that most of the supported frameworks and several of the SageMaker built-in algorithms support distributed training.

Autopilot

If you are working with tabular data and solving regression or classification problems, you may find that you're performing a lot of repetitive work. You may have settled on XGBoost as a high-performing algorithm, always one-hot encoding for low-cardinality categorical features, normalizing numeric features, and so on. Autopilot performs many of these routine steps for you. In the following diagram, you can see the logical steps for an Autopilot job:

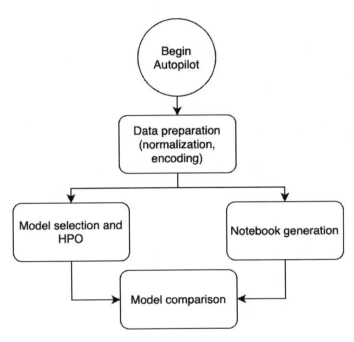

Figure 1.13 – Autopilot process

Autopilot saves you time by automating a lot of that routine process. It will run normal feature preparation tasks, try the three supported algorithms (Linear Learner, XGBoost, and a multilayer perceptron), and run hyperparameter tuning. Autopilot is a great place to start even if you end up needing to refine the output, as it generates a notebook with the code used for the entire process.

HPO

Some ML algorithms accept tens of hyperparameters as inputs. Tuning these by hand is time-consuming. **Hyperparameter Optimization (HPO)** simplifies that process by letting you define the hyperparameters you want to experiment with, the ranges to work over, and the metric you want to optimize. The following screenshot shows example output for an HPO job:

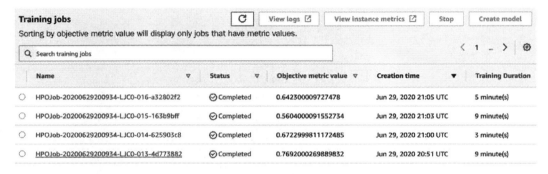

Figure 1.14 – Hyperparameter tuning jobs showing the objective metric of interest

SageMaker Debugger

SageMaker Debugger helps you debug and, depending on your ML framework, profile your training jobs. While making training jobs run faster is always helpful, debugging is particularly useful if you are writing your own deep learning code with neural networks. Problems such as exploding gradients or mysterious NaN in your tensors are quite tough to track down, particularly in distributed training jobs. Debugger can effectively help you set breakpoints to see where things are going wrong. The following figure shows an example of the training and validation loss captured by SageMaker Debugger:

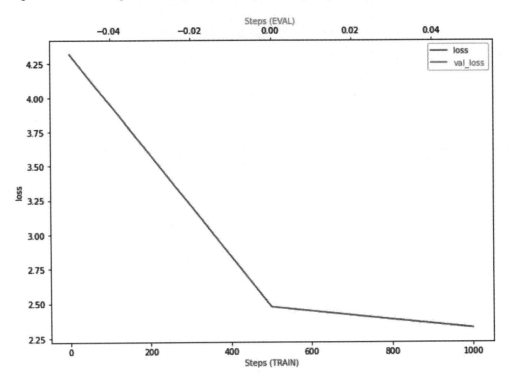

Figure 1.15 – Visualization of tensors captured by SageMaker Debugger

SageMaker Experiments

ML is an iterative process. When you're tuning a model, you may try several variations of hyperparameters, features, and even algorithms. It's important to track that work systematically so you can reproduce your results later on. That's where SageMaker Experiments comes into the picture. It helps you track, organize, and compare different trials. The following screenshot shows an example of SageMaker Experiments information:

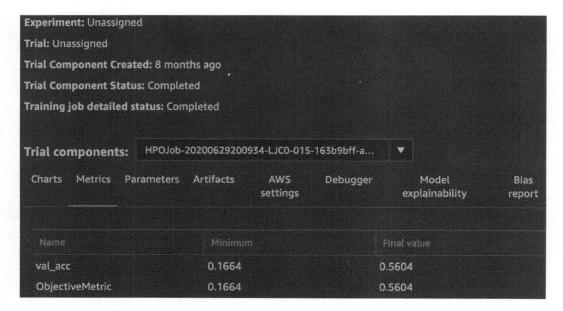

Figure 1.16 – Trial results in SageMaker Experiments

Now that we've introduced several SageMaker capabilities for training and tuning, let's move on to model management and deployment capabilities.

Feature tour of model management and deployment capabilities

In this section, we'll dive into SageMaker's model hosting and monitoring capabilities. By the end of this section, you should understand the basics of SageMaker model endpoints along with the use of **SageMaker Model Monitor**. You'll also learn about deploying models on edge devices with **SageMaker Edge Manager**.

Model Monitor

In some organizations, the gap between the ML team and the operations team causes real problems. Operations teams may not understand how to monitor an ML system in production, and ML teams don't always have deep operational expertise.

Model Monitor tries to solve that problem: it will instrument a model endpoint and collect data about the inputs to, and outputs from, an ML model used for inference. It can then analyze that data for data drift and other quality problems, as well as model accuracy or quality problems. The following diagram shows an example of model monitoring data captured for an inference endpoint:

[30]:		feature_name	constraint_check_type	description
	0	State_CT	data_type_check	Data type match requirement is not met. Expected data type: Integral, Expected match: 100.0%. Observed: Only 99.66633299966632% of data is Integral.
	1	State_MN	data_type_check	Data type match requirement is not met. Expected data type: Integral, Expected match: 100.0%. Observed: Only 99.66633299966632% of data is Integral.
	2	State_KY	data_type_check	Data type match requirement is not met. Expected data type: Integral, Expected match: 100.0%. Observed: Only 99.66633299966632% of data is Integral.
	3	State_NV	data_type_check	Data type match requirement is not met. Expected data type: Integral, Expected match: 100.0%. Observed: Only 99.66633299966632% of data is Integral.
	4	State_RI	data_type_check	Data type match requirement is not met. Expected data type: Integral, Expected match: 100.0%. Observed: Only 99.66633299966632% of data is Integral.
	5	State_CO	data_type_check	Data type match requirement is not met. Expected data type: Integral, Expected match: 100.0%. Observed: Only 99.66633299966632% of data is Integral.
	6	Churn	data_type_check	Data type match requirement is not met. Expected data type: Integral, Expected match: 100.0%. Observed: Only 0.0% of data is Integral.
	7	State_IL	data_type_check	Data type match requirement is not met. Expected data type: Integral, Expected match: 100.0%. Observed: Only 99.66633299966632% of data is Integral.
	8	State_SD	data_type_check	Data type match requirement is not met. Expected data type: Integral, Expected match: 100.0%. Observed: Only 99.66633299966632% of data is Integral.
	9	State_NC	data_type_check	Data type match requirement is not met. Expected data type: Integral, Expected match: 100.0%. Observed: Only 99.66633299966632% of data is Integral.

Figure 1.17 – Model Monitor checking data quality on inference inputs

Model endpoints

In some cases, you need to get a large number of inferences at once, in which case SageMaker provides a batch inference capability. But if you need to get inferences closer to real time, you can host your model in a SageMaker managed endpoint. SageMaker handles the deployment and scaling of your endpoints. Just as important, SageMaker lets you host multiple models in a single endpoint. That's useful both for **A/B testing** (that is, you can direct some percentage of traffic to a newer model) and for hosting multiple models that are tuned for different traffic segments.

You can also host an inference pipeline with multiple containers chained together, which is convenient if you need to preprocess inputs before performing inference. The following screenshot shows a model endpoint with two models serving different percentages of traffic:

Production variants

Model name	Training job	Variant name	Instance type	Elastic Inference	Initial instance count	Initial weight	Actions
sagemaker-xgboost-2021-03-11-20-47-16-354	-	variant-name-1	ml.m4.xlarge	none	1	9	Edit | Remove
sagemaker-xgboost-2020-10-20-16-00-05-724	-	variant-name-2	ml.m4.xlarge	none	1	1	Edit | Remove

Add model

Figure 1.18 – Multiple models configured behind a single inference endpoint

Edge Manager

In some cases, you need to get model inferences on a device rather than from the cloud. You may need a lower response time that doesn't allow for an API call to the cloud, or you may have intermittent network connectivity. In video use cases, it's not always feasible to stream data to the cloud for inference. In such cases, **Edge Manager** and related tools such as **SageMaker Neo** help you compile models optimized to run on devices, deploy them, manage them, and get operational metrics back to the cloud. The following screenshot shows an example of a virtual device managed by Edge Manager:

Figure 1.19 – A device registered to an Edge Manager device fleet

Before we conclude with the summary, let's have a recap of the SageMaker capabilities provided for the following primary ML phases:

- For data preparation:

SageMaker Capability	Use when...
Ground Truth	You need to label data for supervised learning tasks such as classification with the assistance of a human team.
Data Wrangler	You want to explore data and start preparing transformations for feature engineering.
Processing	You want to apply data preparation and feature engineering steps using Spark, sklearn, or your own code.
Feature Store	You want to organize, share, and reuse features.
Clarify	You want to check for bias in your data or model behavior and understand what's driving model predictions.

Figure 1.20 – SageMaker capabilities for data preparation

- For operations:

SageMaker Capability	Use when...
Model Monitor	You want to monitor a production model for data quality and model accuracy problems.
Model endpoints	You want to host a model for real-time inference, possibly using A/B testing as part of a deployment process.
Edge Manager	You want to deploy and manage models on devices rather than in the cloud.

Figure 1.21 – SageMaker capabilities for operations

- For model training:

SageMaker Capability	Use when...
SageMaker Studio	You want a fully integrated ML IDE.
Notebook instances	You want to use managed Jupyter notebooks but don't need the full shared IDE experience of Studio.
SageMaker built-in algorithms	You want to solve an ML use case with a tested and scalable implementation, and SageMaker has a relevant algorithm.
Training jobs	You want to run model training, possibly on very large datasets, without managing the infrastructure.
Autopilot	You want to quickly train a model (for supported problem types) without dealing with routine feature engineering and model tuning.
HPO	You want to systematically search for the best hyperparameter values for your model.

Figure 1.22 – SageMaker capabilities for model training

With this, we have come to the end of this chapter.

Summary

In this chapter, you saw how to map SageMaker capabilities to different phases of the ML life cycle. You got a quick look at important SageMaker capabilities. In the next chapter, you will learn about the technical requirements and the use case that will be used throughout. You'll also learn about setting up managed data science environments for scaling model-building activities.

2
Data Science Environments

In this chapter, we will get an overview of how to create managed data science environments to scale and create repeatable environments for your model-building activities. In this chapter, you will get a brief overview of the **machine learning** (**ML**) use case, including the dataset that will be used throughout the chapters in this book.

The topics that will be covered in this chapter are as follows:

- Machine learning use case and dataset
- Creating data science environments

Technical requirements

You will need an AWS account to run the examples included in this chapter. Full code examples included in the book are available on GitHub at `https://github.com/PacktPublishing/Amazon-SageMaker-Best-Practices/tree/main/Chapter02`. You will need to install a Git client to access them (`https://git-scm.com/`). Portions of the code are included within the chapter to call out specific technical concepts; however, please refer to the GitHub repository for the full code required to complete the hands-on activities that go along with this chapter.

Machine learning use case and dataset

Throughout this book, we will be using examples to demonstrate the best practices that apply across the ML life cycle. For this, we'll focus on a single ML use case and use an open dataset with data relating to the ML use case.

The primary use case we'll explore in this book is predicting air quality readings. Given a location (weather station) and date, we'll try to predict a value for a particular type of air quality measurement (for example, pm25 or o3). We'll treat this as a regression problem and explore XGBoost and neural network-based model approaches.

For this, we'll use a dataset from OpenAQ (`https://registry.opendata.aws/openaq/`) that includes air quality data from public data sources. The dataset that we will use is the `realtime` dataset (`https://openaq-fetches.s3.amazonaws.com/index.html`) and the `realtime-parquet-gzipped` dataset (`https://openaq-fetches.s3.amazonaws.com/index.html`), which includes daily reports from multiple stations.

The daily reports are in JSON format. Each record contains the following:

- A timestamp (both UTC and local)
- Parameter ID (pm25)
- Location (station ID)
- Value (numeric)
- Units for value
- City
- Attribution (link to station website)
- Averaging period (for example, 1 hour)
- Coordinates (lat/lon)
- Country code
- Source name (short version of station name)
- Source type
- Mobile (true/false)

Let's now look at how to create data science environments.

Creating data science environment

In the previous section, we introduced high-level Amazon SageMaker features that can often be used in isolation or together for end-to-end capabilities. In this section, we will focus on creating consistent and repeatable governed data science environments that can take advantage of the features discussed in the first section.

To build, train, and deploy models using Amazon SageMaker, ML builders need access to select AWS resources spanning the ML development life cycle. Because many different personas may be responsible for building ML models, the term ML builder refers to any individual tasked with model building. This could include data scientists, ML engineers, or data analysts.

Data science development environments provide ML builders with the AWS resources they need to build and train models. A data science environment could be as simple as an AWS account with access to Amazon SageMaker as well as AWS services commonly used with Amazon SageMaker, such as Amazon S3, AWS Glue, or Amazon EMR. While this may work for small teams, it does not scale well to larger teams or provide repeatability as new projects get created or new team members join the team.

Amazon SageMaker offers three core options in building, training, and tuning models, including the following:

- **API/SDK**: Training and tuning jobs can be started with the SageMaker API, which can be accessed through the high-level SageMaker Python SDK, lower-level AWS SDKs such as boto3 for Python, or the AWS CLI.

- **Amazon SageMaker Studio**: Amazon SageMaker Studio has built-in notebooks as part of an integrated workbench that includes native integrations with other Amazon SageMaker features and feature visualizations.

- **Amazon SageMaker notebook instances**: SageMaker notebook instances provide a compute instance with attached storage hosting the Jupyter Notebook application. These notebooks come preinstalled with packages, libraries, and kernels.

This section will focus only on Amazon SageMaker Studio and Amazon SageMaker notebook instances for setting up data science environments. Similar approaches can be applied in using the SageMaker API or SDK from a data science environment hosted outside of SageMaker. We'll first highlight the two common approaches using **Infrastructure-as-Code (IaC)/Configuration-as-Code (CaC)** as well as building a common catalog of data science environments. We will expand on each option in more detail in later sections.

To build a repeatable mechanism for creating data science sandbox environments, it is recommended to utilize IaC/CaC to define the intended configuration and controls to implement for your sandbox environments. Let's see what the two processes refer to:

- IaC refers to the process of provisioning and managing infrastructure using code instead of relying on manual setup, which is not only slow but also prone to error and inconsistencies across environments.

- Cac refers to the process of managing the configuration of resources through code. Because this is all defined via code, it can be managed as source code and reused for consistency across environments.

Using Iac/CaC can be taken a step further by providing data science environments through a service, such as AWS Service Catalog, that is purposely built for centrally creating and managing catalogs of IT services that are approved for use on AWS.

Figure 2.1 illustrates the most common approaches for setting up governed data science environments. Each of these options will be discussed in detail in this section. At a minimum, it's recommended to adopt an automated approach, which would include options 2 and 3 in the following diagram:

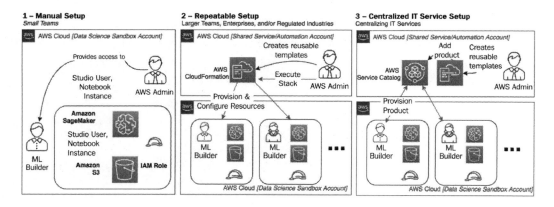

Figure 2.1 – Approaches for creating data science sandbox environments

A manual approach to provisioning and providing access to AWS services for ML builders creates challenges when scaling multiple ML builders and managing governance beyond a small team.

With the introduction of AWS CloudFormation, or an equivalent service providing IaC/CaC capabilities, data science environments can be repeatedly created as well as provide additional capabilities such as the following:

- **Environment governance**: AWS CloudFormation allows you to define the intended state of your data science environment in terms of which resources get provisioned as well as how they get provisioned. This allows you to enforce configurations such as cost allocation tags, encrypted storage, or control access to pre-approved resources such as specific instance types for notebook instance compute.

- **Consistency**: As ML builder teams grow, there is a need to gain operational efficiencies by provisioning environments with reduced manual effort and increased consistency. IaC/CaC allows for data science environments to be automatically provisioned and provides consistency through code and automation.

- **Improved management capabilities**: AWS CloudFormation not only allows you to automatically build a data science environment, but it also allows you to quickly deprovision a data science environment that is no longer in use. This capability reduces environment sprawl and ensures that you are not paying for resources that are no longer in use.

Using IaC/CaC to provision and manage data science environments is often sufficient in being able to consistently enable ML builders. However, providing these data science environments through a central catalog of IT services adds an additional layer of operational efficiencies, such as *reducing manual approvals, reducing hand-offs in siloed teams*, and *providing centralized governance by ensuring environments are provisioned across teams using only approved configurations.*

AWS Service Catalog allows administrators to centrally define and manage a portfolio of approved products or configurations defined through AWS CloudFormation templates. The addition of AWS Service Catalog for managing a portfolio of products used to create data science environments enables additional capabilities over standalone IaC/CaC, including the following:

- **Self-service capabilities**: Using only IaC/CaC to provision and configure AWS resources can often result in delays while requests are approved, tracked, and, ultimately, the environment is provisioned by the AWS Admin. AWS Service Catalog allows ML builders, or approved designated project resources, to automatically request and provision a data science environment that is preconfigured according to standards that you define.

- **Applying constraints and access controls**: With AWS Service Catalog, constraints and access controls can be centrally defined and applied consistently across teams.

- **Service management**: While AWS Service Catalog utilizes AWS CloudFormation, it also includes capabilities to manage the life cycle of these templates or products across versions.

AWS Service Catalog allows ML builders, or an approved resource, to request and instantiate a data science environment using approved products contained in an AWS Service Catalog portfolio. An AWS Service Catalog portfolio can exist in a separate AWS account and be shared across AWS accounts to establish a company or business unit standard for governing the configuration and provisioning of products. Products within a portfolio contain the pre-configured templates, using IaC/CaC, that should be used to provision or instantiate the data science environment for an ML builder:

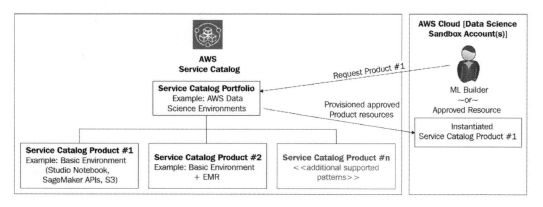

Figure 2.2 – AWS Service Catalog – anatomy of a portfolio

In the rest of this chapter, we'll cover considerations to consistently create data science environments through IaC/CaC, as well as advanced capabilities allowing you to provide those environments across multiple teams through a governed catalog of IT services. Each of these will be covered for both Amazon SageMaker notebook instances as well as Amazon SageMaker Studio. First, we'll cover the use of IaC/CaC to create repeatable data science environments.

Creating repeatability through IaC/CaC

Using AWS CloudFormation to provision and configure the AWS resources and access required for SageMaker model-building activities allows teams to create a repeatable pattern that can be shared across teams and used to consistently create data science environments.

A CloudFormation template lets you programmatically describe the desired AWS resources, configurations, and dependencies that should be provisioned when that template is launched as a stack. Key considerations when building AWS CloudFormation templates for data science environments include what resources should be provisioned, how they should be configured, and what permissions ML builders need for model-building activities.

What resources are required?

AWS CloudFormation lets you define the AWS services to automatically provision via a template using supported resources and resource types. As an example, Amazon SageMaker is a supported resource, and a SageMaker notebook instance is a supported resource type. A CloudFormation resource type is represented in a consistent format, as shown in *Figure 2.3*, whether you are building your CloudFormation template as JSON or YAML:

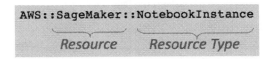

Figure 2.3 – AWS CloudFormation resource type for an Amazon SageMaker notebook instance

This means teams can automatically provision and configure a notebook instance through a CloudFormation template. However, a notebook instance alone is typically not enough for a data science environment. For a basic environment, you typically need a notebook instance, an S3 bucket, and an AWS IAM SageMaker execution role to execute API calls from within your notebook environment.

In addition to a basic environment, there may be a need to provision other resources as part of a data science environment. Additional resources to provision fall into a few key categories:

- **Data preparation resources**: This category includes AWS resources commonly used for data preparation activities such as **Amazon Elastic MapReduce (EMR)**. For this, you can create an EMR cluster to process and analyze vast amounts of data using the AWS::EMR::Cluster resource type.

- **Machine learning pipeline resources**: This category includes AWS resources commonly used in creating machine learning pipelines, such as the following:

  a. **AWS CodeCommit**: Create a source code repository for model training code in AWS CodeCommit using the AWS::CodeCommit::Repository resource type.

b. **Amazon Elastic Container Registry (ECR)**: Create a new container image repository in ECR that can be used for your training and inference container images in the case of using SageMaker's capability to bring your own container image. A new repository can be created using the `AWS::ECR::Repository` resource type.

- **Identity resources**: This category includes any additional policies or service roles that need to be created to use AWS resources. For example, to utilize AWS Step Functions, or the Data Science Python SDK, for creating ML workflows, a service-level IAM execution role needs to be created. The creation of this role can be specified in your CloudFormation template. The role should also include permissions that allow access to AWS services and actions that will be used in your ML workflow, such as AWS Glue for data preparation and Amazon SageMaker for training jobs.

How should the resources be configured?

Each resource that gets provisioned through a CloudFormation template includes a set of properties that define how a resource should be configured. Defining these properties through code allows you to consistently provision resources that are configured according to pre-defined specifications. Properties include important configuration options, such as launching environments with a VPC attached or enforcing controls such as encryption at rest. CloudFormation also allows for **parameters** that can be defined in the template and passed in when launching a CloudFormation stack.

What permissions are needed?

After you've identified the AWS resources and resource types that need to be provisioned for your data science environment, you need to identify the permissions that are also required to be able to access the notebook environment and the underlying APIs required for model building.

There is some variance between Amazon SageMaker notebook instances and Amazon SageMaker Studio discussed in the sections below; however, in both cases, a basic environment requires an IAM SageMaker execution role. Depending on the intent of the CloudFormation template, you need to consider the additional allowed AWS API calls and actions that the SageMaker execution role will need access to. For example, if your data science team uses AWS Glue for data preparation activities, the IAM SageMaker execution role needs to allow access to the corresponding AWS Glue API actions.

To build the AWS CloudFormation templates that will be used to create and consistently enforce controls in your data science environment, a few planning tasks should be considered before building those templates:

1. First, you should identify the patterns for the resources that should be provisioned together.

2. Second, you should identify how those resources should be configured.

3. Finally, you need to identify the minimum permissions that need to be in place for the provisioned resources to integrate seamlessly as well as the permissions required for an ML builder to operate within those provisioned environments.

Typically, several patterns are built supporting different environment patterns that may be needed for varying use cases or multiple teams. The following sections include detailed sample scenarios for both Amazon SageMaker notebook instances and Amazon SageMaker Studio. For either scenario, the sections can be read independently of one another and contain some duplicated information so that they can exist independently.

Amazon SageMaker notebook instances

Building data science environments that utilize Amazon SageMaker notebook instances typically includes the provisioning of the following:

- A notebook instance (required)
- An S3 bucket (optional)
- An IAM execution role (optional if using an existing one)
- Any other resources identified as needed by ML builder teams

An Amazon S3 bucket is noted as optional above because many organizations have existing S3 buckets that are used for data science model-building activities. In these cases, the data science environment may instead include permissions to access an existing S3 bucket. *Figure 2.2* shows a basic data science environment template that provisions a SageMaker notebook instance, an Amazon S3 bucket, and creates a SageMaker execution role that is attached to the notebook instance. The template can be used to instantiate multiple environments:

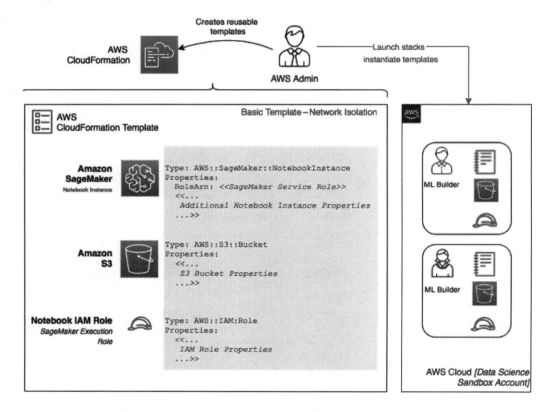

Figure 2.4 – Notebook instance-based data science environment

The following code snippets from a CloudFormation template show a pattern that can be used to quickly provision a data science environment using controls pre-approved by security and administrative teams and implemented through code. In the first section of the template, we identify parameters that are configurable each time a new template is launched. Parameters allow you to pass in data used in the provisioning and configuration of resources:

```
AWSTemplateFormatVersion: '2010-09-09'
Metadata:
```

```
License: Apache-2.0
Description: 'Example data science environment creating a
new SageMaker Notebook Instance using an existing VPC.  This
template also includes the creation of an Amazon S3 Bucket and
IAM Role.  A lifecycle policy is also included to pull the
dataset that will be used in future book chapters.'
Parameters: #These are configuration parameters that are passed
in as input on stack creation
   NotebookInstanceName:
           AllowedPattern: '[A-Za-z0-9-]{1,63}'
           ConstraintDescription: Maximum of 63 alphanumeric
characters. Can include hyphens but not spaces.
           Description: SageMaker Notebook instance name
           MaxLength: '63'
           MinLength: '1'
           Type: String
           Default: 'myNotebook'
   NotebookInstanceType:
     VPCSubnetIds:
     VPCSecurityGroupIds:
     KMSKeyId:
     NotebookVolumeSize:
```

In the next section of the template, we identify the resources to provision and configure
for your data science environment. The Properties of each resource identify the
configuration and controls to provision. These controls can include configuration such as
ensuring the storage volume attached to the notebook instance is encrypted and that the
notebook instance is provisioned with a VPC attached:

```
Resources:
   SageMakerRole:
           Type: AWS::IAM::Role
           Properties:
               AssumeRolePolicyDocument:
                 Version: 2012-10-17
               Statement:
                 - Effect: Allow
                   Principal:
                     Service:
```

```
                        - "sagemaker.amazonaws.com"
            Action:
            - "sts:AssumeRole"
          ManagedPolicyArns:
          - "arn:aws:iam::aws:policy/AmazonSageMakerFullAccess"
          - ...
    SageMakerLifecycleConfig:
        ...
    SageMakerNotebookInstance:
        ...
  S3Bucket:
  ...
```

In the template snippets here, we are asking for a pre-configured VPC as a parameter on input; however, you could also include the creation of a new VPC within your CloudFormation template depending on your needs. We also include the notebook instance type and storage size as parameters that are configurable with each new launched template. Configurations that are likely to change for different ML use cases are good candidates that convert into configurable parameters that can be defined while launching a stack.

Once the template is uploaded to Amazon S3 and validated, it can be launched repeatedly for each new data science environment needed. Launching the stack can be done through the AWS console, AWS CLI, or the AWS SDK. This is most frequently done from an administrative account using cross-account privileges to ensure control in the roles that can define and provision environments versus the users who use the provisioned environments.

After the CloudFormation stack is completed, an ML builder can then access their environment through the provisioned Amazon SageMaker notebook instances via the AWS console. To access the notebook instance, the sign-in credentials for the ML builder must have the IAM permissions to send a CreatePresignedNotebookInstanceUrl API request.

Amazon SageMaker Studio

Building data science environments that utilize Amazon SageMaker Studio includes the provisioning of the following:

- A new user within an existing Studio domain (required)
- An S3 bucket (optional)
- An IAM execution role (optional if using an existing one)
- Any other resources or configurations identified as needed by ML builder teams

An Amazon S3 bucket is noted as optional above because many organizations have existing S3 buckets that are used for data science model-building activities. In these cases, the data science environment may instead include permissions to access an existing S3 bucket. *Figure 2.5* shows a basic data science environment template that provisions a new user in SageMaker Studio, an Amazon S3 bucket, and creates a SageMaker execution role that is attached to the Studio domain user. The template can be used to instantiate multiple user environments:

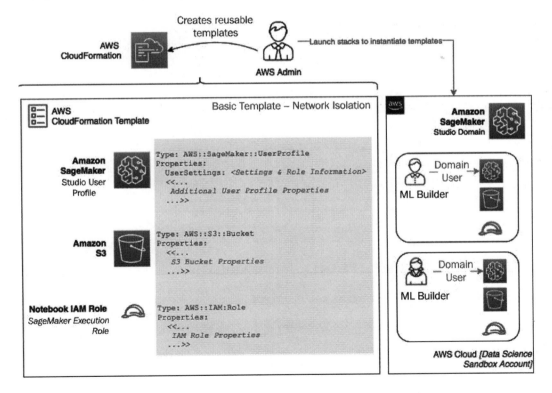

Figure 2.5 – Amazon SageMaker Studio-based data science environment

The CloudFormation template below shows a pattern that can be used to quickly provision an integrated data science workbench environment using Amazon SageMaker Studio, giving ML builders access to Studio notebooks as well as other integrated features inside SageMaker Studio. Again, the first section contains the parameters that allow you to define how to provision and configure the environment:

```
AWSTemplateFormatVersion: '2010-09-09'
Metadata:
  License: Apache-2.0
Description: 'Example data science environment creating a new
SageMaker Studio User in an existing Studio Domain using an
existing VPC.  This template also includes the creation of an
Amazon S3 Bucket and IAM Role.'
Parameters:
  StudioDomainID:
        AllowedPattern: '[A-Za-z0-9-]{1,63}'
        Description: ID of the Studio Domain where user
should be created (ex. d-xxxnxxnxxnxn)
        Default: d-xxxnxxnxxnxn
        Type: String
  Team:
        AllowedValues:
        - weatherproduct
        - weatherresearch
        Description: Team name for user working in
associated environment
        Default: weatherproduct
        Type: String
  UserProfileName:
        Description: User profile name
        AllowedPattern: '^[a-zA-Z0-9](-*[a-zA-Z0-9]){0,62}'
        Type: String
        Default: 'UserName'
  VPCSecurityGroupIds:
    ...
```

In the next section of the template, we identify the resources to provision and configure for your data science environment. Again, the properties of each resource identify the configuration and controls to provision as follows:

```yaml
Resources:
  StudioUser:
        Type: AWS::SageMaker::UserProfile
        Properties:
        DomainId: !Ref StudioDomainID
        Tags:
        - Key: "Environment"
          Value: "Development"
        - Key: "Team"
        Value: !Ref Team
        UserProfileName: !Ref UserProfileName
        UserSettings:
        ExecutionRole: !GetAtt SageMakerRole.Arn
        SecurityGroups: !Ref VPCSecurityGroupIds

  SageMakerRole:
    ...
  S3Bucket:
    ...
```

In the CloudFormation template, we are adding a new user to an existing Studio domain. A **Studio domain** exists at the AWS account level and there is only one domain per AWS region. You can optionally include the creation of a new Studio domain within your CloudFormation template using the AWS:SageMaker:Domain resource type. Creating a Studio domain is a one-time activity per AWS account and per AWS region, so this would be considered a prerequisite to creating users within your Studio domain. In addition, some regulated workloads enforce account-level isolation per ML builder, so in these cases, your CloudFormation template may include the setup of a Studio domain. However, the most common pattern is multiple users per Studio domain.

Once the template is built and validated, it is ready to be deployed after uploading the template to Amazon S3 and launching the stack through the AWS console, AWS CLI, or the AWS SDK. Again, this is most frequently done from an administrative account using cross-account privileges to ensure control in the roles that can define and provision environments versus the users who use the provisioned environments.

After the CloudFormation stack is completed, an ML builder can access the Studio environment and create notebooks through the Studio IDE with AWS IAM sign-in credentials or through AWS SSO credentials and the generated Studio URL.

Providing and creating data science environments as IT services

Creating a governed catalog of IT services that includes data science environments is a way to build on the concepts of using IaC/CaC for repeatability by adding a central catalog of approved IT services across teams. This is especially useful for large companies or enterprises that rely on central IT or infrastructure teams to provision AWS resources. Creating a central catalog using AWS Service Catalog allows the added benefits of ensuring compliance with corporate standards, accelerating the ability of ML builders to quickly gain access to data science environments, managing versions of products offered through the catalog, and integrating with third-party **IT Service Management (ITSM)** software for change control.

For model building using Amazon SageMaker, AWS Service Catalog allows teams to take the AWS CloudFormation templates discussed in the previous section and offer those templates as versioned products inside a central portfolio of products. The approved configurations for those products can be centrally managed and governed. AWS Service Catalog lets teams control the users who have access to launch a product, which means admins can also provide self-service capabilities to ML builders to ensure that they have quick access to governed data science environments:

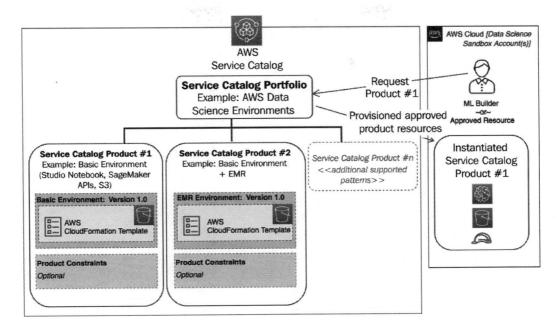

Figure 2.6 – Centrally managed data science environments using AWS Service Catalog

When products are added to a portfolio, you can optionally add product constraints. **Product constraints** allow you to add controls in terms of how an ML builder uses products. Several constraint types are allowed, including launch, notification, template, stack set, and tag update constraints. Each of these constraint types can be applied to any product; however, launch and template constraints have unique considerations for data science environments.

A launch constraint allows you to specify the IAM role that AWS Service Catalog assumes for provisioning AWS resources for a product within a portfolio. This follows the recommended practice of granting least privilege by providing ML builders with access to the resources that get provisioned, but not allowing ML builders access to provision resources outside of AWS Service Catalog.

For data science environments, a launch constraint can be added to a product in the portfolio using a pre-defined IAM role that is assumed for provisioning resources. This means you do not need to grant privileges for actions such as creating a new IAM role or working with AWS CloudFormation to the ML builder directly.

A template constraint is a JSON-formatted text file that defines rules describing when an ML builder can use the templates, and which values they can specify for the parameters defined in the AWS CloudFormation template. Each rule has two properties: *a rule condition* (optional) and *assertions* (required).

The rule condition determines when the rule takes effect, and the assertion describes the values a user can specify for a specific parameter. For data science environments, template constraints can be used for defining allowable configurations such as instance types via assertions. You can also add a rule condition to that assertion that limits the allowed instances within specific environments.

AWS Service Catalog provides added benefits over using AWS CloudFormation by creating a centralized portfolio for *data science environments* that contains managed products for provisioning data science environments. The first step is to create a portfolio, which can be done through the AWS CLI, AWS SDK, or AWS console, as shown below.

Creating a portfolio in AWS Service Catalog

To create a portfolio, perform the following steps:

1. From AWS Service Catalog service, select **Create portfolio**:

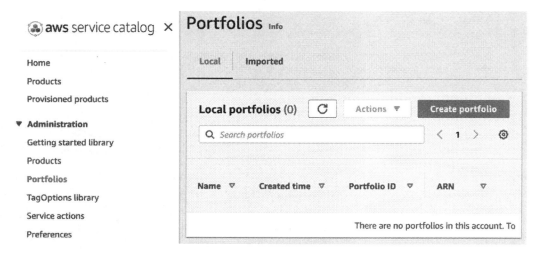

Figure 2.7 – AWS Service Catalog – creating a new portfolio

2. Define your portfolio by entering the following under **Create portfolio**:

    -   **Portfolio name**: Data Science Environments
    -   **Description**: Service catalog portfolio of approved products for provisioning data science environments for ML builders
    -   **Owner**: Your name

3. Click the **Create** button to create the portfolio. You will then see a **Success** message, indicating the portfolio is available to add products.

As products are added to the portfolio and provisioned, AWS Service Catalog provides visibility for admins to view all provisioned products and perform administrative tasks, such as identifying user resource allocation. ML builders also have a central view of all the provisioned products they have requested:

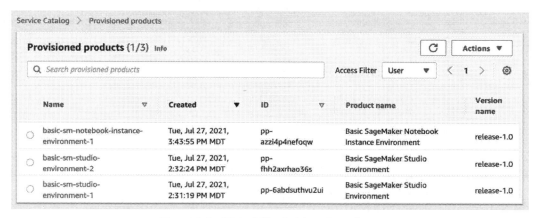

Figure 2.8 – List of all provisioned products

The unique aspects of products for SageMaker notebook instances and SageMaker Studio are largely handled within the CloudFormation templates. The high-level steps to create a product are consistent between the two types of data science environments. The following sections include detailed sample scenarios extending the CloudFormation templates previously created for both Amazon SageMaker notebook instances and Amazon SageMaker Studio.

Amazon SageMaker notebook instances

A new product can be added to an AWS Service Catalog portfolio using the AWS CLI, AWS SDK, or the AWS console. When a new product is added to a portfolio, the CloudFormation template that defines that environment must be uploaded to an S3 bucket and provided as input. In this example, the previous CloudFormation template will be used in addition to several other parameters required on input, as shown in the following:

1. From within the portfolio created, select **Upload new product**:

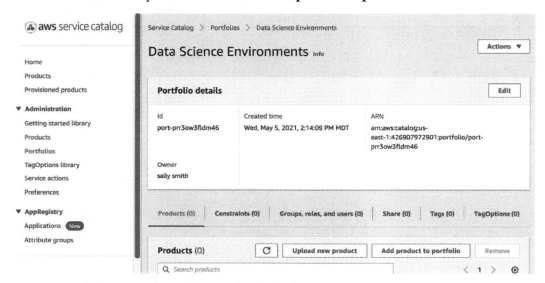

Figure 2.9 – AWS Service Catalog – uploading a new product to the portfolio

2. Under **Enter product details**, there are three sections of information to fill out, including **Product details**, **Version details**, and **Support details**.

    - For **Product details**, this section contains information about the product. Enter the following information in the fields on input and then leave any field not specified blank:

        + **Product name**: Basic SageMaker notebook instance environment.

        + **Description**: Basic data science environment using Amazon SageMaker notebook instances, including (1) **New Notebook Instance** (2) **SageMaker Execution IAM Service Role** (3) **S3 Bucket**.

        + **Owner**: Your name.

- The **Version details** section includes the S3 location of the CloudFormation template combined with version and release details. Enter the following in the fields matching on input, leaving any field not specified blank:

  - **Choose a method**: Select the radio button for **Use a CloudFormation template**.

  - **Use a CloudFormation template**: Enter the S3 URL for the CloudFormation template in the format `https://`....

> **Important note**
>
> The default location for templates used on launched stacks is `https://s3.<region>.amazonaws.com/cf-templates-<hash>-region/notebook-instance-environment.yaml`, or you can upload the CloudFormation template provided for this chapter directly to an S3 bucket you choose.

  - **Version name**: `release-1.0`.

  - **Description**: `Initial product release`.

- The **Support details** section includes the information about the support contacts and support information. Enter the following for each field specified and leave any field not specified blank:

- **Email contact**: Your email@mail.com.

3. After filling in the information as described in the preceding steps, scroll to the bottom, select **Review**, and then **Create Product**.

4. The product will now be visible within the product list for the **Data Science Environments** portfolio.

After adding the product to the portfolio, constraints can be added to the product. **Constraints** are optional but offer additional recommended enforcement of practices, such as least privilege, and additional controls to enforce best practices such as cost optimization. To enforce minimum privileges, a launch constraint can be added to the product by first creating a launch IAM role that will be assumed when provisioning a product as documented in AWS Service Catalog product documentation: `https://docs.aws.amazon.com/servicecatalog/latest/adminguide/constraints-launch.html`.

In this IAM policy for this role, you'll need to add each service that the product provisions to the action list. Therefore, in this case, the following IAM policy may be overly permissive for your needs, in which case you can scope the role down to specific actions, conditions, and resources for your use case:

```
{

{
        "Version": "2012-10-17",
        "Statement": [
            {
        "Effect": "Allow",
            "Action": [
                    "s3:*"
            ],
            "Resource": "*",
            "Condition": {
                    "StringEquals": {
                    "s3:ExistingObjectTag/
servicecatalog:provisioning": "true"
                    }
            }
            },
            {
        "Effect": "Allow",
            "Action": [
                    "...",
            ],
        "Resource": "*"
            }
        ]
}
```

After creating the launch role and the policy to dictate permissions, the role needs to be applied to the product as a launch constraint, as shown in the following screenshot. The detailed instructions to apply a launch constraint are included in the existing AWS product documentation, `https://docs.aws.amazon.com/servicecatalog/latest/adminguide/constraints-launch.html`, under **Applying a Launch Constraint** -> **To assign the role to a product**. After applying the IAM role to the product launch constraint, you'll see the constraint listed for the product, as shown in the following screenshot:

| Products (1) | Constraints (1) | Groups, roles, and users (0) | Share (0) | Tags (0) | TagOptions (0) |

Constraints (1)   [Edit constraint] [Delete constraint] [**Create constraint**]

Description	Type	Product Name	Origin
○ Launch as arn:aws:iam::602974479434:role/ServiceCatalog-DataScienceProducts	LAUNCH	Basic SageMaker Notebook Instance Environment	602974479434

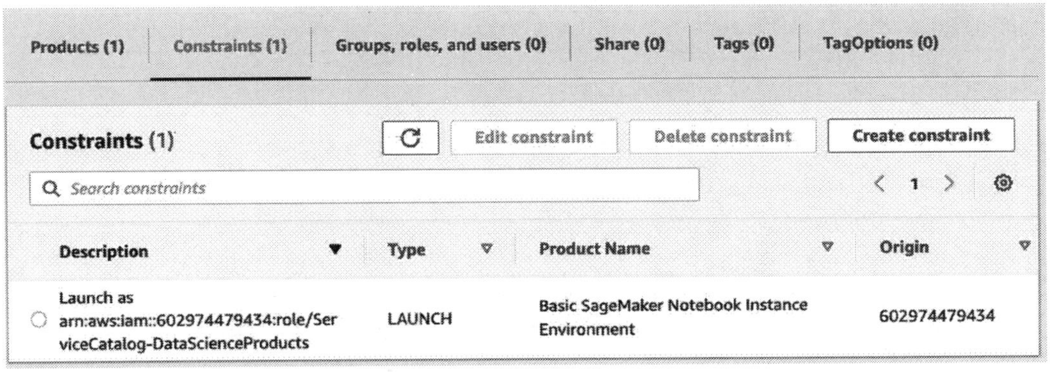

Figure 2.10 – AWS Constraints

The launch constraint tells Service Catalog to assume the `ServiceCatalog-DataScienceProducts` role when an end user launches the product. This role contains the policy we created with the privileges needed to provision and configure all the resources in the `CloudFormation` template for that product.

Finally, we will add a template constraint to limit the options for instance type size that is available to end users. This allows the implementation of cost controls on the type of instance that can be provisioned. You can optionally implement multiple constraints such as storage size. Template constraints are added as documented in the AWS product documentation: `https://docs.aws.amazon.com/servicecatalog/latest/adminguide/catalogs_constraints_template-constraints.html`. The specific template constraint JSON is listed in the following code block, where we are identifying that only the noted instance types are approved and available for use:

```
{
    "Rules": {
            "Rule1": {
            "Assertions": [
                {
                "Assert": {
```

```
            "Fn::Contains": [
                [
                            "ml.t2.large",
                            "ml.t2.xlarge",
                            "ml.t3.large",
                            "ml.t3.xlarge"
                ],
                {
                            "Ref": "NotebookInstanceType"
                }
                ]
            },
            "AssertDescription": "Instance type should have
approved types"
            }
        ]
        }
    }
}
```

After creating the preceding template constraint, you'll now see two constraints for this product in the console:

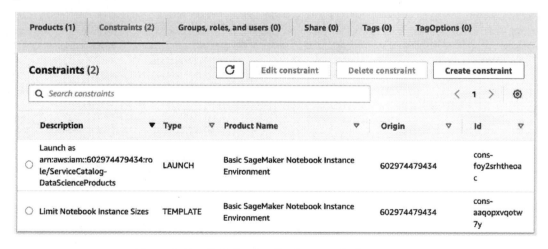

Figure 2.11 – AWS Service Catalog – applied constraint

The product is then available, with the constraints we identified, within the Data Science Environment portfolio and can be made available for self-service provisioning by ML builders.

Amazon SageMaker Studio

In this section, the CloudFormation template to create a data science environment in SageMaker Studio will be used to create a new product inside the data science environment portfolio. Again, a new product can be added to an AWS Service Catalog portfolio using the AWS CLI, AWS SDK, or the AWS console. When a new product is added to a portfolio, the CloudFormation template that defines that environment must be uploaded to an S3 bucket and provided as input. The steps to add a product require administrative privileges in Service Catalog and are performed in the **Administration** view:

1. From within the `Data Science Environments` portfolio, click on **Upload new product**.

2. Under **Enter product details**, there are three sections of information to fill out, including **Product details**, **Version details**, and **Support details**.

   For **Product details**, this section contains information about the product. Enter the following, leaving any field not specified blank:

   a) Product name: `Basic SageMaker Studio Environment`

   b) Description: Basic data science environment using Amazon SageMaker Studio, including (1) **New User in Existing Studio Domain** (2) **SageMaker Execution IAM Service Role** (3) **S3 Bucket**

   c) Owner: Your name

   For **Version details**, this section includes the S3 location of the CloudFormation template combined with version and release details. Enter the following, leaving any field not specified blank:

   d) Choose a method: Select the radio button for **Use a CloudFormation template**.

e) Use a CloudFormation template: Enter the S3 URL for the CloudFormation template in the format `https://...` Note: The default location for templates used on launched stacks is `https://s3.<region>.amazonaws.com/ cf-templates-<hash>-region/studio-environment.yaml`, or you can upload the CloudFormation template provided for this chapter directly to an S3 bucket of your choosing.

f) Version name: `release-1.0`.

g) Description: `Initial product release`.

For **Support details**, this section includes information about the support contacts and support information. Enter the following, leaving any field not specified blank:

Email contact: Your email@mail.com

3. After filling in the information as described in the preceding steps, scroll to the bottom, select **Review**, and then **Create Product**.

4. The product will now be visible within the product list for the **Data Science Environments** portfolio.

After adding the product to the portfolio, constraints can be added to the product. You can then add a launch constraint, to enforce minimum privileges, and template constraints based on your use case using the same steps performed under your notebook instance product steps.

After configuring the products, they can be made available for self-service provisioning by ML builders. ML builders must be granted access to the AWS Service Catalog end user view in the AWS console. Please refer to the following documentation for details on sharing your portfolio and granting access to end users: `https://docs.aws. amazon.com/servicecatalog/latest/adminguide/getstarted-deploy. html`.

This section covered the advantages of using IaC/CaC (AWS CloudFormation) and a centrally managed catalog of IT services (AWS Service Catalog) to create data science environments at scale.

Please head over to the *References* section to find additional reference links that you may find useful after reading this section.

Summary

In this chapter, you saw how to map SageMaker capabilities to different phases of the ML life cycle. You got a quick look at important SageMaker capabilities and saw how to set up your own SageMaker environment.

This chapter further covered the advantages of using IaC/CaC (AWS CloudFormation) as well as a centrally managed catalog of IT services (AWS Service Catalog) to create data science environments at scale. The approaches discussed provide the guidance needed to reduce manual effort, provide consistency, accelerate access to model-building services, and enforce governance controls within model-building environments.

In the next chapter, you will learn more about labeling data for ML projects.

References

The following are some of the references that you might find useful after reading this section:

- Amazon SageMaker notebook instances:
  `https://docs.aws.amazon.com/sagemaker/latest/dg/nbi.html`

- Amazon SageMaker Studio Onboarding:

  `https://docs.aws.amazon.com/sagemaker/latest/dg/gs-studio-onboard.html`

- Amazon SageMaker Studio:

  `https://aws.amazon.com/sagemaker/studio/ https://docs.aws.amazon.com/sagemaker/latest/dg/notebooks.html`

- Notebook Comparison:

  `https://docs.aws.amazon.com/sagemaker/latest/dg/notebooks-comparison.html`

- AWS Service Catalog:

  `https://aws.amazon.com/servicecatalog/`

- AWS CloudFormation:

  `https://aws.amazon.com/cloudformation/`

3
Data Labeling with Amazon SageMaker Ground Truth

One of the biggest barriers to ML projects in most companies is access to labeled training data. At one company we worked with, we were trying to identify consumer-impacting outages. The customer had a lot of data from each layer of their application stack, but they couldn't agree on how to define an outage. Is an outage when a load balancer is down? Probably not – we have redundancy in the infrastructure layer. Is an outage when a customer can't access the service for over 10 minutes? That's probably too granular; a single customer might have problems due to local network connectivity issues. So, what exactly do we mean by an outage? How can we automatically label our training data as *outage* or *not an outage*?

In this chapter, we'll review labeling data using SageMaker Ground Truth. We'll cover common challenges associated with large datasets and potentially biased data.

The following topics will be covered in this chapter:

- Challenges with labeling data at scale
- Addressing unique labeling requirements with custom labeling workflows
- Using active learning to reduce labeling time
- Security and permissions

Technical requirements

You will need an AWS account to run the examples included in this chapter. If you have not set up the data science environment yet, please refer to *Chapter 2, Data Science Environments*, which provides a walk-through of the setup process.

Code examples included in the book are available on GitHub at `https://github.com/PacktPublishing/Amazon-SageMaker-Best-Practices/tree/main/Chapter03`. You will need to install a Git client to access them (`https://git-scm.com/`).

The code for this chapter is in the `CH03` folder of the GitHub repository.

Challenges with labeling data at scale

Besides the conceptual challenges with agreeing on how to label data, we need to consider the logistics. **SageMaker Ground Truth** lets you assign data labeling jobs to a human workforce. But you may face additional challenges such as the following:

- **Unique labeling logic**: If our labeling case requires a custom workflow, we need to model that in Ground Truth.
- **Annotation quality**: The labels applied by workers may be subject to implicit bias that affects the results.
- **Cost and time**: Labeling data requires people for a period of time. If you have a very large dataset, you'll consume a lot of person-hours.
- **Security**: Given that your data may be sensitive, you need to make sure that access to the data is restricted to an authorized workforce.

> **Additional information**
>
> If you need an introduction to Ground Truth, please review *Chapter 2* of *Learn Amazon SageMaker*, written by Julien Simon.

To put these concerns into focus, let's consider our weather data introduced in the previous chapter. Ground Truth doesn't have a built-in workflow that lets us prompt workers to label weather data according to our logic for describing air as *good* or *bad*. The dataset for the entire time span is approximately 499 GB; labeling each entry by hand as *good* or *bad* weather quality will take some time. Finally, our workers may have their own implicit or unconscious bias.

A worker who grew up in a city with severe smog may have a much different perception of air quality than someone who grew up in a rural area with very clean air. In the following sections, we'll discuss how to address these challenges.

Addressing unique labeling requirements with custom labeling workflows

Let's get started with a labeling job for our weather data. We want to label each weather report as *good* or *bad*. In order to help our workers do that, we'll make a nice frontend that shows the location of the weather station on a map and displays the reading from the weather station. We need a custom workflow because this scenario doesn't fall neatly into any of the existing Ground Truth templates.

We will have to set up the following:

- A private workforce backed by a Cognito user pool
- A manifest file that lists the items we want to label
- A custom Ground Truth labeling workflow, consisting of two Lambda functions and a UI template

The notebook `LabelData.ipynb` in the `CH02` folder of our repository walks through these steps.

A private labeling workforce

Although you can use a public workforce, most companies will want to use a private workforce to label their own data. Setting up a private workforce starts by defining a Cognito user pool, which, for real use cases, could link to another identity provider such as Active Directory.

We'll create a user group in Cognito; you could use groups to create teams for different types of labeling jobs. Finally, we'll define a SageMaker work team linked to the Cognito user group. Note that SageMaker creates a labeling domain that we have to set as the callback URL in the Cognito user pool client.

Once the work team is set up, the notebook will add an example worker.

The **Create a private workforce** part of the notebook executes all of these steps for you:

- Creating a Cognito user pool

- Creating a Cognito client for the user pool

- Creating an identity pool for the client

- Creating a user group

- Assigning a domain to the user pool

- Creating a SageMaker work team that uses the Cognito user pool and group

- Adding a sample user

Once you execute the **Create a private workforce** part of the notebook, you should see a private workforce defined, along with the login URL that the workers would use. If you scroll further down this part of the console, you'll also see information about the work team and any workers assigned to the team, as shown in *Figure 3.1*:

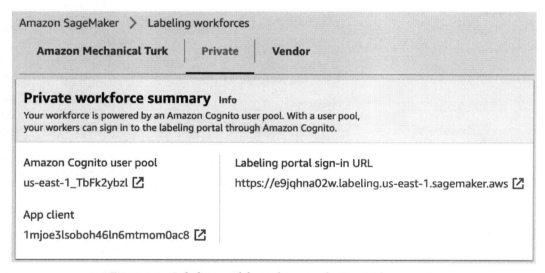

Figure 3.1 – Labeling workforce shown in the SageMaker console

Listing the data to label

We need to create a manifest file that tells Ground Truth how to find the data we want to label. In the manifest, we can list references to files in S3 or we can provide text data directly.

Recall that our source data is in JSON format. Each source file contains multiple entries that look like this:

```
{"date":{"utc":"2021-03-20T19:00:00.000Z","local":
"2021-03-20T23:00:00+04:00"},"parameter":"pm25",
"value":32,"unit":"µg/m³","averagingPeriod":{"val
```

```
ue":1,"unit":"hours"},"location":"US Diplomatic Post:
Dubai","city":"Dubai","country":"AE","coordinates":{"latitude":
25.25848,"longitude":55.309166
```

```
},"attribution":[{"name":"EPA AirNow DOS","url":"http://airnow.
gov/index.cfm?action=airnow.global_summary"}],"sourceName":
"StateAir_Dubai","sourceT
```

```
ype":"government","mobile":false}
```

We cannot pass in links to individual files, as each file contains multiple records to label. Rather, we will summarize each record directly in the manifest file. Each line in the manifest will contain the air quality metric and location:

```
{"source": "pm25,35.8,µg/m³,40.01,116.333"}
```

The `Create a manifest file` notebook section will write out a manifest for a set of records. Since you are the only worker you have, we limit the number of records to 20 by default (more on this in the next section).

Creating the workflow

In order to create a custom workflow, we need the following:

- A *Lambda function that can take one entry from the manifest and inject variables into the UI*. In this case, we will simply map the items in the manifest text entries into a metric label to display along with a geolocation.

- A *UI template that displays the data sensibly for a worker*. In this case, we have a simple UI template that presents the metric along with a map showing the location where the metric was collected.

> **Note**
>
> For the purposes of this book, we are using map tiles from OpenStreetMap. Do not use these tiles for production use cases. Instead, use a commercial provider such as Google Maps or Here.

- A *Lambda function that consolidates annotations from multiple workers.* We simply do a pass-through here since we only have one worker in our sample workforce.

The notebook section `Create a custom workflow` walks you through these steps:

- Defining IAM roles for the workflow and the Lambda function
- Uploading the user interface template and the Lambda processing code to S3
- Creating the pre- and post-processing Lambda functions
- Defining the labeling job

Once the labeling job is created, you can log in to the labeling portal URL (see *Figure 1.1*), using the username and password you specified in the notebook. Once you open the job, you'll see a UI like *Figure 3.2*:

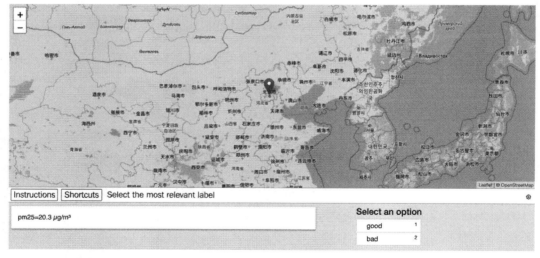

Figure 3.2 – Labeling UI showing the location of a weather station. The locations are shown in the local language

You'll see a map showing the location of the measurement and the actual measurement. You can pick *good* or *bad* to specify whether you think the measurement represents a good or bad air quality day. After you have labeled all of the metrics, your job will show as complete, and you'll see the label for each data point, as shown in *Figure 3.3*:

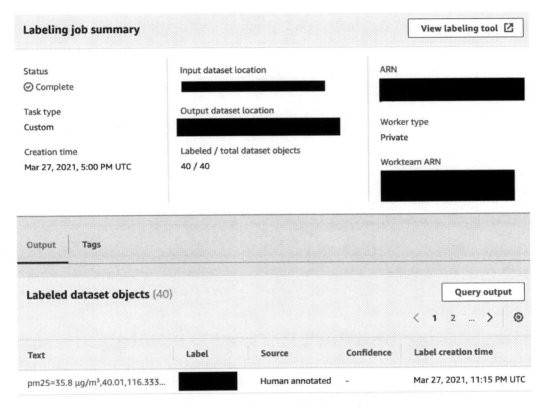

Figure 3.3 – Completed labeling job

We'll describe how to use the labeling output in the next chapter. You'll see examples of the labeling output in the notebook that goes with this chapter.

Improving labeling quality using multiple workers

Relying on a single opinion for a subjective evaluation is risky. In some cases, labeling seems straightforward; telling a car from an airplane when labeling transportation pictures is pretty simple. But let's go back to our weather data. If we're labeling air quality as good or bad based on a measurement that's not intuitive, such as the level of particulate matter (PM25), we may find that a worker's opinion depends greatly on the advice we give them and their preconceptions. If a worker believes that a certain city or country has *dirty air*, they are likely to favor a *bad* label in ambiguous cases. And these biases have real consequences – some governments are very sensitive to the idea that their air quality is bad!

One way to combat this problem is to use multiple workers to label each item and somehow combine the scores. In the notebook section called `Add another worker`, we'll add a second worker to our private workforce. Then in the `Launch labeling job for multiple workers` section, we'll create a new labeling job. Once the new job is ready, log in as both workers and label the small set of data we've selected.

What happens now? We'll need to adjust our post-processing Lambda to consolidate the annotations. We could use a variety of strategies for the consolidation. For example, we could use a majority voting scheme, with ties being assigned to a *mixed* category. In this chapter, we'll simply use the latest annotation as the winner since we only have two workers.

Using active learning to reduce labeling time

Now that we've set up a labeling workflow, we need to think about scale. If our dataset has more than 5,000 records, it's likely that Ground Truth can learn how to label for us. (You need at least 1,250 labeled records for automatic labeling, but at least 5,000 is a good rule of thumb.) This happens in an iterative process, as shown in the following diagram:

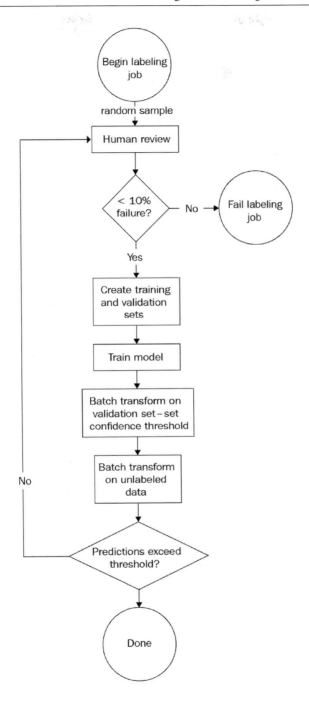

Figure 3.4 – Auto-labeling workflow

When you create a labeling job using automatic labeling, Ground Truth will select a random sample of input data for manual labeling. If at least 90% of these items are labeled without error, Ground Truth will split the labeled data into a training and validation set. It will train a model and compute a confidence score, then attempt to label the remaining data. If the automatically generated labels are beneath the confidence threshold, it will refer them to workers for human review. This process repeats until the entire dataset is labeled. While this process is difficult to simulate, it provides an iterative method to improve automatic labeling with human input.

As a concluding note to this section, you may wonder what the difference is between a model that can automatically label data and a more general-purpose ML model. There's a fine line here. Keep in mind that the data we use for Ground Truth may not be completely representative of the data we see in production. Our goal for a generic ML model is a model that can produce accurate inferences without any human input.

Security and permissions

While some data is not sensitive, most companies would not want to expose their data to the public during the labeling process. In this section, we'll cover data access control, encryption, and workforce management for data labeling.

You should follow the principle of least-privileged access when using Ground Truth (or any other cloud service). Restrict the users who are allowed to create labeling jobs, and restrict users allowed to create labeling jobs using non-private workforces. In a custom labeling job, explicitly provide invoke permissions to your Lambda functions. Restrict labeling job access to only the appropriate S3 buckets and prefixes.

When you run a labeling job, Ground Truth will always encrypt the output in S3. You can use the S3-managed key or provide your own KMS key. For non-sensitive data, the default S3 managed key is adequate. If you have sensitive data, consider using separate KMS keys for different datasets, as that provides another layer of security. You can also use a KMS key to encrypt the storage volumes on instances used for automatic labeling.

When managing your workforce, you should restrict access to a known-good IP address range (CIDR block). You should also use the worker tracking features to log which workers are accessing data. When using Cognito for authentication, make use of strong password policies and multi-factor authentication. In most cases, large companies will prefer to use their own identity provider for workforce management.

Finally, note that you'll need to add **CORS (cross-origin resource sharing)** configuration to your S3 buckets involved in labeling jobs, as described in the documentation (`https://docs.aws.amazon.com/sagemaker/latest/dg/sms-cors-update.html`).

Before we head toward the summary, do have a look at the following table as it summarizes some of the best practices for data labeling:

If you have...	Then do this...
Ambiguous labeling cases	• Augment the data with a custom workflow to help workers label properly. Make sure the UI provides contextual information to improve accuracy. • Use multiple workers to fight bias in labeling.
More than 10,000 items to label	• Use automatic labeling to speed up the process.
Sensitive data to label	• Use a private workforce. • Use data encryption. • Follow the principle of least-privileged access for the data.

Figure 3.5 – Summary of data labeling best practices

With this, we now come to the end of the chapter.

Summary

In this chapter, we started digging into our weather dataset, focusing on the problem of data labeling. We learned how to use SageMaker Ground Truth to label large datasets using a combination of human review and automation, how to use custom workflows to aid the labeling process, and how to fight labeling bias by using multiple opinions. We ended with some advice on making sure that the labeling process is secure.

In the next chapter, we'll explore data preparation. We'll run a feature engineering processing job on the full dataset.

4

Data Preparation at Scale Using Amazon SageMaker Data Wrangler and Processing

So far, we've identified our dataset and explored both manual and automated labeling. Now it's time to turn our attention to preparing the data for training. Data scientists are familiar with the steps of feature engineering, such as **scaling numeric features, encoding categorical features,** and **dimensionality reduction**.

As motivation, let's consider our weather dataset. What if our input dataset is imbalanced or not really representative of the data we'll encounter in production? Our model will not be as accurate as we'd like, and the consequences can be profound. Some facial recognition systems have been trained on datasets weighted toward white faces, with distressing consequences (`https://sitn.hms.harvard.edu/flash/2020/racial-discrimination-in-face-recognition-technology/?web=1&wdLOR=cB09A9880-DF39-442C-A728-B00E70AF1CA9`).

We need to understand what input features are affecting the model. That's important from a business standpoint as well as a legal or regulatory standpoint. Consider a model that predicts operational outages for an application. Understanding why outages happen is perhaps more valuable than predicting when an outage will occur – is the problem in our application or due to some external factor such as a network hiccup? Then, in some industries such as financial services, we cannot use a model without being able to demonstrate that it doesn't violate regulations against discriminatory lending, say.

The smaller version of our dataset (covering 1 month) is about 5 GB of data. We can analyze that dataset on a modern workstation without too much difficulty. But what about the full dataset, which is closer to 500 GB? If we want to prepare the full dataset, we need to work with horizontally scalable cluster computing frameworks. Furthermore, activities such as encoding categorical variables can take quite some time if we use inefficient processing frameworks.

In this chapter, we'll look at the challenges involved in data preparation when processing a large dataset and examining the **SageMaker** features that help us with large-scale feature engineering.

In this chapter, we will cover the following topics:

- Visual data preparation with Data Wrangler
- Bias detection and explainability with Data Wrangler
- Data preparation at scale with SageMaker Processing

Technical requirements

You will need an AWS account to run the examples included in this chapter. If you have not set up the data science environment yet, please refer to *Chapter 2, Data Science Environments*, which walks you through the setup process.

The code examples included in the book are available on GitHub at `https://github.com/PacktPublishing/Amazon-SageMaker-Best-Practices/tree/main/Chapter04`. You will need to install a Git client to access them (`https://git-scm.com/`).

The code for this chapter is in the `CH04` folder of the GitHub repository.

Visual data preparation with Data Wrangler

Let's start small with our 1-month dataset. Working with a small dataset is a good way to get familiar with the data before diving into more scalable techniques. SageMaker Data Wrangler gives us an easy way to construct a data flow, a series of data preparation steps powered by a visual interface.

In the rest of this section, we'll use Data Wrangler to inspect and transform data, and then export the Data Wrangler steps into a reusable flow.

Data inspection

Let's get started with Data Wrangler for data inspection, where we look at the properties of our data and determine how to prepare it for model training. Begin by adding a new flow in SageMaker Studio; go to the **File** menu, then **New**, then **Flow**. After the flow starts up and connects to Data Wrangler, we need to import our data. The following screenshot shows the data import step in Data Wrangler:

Figure 4.1 – Import data source in Data Wrangler

Because our dataset consists of multiple small JSON files scattered in date-partitioned folders, we'll use **Athena** (a managed version of **Presto**) for the import. The PrepareData.ipynb notebook walks you through creating a Glue database and table and registering the partitions in the section called Glue Catalog. Once that's done, click on **Athena** to start importing the small dataset.

On the next screen, specify the database you created in the notebook. Enter the following query to import 1 month's worth of data:

```
select * from openaq where aggdate like '2019-01%'
```

The following screenshot shows the import step in Data Wrangler:

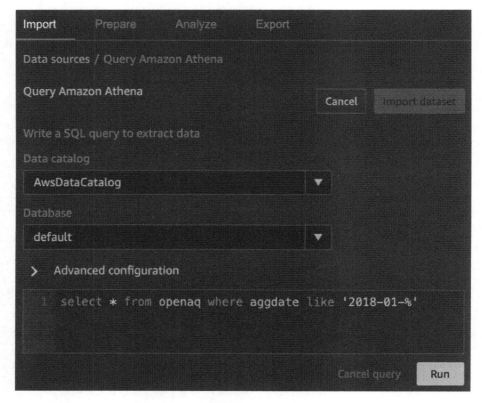

Figure 4.2 – Athena import into Data Wrangler

Run the query and click on **Import dataset**.

Now we're ready to perform some analysis and transformation. Click the + symbol next to the last box in the data flow and select **Add analysis**. You'll now have a screen where you can choose one of the available analyses, as you can see in the following screenshot:

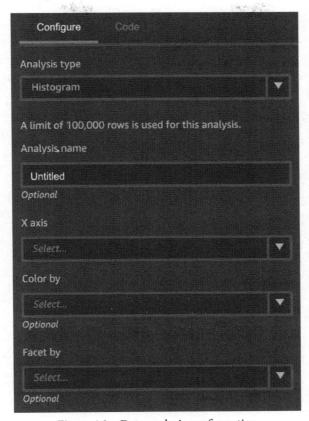

Figure 4.3 – Data analysis configuration

Start with a **Table summary** step, which shows some statistical properties of numeric features, as you can see in the following screenshot:

Create Analysis

Create an analysis of your data. Learn more. ☐

Table Summary: Summary

summary	parameter	location	unit	city
count	50000	50000	50000	50000
mean	None	None	None	None
stddev	None	None	None	None
min	bc	21 de Mayo	ppm	A Coruña
max	so2	龙赛医院	µg/m³	高雄市

Figure 4.4 – Table summary

Next, let's try a scatter plot to help us visualize the distribution of the measurement values. Set the y axis to `value`, the x axis to `aggdate`, color by `country`, and facet by `parameter`. We can see in the following preview chart that the value for nitrogen dioxide is relatively steady over time, while the value for carbon monoxide shows more variability for some countries:

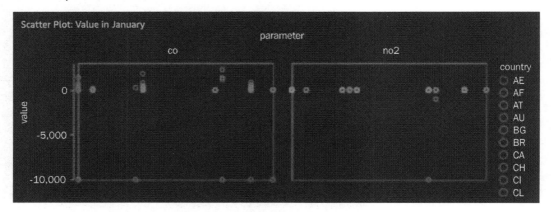

Figure 4.5 – Scatter plot showing measurement values by date, color-coded by country, and faceted by parameter

Feel free to add more scatter plots or try a histogram. We'll explore the bias report and quick mode in the *Bias detection and explainability with Data Wrangler and Clarify* section.

Now that we've done some basic data inspection, we move on to data transformation.

Data transformation

In this section, we will convert the data from the raw format into a format usable for model training. Recall the basic format of our raw data:

```
{"date":{"utc":"2021-03-20T19:00:00.000Z","local":"2021-03-
20T23:00:00+04:00"},"parameter":"pm25","value":32,"unit":"µg/
m³","averagingPeriod":{"val
```

```
ue":1,"unit":"hours"},"location":"US Diplomatic
Post:Dubai","city":"Dubai","country":"AE","coordinates":
{"latitude":25.25848,"longitude":55.309166
```

```
},"attribution":[{"name":"EPA AirNow DOS","url":
"http://airnow.gov/index.cfm?action=airnow.global_
summary"}],"sourceName":"StateAir_Dubai","sourceT
```

```
ype":"government","mobile":false}
```

We'll perform the following steps using Data Wrangler:

- Scale numeric values.

- Encode categorical values.

- Add features related to the date (for example, day of the week, day in a month).

- Drop unwanted columns (`source name`, `coordinates`, `averaging period`, `attribution`, `units`, and `location`). These columns are either redundant (for example, the important part of the location is in the city and country columns) or not usable as features.

Back to the *Preparation* part of the flow, click the + symbol next to the last box in the data flow panel and select **Add Transform**. You'll see a preview of the dataset and a list of the available transforms as follows:

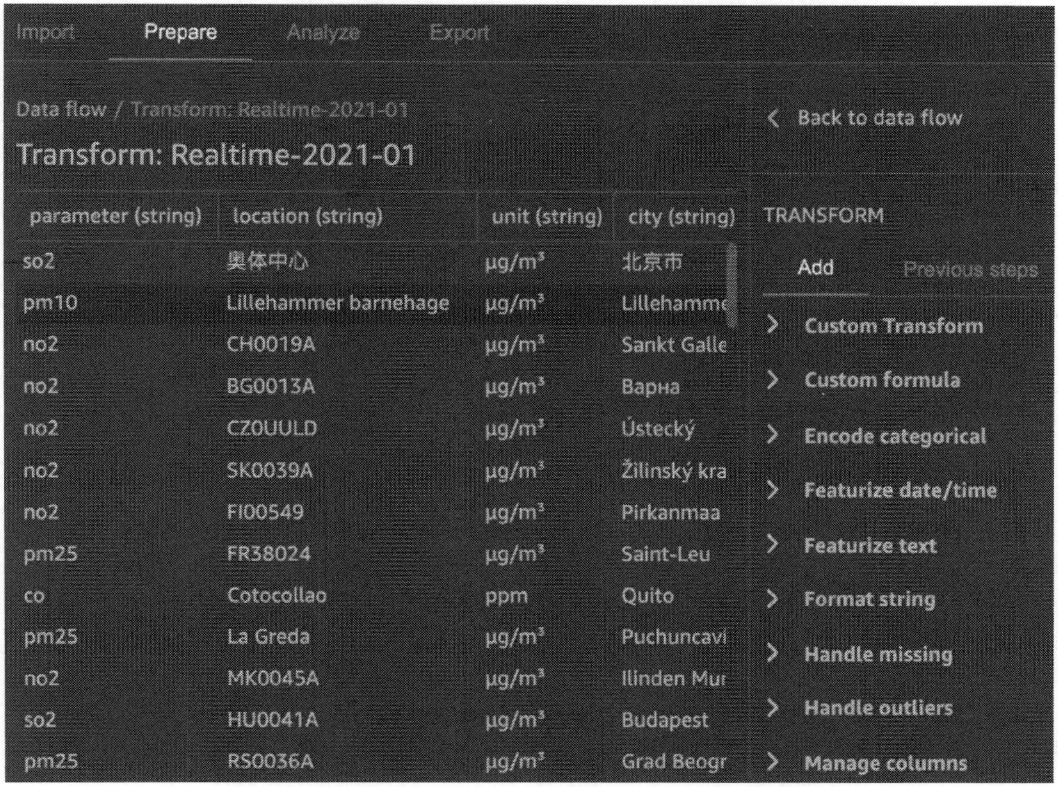

parameter (string)	location (string)	unit (string)	city (string)
so2	奥体中心	µg/m³	北京市
pm10	Lillehammer barnehage	µg/m³	Lillehamme
no2	CH0019A	µg/m³	Sankt Galle
no2	BG0013A	µg/m³	Варна
no2	CZOUULD	µg/m³	Ústecký
no2	SK0039A	µg/m³	Žilinský kra
no2	FI00549	µg/m³	Pirkanmaa
pm25	FR38024	µg/m³	Saint-Leu
co	Cotocollao	ppm	Quito
pm25	La Greda	µg/m³	Puchuncavi
no2	MK0045A	µg/m³	Ilinden Mur
so2	HU0041A	µg/m³	Budapest
pm25	RS0036A	µg/m³	Grad Beogr

TRANSFORM

Add   Previous steps

> Custom Transform
> Custom formula
> Encode categorical
> Featurize date/time
> Featurize text
> Format string
> Handle missing
> Handle outliers
> Manage columns

Figure 4.6 – Data transformations in Data Wrangler

For our first transformation, select **Encode categorical**. In the transformation options panel, pick **One-hot encode** as the transformation, specify sourcetype as the column, set **Output Style** to **Columns**, and add a prefix for the new column names:

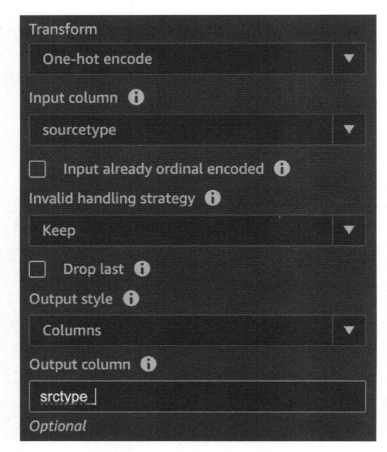

Figure 4.7 – One-hot encoding in Data Wrangler

When you're done setting up the transformation, click **Preview** and then **Add** to add the transform. You can now add additional transformations to drop the unwanted columns, scale the numeric columns, and featurize the date. You can also provide your own custom code if you like.

Exporting the flow

Data Wrangler is very handy when we want to quickly explore a dataset. But we can also export the results of a flow into Amazon SageMaker **Feature Store**, generate a **SageMaker pipeline**, create a Data Wrangler job, or generate **Python** code. We will not use these capabilities now, but feel free to experiment with them.

Bias detection and explainability with Data Wrangler and Clarify

Now that we've done some initial work in exploring and preparing our data, let's do a sanity check on our input data. While bias can mean many things, one particular symptom is a dataset that has many more samples of one type of data than another, which will affect our model's performance. We'll use Data Wrangler to see if our input data is imbalanced and understand which features are most important to our model.

To begin, add an analysis to the flow. Choose **Bias Report** from the list of available transformations and use the `mobile` column as the label, with `1` as the predicted value. Choose `city` as the column to use for bias analysis, then click **Check for bias**. In this scenario, we want to determine whether our dataset is somehow imbalanced with respect to the city and whether the data was collected at a mobile station. If the quality of data from mobile sources is inferior to non-mobile sources, it'd be good to know if the mobile sources are unevenly distributed among cities.

Next, we'll examine **feature importance**. Feature importance is one aspect of model explainability. We want to understand which parts of the dataset are most important to model behavior. Another aspect, which we'll visit in *Chapter 11, Monitoring Production Models with Amazon SageMaker Model Monitor and Clarify*, in the *Monitor bias drift and feature importance drift using Amazon SageMaker Clarify* section, is understanding which features contributed to a specific inference.

Add another analysis in the last step of the flow. Select **Quick Model** for the `value` column (Data Wrangler will infer that this is a regression problem). Preview and create the analysis. You should see a screen that looks similar to the following screenshot:

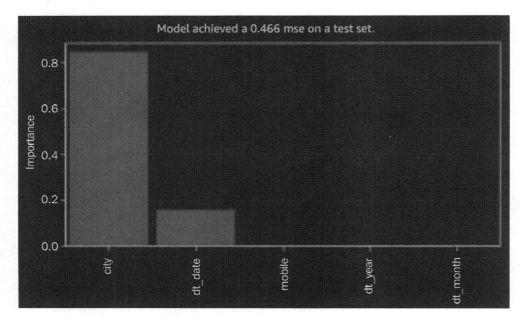

Figure 4.8 – Feature importance generated by Data Wrangler

This analysis generates a random forest model, evaluates performance using a test set with 30% of the data, and calculates a **Gini importance score** for each feature. As you can see in *Figure 4.8*, the city and day of the month are the most important features.

So far we've used Data Wrangler for visual inspection and transformation. Now, we'll look at how to handle larger datasets using SageMaker Processing.

Data preparation at scale with SageMaker Processing

Now let's turn our attention to preparing the entire dataset. At 500 GB, it's too large to process using `sklearn` on a single EC2 instance. We will write a SageMaker processing job that uses **Spark ML** for data preparation. (Alternatively, you can use **Dask**, but at the time of writing, SageMaker Processing does not provide a Dask container out of the box.)

The `Processing Job` part of this chapter's notebook walks you through launching the processing job. Note that we'll use a cluster of 15 EC2 instances to run the job (if you need limits raised, you can contact AWS support).

Also note that up until now, we've been working with the uncompressed JSON version of the data. This format containing thousands of small JSON files is not ideal for Spark processing as the **Spark executors** will spend a lot of time doing I/O. Luckily, the OpenAQ dataset also includes a **gzipped Parquet version** of the data. Compression will save on storage space and is a good idea unless our processing job is CPU-bound rather than I/O-bound. Note, however, that gzip is not a preferred compression format as it is not splittable; if you have a choice, use the Snappy compression format.

We will use the gzipped Parquet version of our data for the larger data preparation job:

1. First, we will define the processor class, using **Spark 3.0**. We will set the max runtime to 7200 seconds (2 hours). Two hours is more than sufficient to process at least one of the 8 tables in the Parquet dataset. If you want to process all eight of them, change the timeout to 3 hours and make an adjustment in the preprocess. py script:

```
spark_processor = PySparkProcessor(
    base_job_name="spark-preprocessor",
    framework_version="3.0",
    role=role,
    instance_count=15,
    instance_type="ml.m5.4xlarge",
    max_runtime_in_seconds=7200,
)
```

2. Next, we'll set the Spark configuration, following the formulas defined in an EMR blog (https://aws.amazon.com/blogs/big-data/best-practices-for-successfully-managing-memory-for-apache-spark-applications-on-amazon-emr/):

```
configuration = [
    {
        "Classification": "spark-defaults",
        "Properties": {"spark.executor.memory": "18g",
            "spark.yarn.executor.memoryOverhead": "3g",
            "spark.driver.memory": "18g",
            "spark.yarn.driver.memoryOverhead": "3g",
            "spark.executor.cores": "5",
            "spark.driver.cores": "5",
            "spark.executor.instances": "44",
```

```
                          "spark.default.parallelism": "440",
                "spark.dynamicAllocation.enabled": "false"
                           },
            },
            {
        "Classification": "yarn-site",
        "Properties": {"yarn.nodemanager.vmem-check-enabled":
"false",
            "yarn.nodemanager.mmem-check-enabled": "false"},
        }
    ]
```

3. Finally, we'll launch the job. We need to include a JSON `serde` class:

```
spark_processor.run(
    submit_app="scripts/preprocess.py",
    submit_jars=["s3://crawler-public/json/serde/json-
serde.jar"],
    arguments=['--s3_input_bucket', s3_bucket,
               '--s3_input_key_prefix', s3_prefix_parquet,
               '--s3_output_bucket', s3_bucket,
               '--s3_output_key_prefix', s3_output_prefix],
    spark_event_logs_s3_uri="s3://{}/{}/spark_event_
logs".format(s3_bucket, 'sparklogs'),
    logs=True,
    configuration=configuration
)
```

The processing script, `CH04/scripts/preprocess.py`, walks through several steps, which we'll explain in the subsequent sections.

Loading the dataset

We will load one or more of the Parquet table sets from S3. If you want to process more than one, modify the get_tables function to return more table names in the list as follows:

```
# the helper function `get_tables` lists the tables we want to
include
tables = get_tables()
df = spark.read.parquet(
    f"s3://{args.s3_input_bucket}/" +
    f"{args.s3_input_key_prefix}/{tables[0]}/")
for t in tables[1:]:
    df_new = spark.read.parquet(
        f"s3://{args.s3_input_bucket}/" +
        f"{args.s3_input_key_prefix}/{t}/")
    df = df.union(df_new)
```

The next step in the processing script is dropping unnecessary columns from the dataset.

Drop columns

We'll repeat most of the steps we did in Data Wrangler using **PySpark**. We need to drop some columns that we don't want, as follows:

```
df = df.drop('date_local') \
.drop('unit') \
.drop('attribution') \
.drop('averagingperiod') \
.drop('coordinates')
```

Converting data types

We'll convert the mobile field to an integer:

```
df = df.withColumn("ismobile",col("mobile").
cast(IntegerType())) \
.drop('mobile')
```

Scaling numeric fields

We'll use the Spark ML standard scaler to transform the value field:

```
value_assembler = VectorAssembler(inputCols=["value"],
outputCol="value_vec")
value_scaler = StandardScaler(inputCol="value_vec",
outputCol="value_scaled")
value_pipeline = Pipeline(stages=[value_assembler, value_
scaler])
value_model = value_pipeline.fit(df)
xform_df = value_model.transform(df)
```

Featurizing the date

The date by itself isn't that useful, so we'll extract several new features from it indicating the day, month, quarter, and year:

```
xform_df = xform_df.withColumn('aggdt',
              to_date(unix_timestamp(col('date_utc'),
"yyyy-MM-dd'T'HH:mm:ss.SSSX").cast("timestamp")))
xform_df = xform_df.withColumn('year',year(xform_df.aggdt)) \
      .withColumn('month',month(xform_df.aggdt)) \
      .withColumn('quarter',quarter(xform_df.aggdt))
xform_df = xform_df.withColumn("day", date_format(col("aggdt"),
"d"))
```

Simulating labels for air quality

Although we used ground truth in *Chapter 3, Data Labeling with Amazon SageMaker Ground Truth*, for labeling, for the sake of this demonstration we'll use a simple heuristic to assign these labels instead:

```
isBadAirUdf = udf(isBadAir, IntegerType())
xform_df = xform_df.withColumn('isBadAir', isBadAirUdf('value',
'parameter'))
```

Encoding categorical variables

Now we'll encode the categorical features. Most of these features have fairly high cardinality, so we'll perform ordinal encoding here and learn embeddings later in our training process. We will only use one-hot encoding for the parameter, which only has seven possible choices:

```
parameter_indexer = StringIndexer(inputCol="parameter", \
outputCol="indexed_parameter", handleInvalid='keep')
location_indexer = StringIndexer(inputCol="location", \
outputCol="indexed_location", handleInvalid='keep')
city_indexer = StringIndexer(inputCol="city", \
outputCol="indexed_city", handleInvalid='keep')
country_indexer = StringIndexer(inputCol="country", \
outputCol="indexed_country", handleInvalid='keep')
sourcename_indexer = StringIndexer(inputCol="sourcename", \
outputCol="indexed_sourcename", handleInvalid='keep')
sourcetype_indexer = StringIndexer(inputCol="sourcetype", \
outputCol="indexed_sourcetype", handleInvalid='keep')
enc_est = OneHotEncoder(inputCols=["indexed_parameter"], \
outputCols=["vec_parameter"])
enc_pipeline = Pipeline(stages=[parameter_indexer, location_
indexer,
        city_indexer, country_indexer, sourcename_indexer,
        sourcetype_indexer, enc_est])
enc_model = enc_pipeline.fit(xform_df)
enc_df = enc_model.transform(xform_df)
param_cols = enc_df.schema.fields[17].metadata['ml_attr']
['vals']
```

Splitting and saving the dataset

After some final cleanup of the dataset, we can split the dataset into train, validation, and test sets, and save them to S3:

```
(train_df, validation_df, test_df) = final_df.randomSplit([0.7,
0.2, 0.1])
train_df.write.option("header",True).csv('s3://' + \
os.path.join(args.s3_output_bucket,
      args.s3_output_key_prefix, 'train/'))
validation_df.write.option("header",True).csv('s3://' + \
os.path.join(args.s3_output_bucket,
      args.s3_output_key_prefix, 'validation/'))
test_df.write.option("header",True).csv('s3://' + \
os.path.join(args.s3_output_bucket,
      args.s3_output_key_prefix, 'test/'))
```

In this section, we saw how to use a SageMaker Processing job to perform data preparation on a larger dataset using Apache Spark. In the field, many datasets are large enough to require a distributed processing framework, and now you understand how to integrate a Spark job into your SageMaker workflow.

Summary

In this chapter, we tackled feature engineering for a large (~ 500 GB) dataset. We looked at challenges including scalability, bias, and explainability. We saw how to use SageMaker Data Wrangler, Clarify, and Processing jobs to explore and prepare data.

While there are many ways to use these tools, we recommend using Data Wrangler for interactive exploration of small to mid-sized datasets. For processing large datasets in their entirety, switch to programmatic use of processing jobs using the Spark framework to take advantage of parallel processing. (At the time of writing, Data Wrangler does not support running on multiple instances, but you can run a processing job on multiple instances.) You can always export a Data Wrangler flow as a starting point.

If your dataset is many terabytes, consider running a Spark job directly in **EMR** or Glue and invoking SageMaker using the SageMaker Spark SDK. EMR and Glue have optimized Spark runtimes and more efficient integration with S3 storage.

At this point, we have our data ready for model training. In the next chapter, we'll explore using Amazon SageMaker Feature Store to help us manage prepared feature data.

5
Centralized Feature Repository with Amazon SageMaker Feature Store

Let's begin with the basic questions – what is a feature store and why is it necessary? A feature store is a repository that persists engineered features. A lot of time goes into feature engineering, sometimes involving multi-step data processing pipelines executed over hours of compute time. ML models depend on these engineered features that often come from a variety of data sources. A feature store accelerates this process by reducing repetitive data processing that is required to convert raw data into features. A feature store not only allows you to share engineered features during model-building activities, but also allows consistency in using engineered features for inference.

Amazon SageMaker Feature Store is a managed repository with capabilities to store, update, retrieve, and share features. SageMaker Feature Store provides the ability to reuse the engineered features in two different scenarios. First, the features can be shared between the training and inference phases of a single ML project resulting in consistent model inputs and reduced training-serving skew. Second, features from SageMaker

Feature Store can also be shared across multiple ML projects, leading to improved data scientist productivity.

By the end of this chapter, you will be able to use Amazon SageMaker Feature Store capabilities and apply best practices to implement solutions to address the challenges of reducing data processing time and architecting features for near real-time ML inferences.

In this chapter, we are going to cover the following main topics:

- Basic concepts of Amazon SageMaker Feature Store
- Creating reusable features to reduce feature inconsistencies and inference latency
- Designing solutions for near real-time ML predictions

Technical requirements

You will need an AWS account to run the examples included in this chapter. If you have not set up the data science environment yet, please refer to *Chapter 2, Data Science Environments*, which provides a walk-through of the setup process.

Code examples included in the book are available on GitHub at `https://github.com/PacktPublishing/Amazon-SageMaker-Best-Practices/tree/main/Chapter05`. You will need to install a Git client to access them (`https://git-scm.com/`).

Amazon SageMaker Feature Store essentials

In this section, you will learn the basic terminology and capabilities of Amazon SageMaker Feature Store. Amazon SageMaker Feature Store provides a centralized repository with capabilities to store, update, retrieve, and share features. Scalable storage and near real-time feature retrieval are at the heart of Amazon SageMaker Feature Store. Utilizing Amazon SageMaker Feature Store involves three high-level steps, as shown in the following diagram:

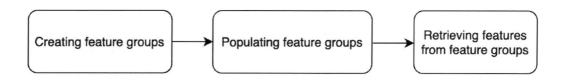

Figure 5.1 – High-level steps with Amazon SageMaker Feature Store

Let's see what is involved in each of these steps in a bit more detail.

Creating feature groups

In Amazon SageMaker Feature Store, features are stored in a collection called a **feature group**. A feature group, in turn, is composed of records of features and feature values. Each record is a collection of feature values, identified by a unique `RecordIdentifier` value. Every record belonging to a feature group will use the same feature as `RecordIdentifier`. For example, the record identifier for the feature store created for the weather data could be `parameter_id` or `location_id`. Think of `RecordIdentifier` as a primary key for the feature group. Using this primary key, you can query feature groups for the fast lookup of features. It's also important to note that each record of a feature group must, at a minimum, contain a `RecordIdentifier` and an event time feature. The event time feature is identified by `EventTimeFeatureName` when a feature group is set up. When a feature record is ingested into a feature group, SageMaker adds three features – `is_deleted`, `api_invocation` time, and `write_ time` – for each feature record. `is_deleted` is used to manage the deletion of records, `api_invocation_time` is the time when the API call is invoked to write a record to a feature store, and `write_time` is the time when the feature record is persisted to the offline store.

Figure 5.2 shows a high-level view of how a feature store is structured:

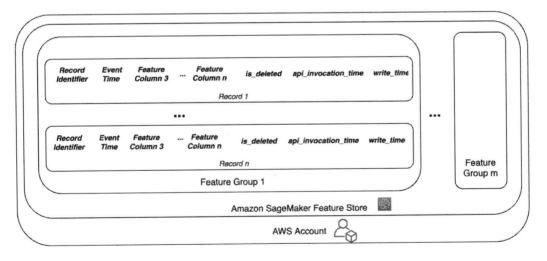

Figure 5.2 – Amazon SageMaker feature store structure

While each feature group is managed and scaled independently, you can search and discover features from multiple feature groups as long as the appropriate access is in place.

When you create a feature store group with SageMaker, you can choose to enable an offline store, online store, or both. When both online and offline stores are enabled, the service replicates the online store contents into the offline store maintained in Amazon S3.

The following code blocks show the process of creating a feature store:

1. First define the feature group name:

```
#Feature group name
weather_feature_group_name_offline = 'weather-feature-
group-offline' + strftime('%d-%H-%M-%S', gmtime())
```

2. Then, create the feature definitions that capture the feature name and the type:

```
##Create FeatureDefinitions
fd_location=FeatureDefinition(feature_name='location',
feature_type=FeatureTypeEnum('Integral'))
fd_event_time=FeatureDefinition(feature_name='EventTime',
feature_type=FeatureTypeEnum('Fractional'))
...


weather_feature_definitions = []
weather_feature_definitions.append(fd_location)
weather_feature_definitions.append(fd_event_time)
...
```

3. Next, define the record identifier feature:

```
##Define unique identifier
record_identifier_feature_name = "location"
```

4. Finally, create the feature group using the create() API, which, by default, creates a feature group with an offline store:

```
#Create offline feature group
weather_feature_group_offline =        \
    FeatureGroup(name=weather_feature_group_name_offline,
        feature_definitions=weather_feature_definitions,
            sagemaker_session=sagemaker_session)
weather_feature_group_offline.create(
        s3_uri=f"s3://{s3_bucket_name}/{prefix}",
        record_identifier_name="location",
```

```
        event_time_feature_name="EventTime",
        role_arn=role
)
```

5. To enable an online store in addition to an offline store, use enable_online_store, as shown in the following code:

```
weather_feature_group_offline_online.create(
        s3_uri=f"s3://{s3_bucket_name}/{prefix}",
    record_identifier_name="location",
        event_time_feature_name="EventTime",
        role_arn=role,
        enable_online_store=True
)
```

6. To create a feature group with only an online store enabled, set s3_uri to False, as shown in the following code:

```
weather_feature_group_online.create(
        s3_uri=False,
        record_identifier_name="location",
        event_time_feature_name="EventTime",
        role_arn=role,
        enable_online_store=True
)
```

Note that you can also create a feature group using **SageMaker Studio**. Once feature groups are created either using the APIs or SageMaker Studio, you can view them along with their status in SageMaker Studio. *Figure 5.3* shows a list of feature groups in SageMaker Studio:

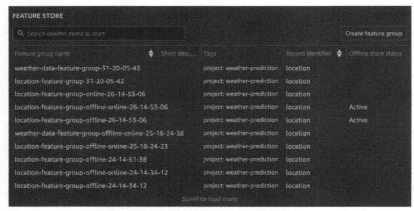

Figure 5.3 – Feature groups list in SageMaker Studio

To wrap up the feature group creation discussion, the following table summarizes the differences between the online and offline feature stores:

	Online feature store	**Offline feature store**
Primary use	Real-time predictions such as real-time fraud detection	Batch predictions and training models
Feature data versions	Only maintains the latest version of feature data	Maintains a historical record of all versions of the feature data
Access to underlying storage	Only accessible through the Feature Store APIs	Accessible through Feature Store APIs and directly from an S3 bucket
Write throughput	High-throughput writes	High-throughput writes
Read latency	Latency reads of a few milliseconds	S3 latency in tens to hundreds of milliseconds, with < 15 min read after write latency

Figure 5.4 – Comparison of online and offline feature stores

Now that you can create feature groups in the feature store, let's take a look at how to populate them.

Populating feature groups

After creating the feature groups, you will populate them with features. You can ingest features into a feature group using either **batch ingestion** or **streaming ingestion**, as shown in *Figure 5.5*:

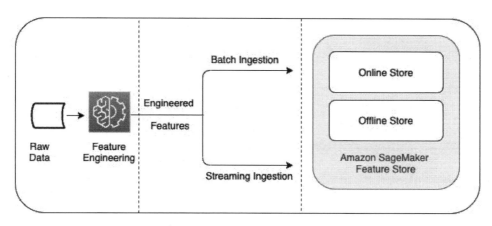

Figure 5.5 – Ingesting features into feature groups

To ingest features into the feature store, you create a feature pipeline that can populate the feature store. A **feature pipeline** can include any service or capability that accepts raw data and then transforms that raw data into engineered features and puts the features in a designated feature group. Features can be ingested either in bulk in batches or streamed individually. The PutRecord API call is the core SageMaker API for ingesting features. This is used for both online and offline feature stores as well as ingesting through batch or streaming methods.

The following code block shows the usage of the PutRecord API:

```
##Create a record to ingest into the feature group
record = []
event_time_feature = {'FeatureName':
'EventTime','ValueAsString': str(int(round(time.time())))}
location_feature =   {'FeatureName':
'location','ValueAsString': str('200.0')}
ismobile_feature
=   {'FeatureName':   'ismobile','ValueAsString': str('0')}
```

```
value_feature ={'FeatureName': 'value','ValueAsString':
str('34234.0')}
```

```
record.append(event_time_feature)
```

```
record.append(location_feature)
```

```
record.append(ismobile_feature)
```

```
record.append(value_feature)
```

```
response = sagemaker_fs_runtime_client.put_record(
        FeatureGroupName=weather_feature_group_online,
                                        Record=record)
```

You can also use a wrapper API, fg.ingest, which takes in a pandas dataframe as input and allows you to configure multiple workers and processes to ingest features in parallel. The following code block shows how to use the ingest() API:

```
#Read csv directly from S3 into a dataframe
weather_df = pd.read_csv(s3_path)
```

```
#Ingest features into the feature group
weather_feature_group_offline.ingest(
        data_frame=weather_df, max_workers=3, wait=True
)
```

For batch ingestion, you can author features (for example, using **Amazon Data Wrangler**) and ingest features in batches using a **SageMaker Processing** job. This allows batch ingestion into the offline store and the online store. For streaming ingestion, records can be pushed synchronously using the PutRecord API call. When ingesting records to the online feature store, you maintain only the latest feature values for a given record identifier. Historical values are only maintained in the replicated offline store if the feature group is configured for both online and offline stores. *Figure 5.6* outlines the methods to ingest features as they relate to the online and offline feature stores:

Ingestion Method	Ingestion Type		Feature Group Type	
	Batch	Streaming	Online	Offline
SageMaker API: PutRecord (https://docs.aws.amazon.com/ sagemaker/latest/APIReference/ API_feature_store_PutRecord. html) The base API used for data ingestion.	Yes	Yes	Yes	Yes
SageMaker Python SDK: The ingest() method (https://sagemaker.readthedocs. io/en/stable/api/prep_data/ feature_store.html) The method that uses the underlying PutRecord API to ingest records into a pandas DataFrame and uses multiple workers/processes to put records.	Yes	Yes	Yes	Yes
SageMaker Processing Job (PySpark) (https://docs.aws.amazon.com/ sagemaker/latest/dg/feature- store-ingest-data.html#feature- store-data-wrangler- integration) Provided by SageMaker Data Wrangler to ingest batched data using PySpark parallelism.	Yes	No	Yes	Yes
Put to S3 Directly populate S3 for offline stores. Use caution with this option but it represents a common approach for backfilling data.	Yes	No	No	Yes

Figure 5.6 – Ingesting feature store records

With the ingestion APIs in hand, let's take a look at a generic batch ingestion architecture. *Figure 5.7* shows the architecture for batch ingestion with **Amazon SageMaker Processing**:

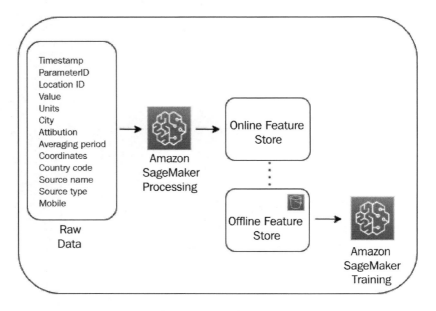

Figure 5.7 – Batch ingestion with SageMaker Processing

Here are the high-level steps involved in the batch ingestion architecture:

1. Bulk raw data is available in an S3 bucket.

2. The Amazon SageMaker Processing job takes raw data as input and applies feature engineering techniques to the data. The processing job can be configured to run on a distributed cluster of instances to process data at scale.

3. The processing job also ingests the engineered features ingested into the online store of the feature group, using the PutRecord API. Features are then automatically replicated to the offline store of the feature group.

4. Features from the offline store can then be used for training other models and by other data science teams to address a wide variety of other use cases. Features from the online store can be used for feature lookup during real-time predictions.

Note that if the feature store used in this architecture is offline only, the processing job can directly write into the offline store using the PutRecord API.

Next, let's take a look at a possible streaming ingestion architecture in *Figure 5.8*. This should look very similar to batch ingestions, except instead of using a processing job, you use a single compute instance or an **AWS Lambda function**:

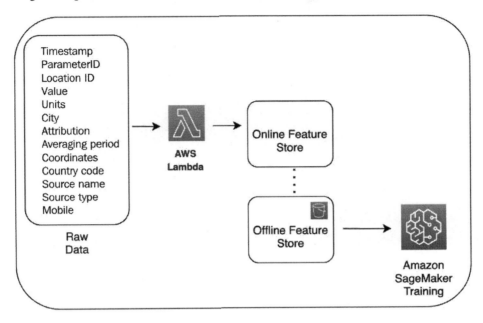

Figure 5.8 – Streaming ingestion with AWS Lambda

Here are the high-level steps involved in the streaming ingestion architecture:

1. Raw data lands in an S3 bucket, which triggers an AWS Lambda function.

2. The Lambda function processes data and inserts features into the online store of the feature group, using the `PutRecord` API.

3. Features are then automatically replicated to the offline store of the feature group.

4. Features from the offline store can then be used for training other models and by other data science teams to address a wide variety of other use cases. Features from the online store can be used for feature lookup during real-time predictions.

In addition to using the ingestion APIs to populate the offline store, you can populate the underlying S3 bucket directly. If you don't have a need for real-time inference and have huge volumes of historical feature data (terabytes or even hundreds of gigabytes) that you want to migrate to an offline feature store to be used for training models, you can directly upload them to the underlying S3 bucket. To do this effectively, it is important to understand the S3 folder structure of the offline bucket. Feature groups in the offline store are organized in the structure s3:

```
s3://<bucket-name>/<customer-prefix>/<account-id>/
sagemaker/<aws-region>/offline-store/<feature-group-name>-
<feature-group-creation-time>/data/year=<event-time-year>/
month=<event-time-month>/day=<event-time-day>/hour=<event-
time-hour>/<timestamp_of_latest_event_time_in_file>_<16-random-
alphanumeric-digits>.parquet
```

Also note that, when you use ingestion APIs, the features isdeleted, api_invocation_time, and write-time are included automatically in the feature record, but when you write directly to the offline store, you are responsible for including them.

Retrieving features from feature groups

Once feature groups are populated, to retrieve features from the feature store, there are two APIs available – get_record and batch_get_record. The following code block shows retrieving a single record from a feature group using the get_record API:

```
record_identifier_value = str('300')
response = sagemaker_fs_runtime_client.get_record
(FeatureGroupName=weather_feature_group_name_online,
RecordIdentifierValueAsString=record_identifier_value)
response
Response from the code block looks similar to the following
figure:
{'ResponseMetadata': {'RequestId': '195debf2-3b10-4116-98c7-
142dc13e9df3',
  'HTTPStatusCode': 200,
  'HTTPHeaders': {'x-amzn-requestid': '195debf2-3b10-4116-98c7-
142dc13e9df3',
   'content-type': 'application/json',
   'content-length': '214',
   'date': 'Wed, 14 Jul 2021 04:27:11 GMT'},
```

```
  'RetryAttempts': 0},
 'Record': [{'FeatureName': 'value', 'ValueAsString':
'4534.0'},
   {'FeatureName': 'ismobile', 'ValueAsString': '0'},
   {'FeatureName': 'location', 'ValueAsString': '300'},
   {'FeatureName': 'EventTime', 'ValueAsString': '1626236799'}]}
```

Similarly, the following code shows retrieving multiple records from one or more feature groups using the batch_get_record API:

```
record_identifier_values = ["200", "250", "300"]
response=sagemaker_fs_runtime_client.batch_get_record(
            Identifiers=[
          {"FeatureGroupName": weather_feature_group_name_
online, "RecordIdentifiersValueAsString": record_identifier_
values}
            ]
)
response
```

The response from the code block should look similar to the following response:

```
{'ResponseMetadata': {'RequestId': '3c3e1f5f-3a65-4b54-aa18-
8683c83962c5',
  'HTTPStatusCode': 200,
  'HTTPHeaders': {'x-amzn-requestid': '3c3e1f5f-3a65-4b54-aa18-
8683c83962c5',
   'content-type': 'application/json',
   'content-length': '999',
   'date': 'Wed, 14 Jul 2021 04:29:47 GMT'},
  'RetryAttempts': 0},
 'Records': [{'FeatureGroupName': 'weather-feature-group-
online-13-19-23-46',
   'RecordIdentifierValueAsString': '300',
   'Record': [{'FeatureName': 'value', 'ValueAsString':
'4534.0'},
           {'FeatureName': 'ismobile', 'ValueAsString': '0'},
           {'FeatureName': 'location', 'ValueAsString': '300'},
           {'FeatureName': 'EventTime', 'ValueAsString':
'1626236799'}]},
```

```
    {'FeatureGroupName': 'weather-feature-group-
online-13-19-23-46',
    'RecordIdentifierValueAsString': '200',
    'Record': [{'FeatureName': 'value', 'ValueAsString':
'34234.0'},
            {'FeatureName': 'ismobile', 'ValueAsString': '0'},
          {'FeatureName': 'location', 'ValueAsString': '200'},
        {'FeatureName': 'EventTime', 'ValueAsString':
'1626236410'}]}],
 'Errors': [],
 'UnprocessedIdentifiers': []}
```

The get_record and batch_get_record APIs should be used with online stores. Additionally, since the underlying storage for an offline store is an S3 bucket, you can query the offline store directly using Athena or other ways of accessing S3. The following code shows a sample Athena query that retrieves all feature records directly from the S3 bucket supporting the offline store:

```
weather_data_query = weather_feature_group.athena_query()
weather_table = weather_data_query.table_name


#Query string
query_string = 'SELECT * FROM "'+ weather_table + '"'
print('Running ' + query_string)


#run Athena query. The output is loaded to a Pandas dataframe.
weather_data_query.run(query_string=query_string, output_
location='s3://'+s3_bucket_name+'/'+prefix+'/query_results/')
weather_data_query.wait()
dataset = weather_data_query.as_dataframe()
```

For the dataset used in this book, we will use two feature groups – location and weather data. The location feature group will have location_id as the record identifier and capture features related to the location such as the city name. The weather data feature group will also have location_id as the record identifier and capture weather quality measurements such as pm25. This allows us to use the feature groups across multiple ML projects.

For example, features from both location and weather data feature groups are used for a regression model to predict future weather measurements for a given location. On the other hand, features from the weather data feature group can also be used for a clustering model to find stations with similar measurements.

> **Important note**
>
> The example notebook provides a walk-through of the key Amazon SageMaker Feature Store APIs for creating a feature group, ingesting features into feature groups, and retrieving features from a feature group. To see all the feature store capabilities in action, we recommend that you execute the sample notebook in the data science environment you set up in *Chapter 2, Data Science Environments*:
>
> ```
> https://gitlab.com/randydefauw/packt_book/-/blob/
> main/CH05/feature_store_apis.ipynb.
> ```

Now that you have learned the capabilities of SageMaker Feature Store, in the next two sections, you will learn how to use these capabilities to solve feature design challenges that data scientists and organizations face.

Creating reusable features to reduce feature inconsistencies and inference latency

One of the challenges data scientists face is the long data processing time – hours and sometimes days – necessary for preparing features to be used for ML training. Additionally, the data processing steps applied in feature engineering need to be applied to the inference requests during prediction time, which increases the inference latency. Each data science team will need to spend this data processing time even when they use the same raw data for different models. In this section, we will discuss best practices to address these challenges by using Amazon SageMaker Feature Store.

For use cases that require low latency features for inference, an online feature store should be configured, and it's generally recommended to enable both the online and offline feature store. A feature store enabled with both online and offline stores allows you to reuse the same feature values for the training and inference phases. This configuration reduces the inconsistencies between the two phases and minimizes training and inference skew. In this mode, to populate the store, ingest features into the online store either using batch or streaming.

As you ingest features into an online store, SageMaker automatically replicates feature values to an offline store, continuously appending the latest values. It's important to note that for the online feature store, only the most current feature record is maintained and the `PutRecord` API is always processed as `insert/upsert`. This is key because if you need to update a feature record, the process to do so is to re-insert or overlay the existing record. This is to allow the retrieval of features with the minimum possible latency for inference use cases.

Although the online feature store maintains only the latest record, the offline store will provide a full history of feature values over time. Records will stay in the offline store until they are explicitly removed. As a result, you should establish a process to prune unnecessary records in the offline feature store using the standard mechanisms provided for S3 archival.

> **Important note**
>
> The example notebook from the GitHub repository shows the end-to-end flow of creating a feature store, ingesting features, retrieving features, and further using the features for training the model, deploying the model, and using the features from the feature store during inference: `https://gitlab.com/ randydefauw/packt_book/-/blob/main/CH04/feature_ store_train_deploy_models.ipynb`.

Another best practice is to set up standards for versioning features. As features evolve, it is important to keep track of feature versions. Consider versioning at two levels – versions of the feature group itself and versions of features within a feature group. You need to create a new version of the feature group for when the schema of the features change, such as when feature definitions need to be added or deleted.

At the time of this book's publication, feature groups are immutable. To add or remove features, you will need to create a new feature group. To address the requirement of multiple versions of a feature group with different numbers of features, establish and stick to naming conventions. For example, you could create a `weather-conditions-v1` feature group initially. When that feature group needs to be updated, you can create a new `weather-conditions-v2` feature group. You can also consider adding descriptive labels on data readiness or usage, such as `weather-conditions-latest-v2` or `weather-conditions-stable-v2`. You also can tag feature groups to provide metadata. Additionally, you should also establish standards for how many concurrent versions to support and when to deprecate old versions.

For the versioning of the individual features, the offline store keeps a history of all values of the features in a feature group. Each feature record is required to have an `eventTime`, which supports the ability to access feature versions by date. To retrieve previous version values of features from the offline store, use an Athena query with a specific timestamp, as shown in the following code block:

```
#Query string with specific date/time
timestamp = int(round(time.time()))
time_based_query_string = f"""
SELECT *
FROM "{weather_table}"
where eventtime <= {timestamp} and city=1080.0
"""
# Run Athena query. The output is loaded to a Pandas dataframe.
weather_query.run(query_string=time_based_query_string, output_
location='s3://'+s3_bucket_name+'/'+prefix+'/query_results/')
weather_query.wait()
dataset = weather_query.as_dataframe()
```

Note that you can further fine-tune the Athena query to include `write-time` and `api_call_time` to extract very specific versions of the features. Please see the references section for a link to a detailed blog on point-in-time queries with SageMaker Feature Store.

Additionally, when a record is deleted from the online store, the corresponding record in the offline store is only logically deleted, which is typically referred to as a tombstone. When you query the offline store, you may see a tombstone in the results. Use the `is_deleted` feature of the record to filter these records from the results.

Now that you have the feature groups created and populated, how do teams in your organization discover and reuse the features? All authorized users of the Amazon SageMaker Feature Store can view and browse through a list of feature groups in a feature store in a SageMaker Studio environment. You can also search for specific feature groups by name, description, record identifier, creation date, and tags, as shown in *Figure 5.9*:

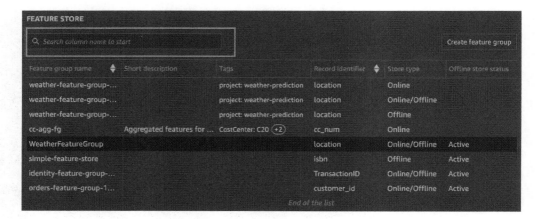

Figure 5.9 – Search and discover feature groups

You can go a step further, view feature definitions of the feature group, and search for specific features as shown in *Figure 5.10*:

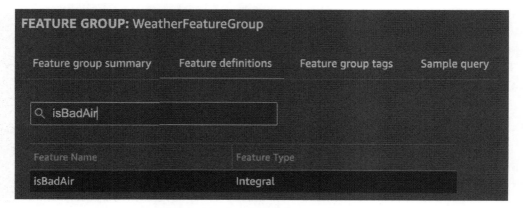

Figure 5.10 – Search and discover features

In the next section, you will learn about designing an ML system that provides near real-time predictions.

Designing solutions for near real-time ML predictions

Sometimes machine learning applications demand high-throughput updates to features and near real-time access to the updated features. Timely access to fast-changing features is critical for the accuracy of predictions made by these applications. As an example, consider a machine learning application in a call center that predicts how to route the incoming customer calls to available agents. This application needs to have knowledge of the customer's latest web session clicks to make accurate routing decisions. If you capture a customer's web-click behavior as features, the features need to be updated instantly and the application needs access to the updated features in near-real time. Similarly, for weather prediction problems, you may want to capture the weather measurement features frequently for accurate weather predictions and need the ability to look up features in real time.

Let's look at some best practices in designing a reliable solution that meets the requirement of high-throughput writes and low-latency reads. At a high level, this solution will couple streaming ingestion into a feature group with streaming predictions. We will discuss the best practices to apply to ingestion into and serving from a feature store.

For ingesting features, the decision to choose between batch and streaming ingestion should be based on how often feature values in the feature store need to be updated for use by downstream training or inference. While simple machine models may need features from a single feature group, if you are working with data from multiple sources, you will find yourself using features from multiple feature groups. Some of these features need to be updated on a periodic basis (hourly, daily, weekly) and others must be streamed in near-real time.

Feature update frequency and inference access patterns should also be used as a consideration for creating different feature groups and isolating features. By isolating features that need to be inserted on different schedules, the ingestion throughput for streaming features can be improved independently. However, retrieving values from multiple feature groups increases the number of API calls and can increase overall retrieval times.

Your solution needs to balance feature isolation and retrieval performance. If your models require features from a large number of different feature groups at inference, design the solution to utilize larger feature groups or to retrieve from the feature store in parallel to meet the near real-time SLAs for predictions. For example, if your model requires features from three feature groups for inference, you can issue three API calls to get the feature record data in parallel before merging that data for model inference. This can be done through a typical inference workflow executing through an AWS service such as **AWS Step Functions**. Optionally, if that same set of features are always used together for inference, you may want to consider combining those into a single feature group.

Figure 5.11 shows the end-to-end architecture for streaming ingestion and streaming inferences to support high-throughput writes and low-latency reads:

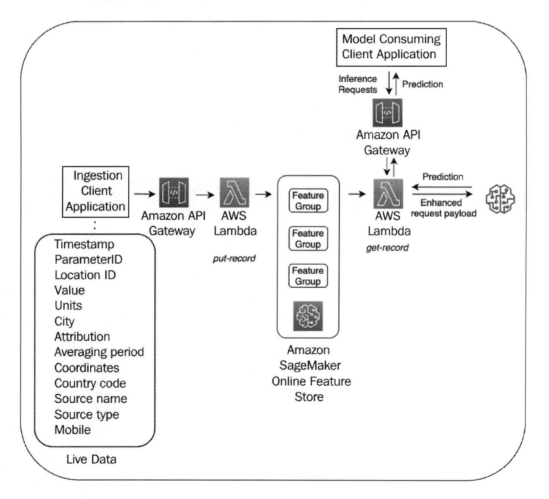

Figure 5.11 – End-to-end architecture for real-time feature ingestion and retrieval

Here are the high-level steps involved in this architecture:

On the ingestion side:

1. The client application collects and processes the live data. For streaming applications, one option is to use **Kinesis Data Streams**. To ingest features, the client application calls an ingestion API hosted by an API Gateway.

2. An API Gateway invokes the lambda function that uses the `put_record` API to push features into the online feature store. As necessary, the lambda function can also perform additional processing on the raw data before pushing features to the feature store.

On the prediction side:

1. A model-consuming client application calls a prediction API hosted by an API Gateway. An API Gateway invokes a lambda function that looks up the features related to inference requests from the online feature store and creates an enhanced request.

2. The enhanced request is sent to the SageMaker deployed endpoint. The prediction from the endpoint traverses back to the client application.

Using these techniques and best practices, you can design real-time ML systems.

Summary

In this chapter, you reviewed the basic capabilities of Amazon SageMaker Feature Store along with the APIs to use. By combining different capabilities, you learned how to reuse engineered features across training and inference phases of a single machine learning project and across multiple ML projects. Finally, you combined streaming ingestion and serving to design near real-time inference solutions. In the next chapter, you will use these engineered features to train and tune machine learning models at scale.

References

For additional reading material, please review these references:

- Using streaming ingestion with Amazon SageMaker Feature Store to make ML-backed decisions in near-real time:

  ```
  https://aws.amazon.com/blogs/machine-learning/using-
  streaming-ingestion-with-amazon-sagemaker-feature-store-
  to-make-ml-backed-decisions-in-near-real-time/
  ```

- Enable feature reuse across accounts and teams using Amazon SageMaker Feature Store:

  ```
  https://aws.amazon.com/blogs/machine-learning/enable-
  feature-reuse-across-accounts-and-teams-using-amazon-
  sagemaker-feature-store/
  ```

- Build accurate ML training datasets using point-in-time queries with Amazon SageMaker Feature Store and Apache Spark:

  ```
  https://aws.amazon.com/blogs/machine-learning/build-
  accurate-ml-training-datasets-using-point-in-time-queries-
  with-amazon-sagemaker-feature-store-and-apache-spark/
  ```

- Ingesting historical feature data into Amazon SageMaker Feature Store:

  ```
  https://towardsdatascience.com/ingesting-historical-
  feature-data-into-sagemaker-feature-store-5618e41a11e6
  ```

Section 2: Model Training Challenges

This section tackles the challenge of training at scale including using large datasets while saving costs, monitoring training resources to identify bottlenecks, speeding up long training jobs, and tracking multiple models trained for a common goal.

This section comprises the following chapters:

- *Chapter 6, Training and Tuning at Scale*
- *Chapter 7, Profile Training Jobs with Amazon SageMaker Debugger*

6

Training and Tuning at Scale

Machine learning (ML) practitioners face multiple challenges when training and tuning models at scale. **Scale challenges** come in the form of high volumes of training data and increased model size and model architecture complexity. Additional challenges come from having to run a large number of tuning jobs to identify the right set of hyperparameters and keeping track of multiple experiments conducted with varying algorithms for a specific ML objective. Scale challenges lead to long training times, resource constraints, and increased costs. This can reduce the productivity of teams, and potentially create a bottleneck for ML projects.

Amazon SageMaker provides managed distributed training and tuning capabilities to improve training efficiency, and capabilities to organize and track ML experiments at scale. SageMaker enables techniques such as streaming data into algorithms by using pipe mode for training with data at scale and Managed Spot Training for reduced training costs. Pipe mode and managed spot training are discussed in detail in *Learn Amazon SageMaker: A guide to building, training, and deploying machine learning models for developers and data scientists*, by Julien Simon.

In this chapter, we will discuss advanced topics of distributed training, best practices for hyperparameter tuning, and how to organize ML experiments at scale. By the end of this chapter, you will be able to use Amazon SageMaker's managed capabilities to train and tune at scale in a cost-effective manner and keep track of a large number of training experiments.

In this chapter, we will cover the following main topics:

- ML training at scale with SageMaker distributed libraries
- Automated model tuning with SageMaker hyperparameter tuning
- Organizing and tracking training jobs with SageMaker Experiments

Technical requirements

You will need an **AWS** account to run the examples included in this chapter. If you have not set up the data science environment yet, please refer to *Chapter 2, Data Science Environments*, which walks you through the setup process.

Code examples included in the book are available on GitHub at `https://github.com/PacktPublishing/Amazon-SageMaker-Best-Practices/tree/main/Chapter06`. You will need to install a Git client to access them (`https://git-scm.com/`).

ML training at scale with SageMaker distributed libraries

Two common scale challenges with ML projects are scaling training data and scaling model size. While increased training data volume, model size, and complexity can potentially result in a more accurate model, there is a limit to the data volume and the model size that you can use with a single compute node, CPU, or GPU. Increased training data volumes and model sizes typically result in more computations, and therefore training jobs take longer to finish, even when using powerful compute instances such as **Amazon Elastic Compute Cloud** (EC2) p3 and p4 instances.

Distributed training is a commonly used technique to speed up training when dealing with scale challenges. Training load can be distributed either across multiple compute instances (nodes), or across multiple CPUs and GPUs (devices) on a single compute instance. There are two strategies for distributed training – **data parallelism** and **model parallelism**. Their names are a good indication of what is involved with each strategy. With data parallelism, the training data is split up across multiple nodes (or devices). With model parallelism, the model is split up across the nodes (or devices).

> **Note**
>
> **Mixed-precision training** is a popular technique to handle training at scale and reduce training time. Typically used on compute instances equipped with NVIDIA GPUs, mixed-precision training converts network weights from FP32 representation to FP16, calculates the gradients, converts weights back to FP32, multiplies by the learning rate, and finally updates the optimizer weights.

In the data parallelism distribution strategy, the ML algorithm or the neural network-based model is replicated on all devices, and each device processes a batch of data. Results from all devices are then combined. In the model parallelism distribution strategy, the model (which is the neural network) is split up across the devices. Batches of training data are sent to all devices so that the data can be processed by all parts of the model. The following diagram shows an overview of data and model parallelism:

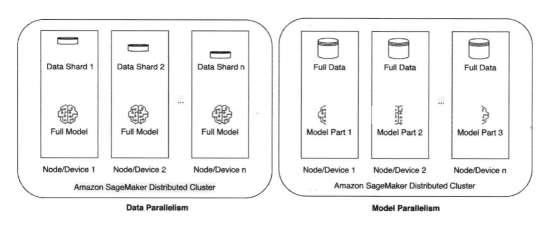

Figure 6.1 – Distribution strategies

Both data and model parallelism distribution strategies come with their own complexities. With data parallelism, each node (or device) is trained on a subset of data (called a mini-batch), and a mini-gradient is calculated. However, within each node, a mini-gradient average, with gradients coming from other nodes, should be calculated and communicated to all other nodes. This step is called **all reduce**, which is a communication overhead that grows as the training cluster is scaled up.

While model parallelism addresses the requirements of a model not fitting in a single device's memory by splitting it across devices, partitioning the model across multiple GPUs may lead to under-utilization. This is because training on GPUs is sequential in nature, where only one GPU is actively processing data while the other GPUs are waiting to be activated. To be effective, model parallelism should be coupled with a pipeline execution schedule to train the model across multiple nodes, and in turn, maximize GPU utilization. Now that you know two different distribution strategies, how do you choose between data and model parallelism?

Choosing between data and model parallelism

When choosing a distributed strategy to implement, keep in mind the following:

- Training on multiple nodes inherently causes inter-node communication overhead.

- Additionally, to meet security and regulatory requirements, you may choose to protect the data transmitted between the nodes by enabling inter-container encryption.

- Enabling inter-container encryption will further increase the training time.

Due to these reasons, use data parallelism if the trained model can fit in the memory of a single device or node. In situations where the model does not fit in the memory due to its size or complexity, you should experiment further with data parallelism before deciding on model parallelism.

You can experiment with the following to improve data parallelism performance:

- **Tuning the model's hyperparameters**: Tuning parameters such as the number of layers of a neural network, or the optimizer to use, affects the model's size considerably.

- **Reducing the batch size**: Experiment by incrementally reducing the batch size until the model fits in the memory. This experiment should balance out the model's memory needs with optimal batch size. Make sure you do not end up with a suboptimal small batch size just because training with a large batch size takes up most of the device memory.

- **Reducing the model input size**: If the model input is tabular, consider embedding vectors of reduced dimensions. Similarly, for **natural language processing (NLP)** models, reduce the input NLP sequence length, and if the input is an image, reduce image resolution.

- **Using mixed-point precision**: Experiment with mixed-precision training, which uses FP16 representation of weights during gradient calculation, to reduce memory consumption.

The following flowchart shows the sequence of decisions and experiments to follow when choosing a distribution strategy to implement:

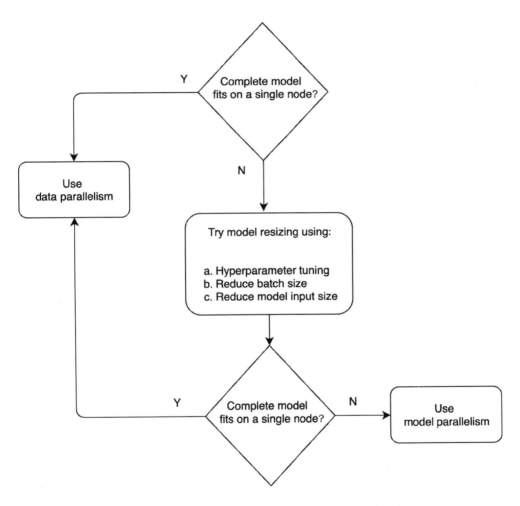

Figure 6.2 – Choose a distribution strategy

While data parallelism addresses the challenge of training data scale, model parallelism addresses the challenge of increased model size and complexity. A hybrid distribution strategy can also be implemented to include both data and model parallelism. *Figure 6.3* walks you through a hybrid distribution strategy with two-way data parallelism and four-way model parallelism:

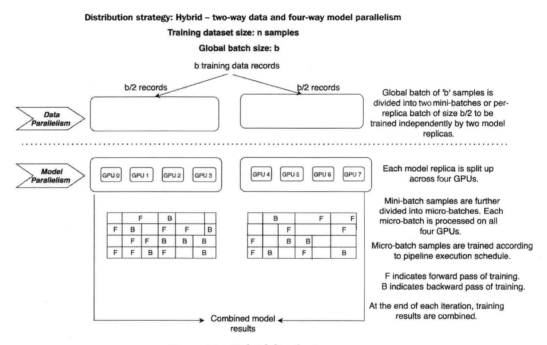

Figure 6.3 – Hybrid distribution strategy

Scaling the compute resources

Both the distributed training strategies depend on a cluster of compute resources to spread the training load. When scaling the distributed cluster to meet the training demands, the recommended best practices are as follows:

- First, scale vertically. That is, scale from a single GPU to multiple GPUs on a single instance. For example, let's say you started with the instance type p3.2xlarge, which has a single GPU for training your model, and you find yourself needing a greater number of GPUs to increase the training time. Change the instance type to p3.16xlarge, which has eight GPUs. This will result in a nearly eight-times decrease in the training, a near-linear speedup. Keeping the training job on a single scaled-up instance results in better performance than using multiple instances while keeping the cost low.

- Next, scale from a single instance to multiple instances. When you reach limits of the instance types offered and still need to scale your training even further, then use multiple instances of the same type, that is, scale from a single `p3.16xlarge` to two `p3.16xlarge` instances. This will give you double the compute capacity, going from 8 GPUs on a single instance, to 16 GPUs across two instances. Keep in mind that when you use multiple instances in the training cluster, all instances should be in the same **Availability Zone**. For example, instances in `us-west-2` must all be in `us-west-2a` or all in `us-west-2b`. Your training data should also be in the same region, `us-west-2`.

When moving from a single instance to multiple instances, it is recommended that you observe the model convergence and increase the batch size as necessary. Since the batch size you use is split across GPUs, each GPU is processing a lower batch size, which could lead to a high error rate and disrupt the model convergence.

For example, let's say you start with a single GPU on a `p3.2xlarge` instance using a batch size of 64, then scale up to four `p3dn.24xlarge`, which gives you 32 GPUs. After this move, each GPU only processes a batch size of two, which is very likely to break the model convergence you observed with the original training.

SageMaker distributed libraries

For easy implementation of data and model parallelism in your training jobs, SageMaker provides two different distributed training libraries. The libraries address the issues of inter-node and inter-GPU communications overhead using a combination of software and hardware technologies. To implement the distributed libraries and take advantage of data and model parallelism, you will need to make minor code changes to your training scripts.

> **Important note**
>
> At the time of the book publication, the SageMaker distributed libraries support two frameworks—**TensorFlow** and **PyTorch**.
>
> While in this chapter we are focusing on the SageMaker native libraries for distributed training, you can also choose to use **Horovod**, the most popular open source distributed training framework, or the native distributed training strategies in frameworks such as TensorFlow and PyTorch. Please see the blog link in the references section for details on using Horovod with TensorFlow on SageMaker.

SageMaker distributed data parallel library

Let's first dive into the SageMaker distributed data parallel library.

The SageMaker distributed data parallel library provides the capabilities to achieve near-linear scaling efficiency and fast training times on deep learning models. The library addresses the challenge of communications overhead in a distributed cluster using two approaches:

- It automatically performs the `AllReduce` operation responsible for the overhead.
- It optimizes node-to-communication by utilizing AWS's network infrastructure and Amazon EC2 instance topology.

SageMaker data parallelism can be used with both single-node, multi-device setup, and with multi-node setup. However, its value is more apparent in training clusters with two or more nodes. In this multi-node cluster, the `AllReduce` operation implemented as part of the library gives you significant performance improvement.

To use the distributed libraries with the SageMaker training jobs, first enable the strategy you want when you construct the `estimator` object. The following code block shows how to create an `estimator` object using a `PyTorch` container with the data parallel strategy enabled:

```
from sagemaker.pytorch import PyTorch

pt_dist_estimator = PyTorch(
                entry_point="train_pytorch_dist.py",
                ...
                distribution={
                        "smdistributed": {"dataparallel":
{"enabled": True}}
                }
)
```

Additionally, there are a few changes that are needed to the training script, `train_pytorch_dist`, in this example. The next few code blocks show the changes required to the training script:

1. First, import and initialize the SageMaker distributed library:

```
import smdistributed.dataparallel.torch.distributed as
dist
from smdistributed.dataparallel.torch.parallel.
```

```
distributed import DistributedDataParallel as DDP
dist.init_process_group()
```

2. Next, pin each GPU to a single SageMaker data parallel library process with `local_rank`, which is a relative rank of the process within a given node:

```
torch.cuda.set_device(dist_get_local_rank())
```

3. Next, resize the batch size to be handled by each worker:

```
batch_size //= dist.get_world_size()
batch_size = max(batch_size, 1)
```

4. Next, wrap the trained model artifact with the DDP class from the distributed library:

```
model = DDP(model)
```

5. Finally, once all of the changes are in place, simply call the `fit()` method on the estimator to kick off training with the training script:

```
pt_dist_estimator.fit()
```

To observe the benefits of the distributed training, we ran two different training jobs on the same dataset. Both the jobs were run on a single `ml.p3.16xlarge`, the first job without distributed training, and the second job with `smdistributed dataparallel` enabled. In this experiment, the first job was completed in 12041 seconds, and the second job was completed in 4179 seconds, resulting in a 65.29% improvement in the training time.

> **Note**
>
> Comparison of the two training jobs with and without `smdistributed dataparallel` enabled is captured in the notebook in the GitHub repo: `https://gitlab.com/randydefauw/packt_book/-/blob/main/CH05/train-distributed.ipynb`.

SageMaker distributed model parallel library

Next, let's look into the SageMaker distributed model parallel library. This provides the capability to train large, complex deep learning models that can potentially increase prediction accuracy. The library automatically and efficiently splits a model across multiple GPUs, providing an option for both manual and automatic partitioning. It further coordinates training through a pipelined execution by building an efficient computation schedule where different nodes can simultaneously work on forward and backward passes for different data samples.

The following code block shows creating an `estimator` object using a `PyTorch` container with the model parallel strategy enabled:

```
mpi_options = {
    "enabled": True,
    "processes_per_host": 4
   }


dist_options = {
    "modelparallel":{
        "enabled": True,
        "parameters": {
            "partitions": 4,  # we'll partition the model among
the 4 GPUs
            "microbatches": 8,  # Mini-batchs are split in
micro-batch to increase parallelism
            "optimize": "memory" # The automatic model
partitioning can optimize speed or memory
            }
        }
}
pt_model_dist_estimator = PyTorch(
    entry_point="train_pytorch_model_dist.py",
    ...
    distribution={"mpi": mpi_options, "smdistributed": dist_
options}
)
```

As with the data parallel strategy, there are a few code changes necessary to the training script. Important changes are discussed in the next few code blocks:

1. First, import and initialize the SageMaker distributed library:

```
import smdistributed.modelparallel.torch as smp
smp.init()
```

2. Next, wrap the model artifact in the DistributedModel class from the distributed library, and wrap the optimizer in the DistributedOptimizer class:

```
model = smp.DistributedModel(model)
optimizer = smp.DistributedOptimizer(optimizer)
```

3. Next, add the forward and backward logic to a function and decorate it with smp.step:

```
@smp.step
def train_step(model, data, target):

    output = model(data)
    long_target = target.long()
    loss = F.nll_loss(output, long_target,
reduction="mean")
    model.backward(loss)
    return output, loss
```

4. Finally, call the fit() method on the estimator object to kick off training:

```
pt_dist_estimator.fit()
```

> **Important Note**
> An example notebook that provides a complete walk-through of using the ModelParallel distribution strategy with a PyTorch container is provided in the GitHub repository: https://gitlab.com/randydefauw/packt_book/-/blob/main/CH06/train.ipynb.

While the SageMaker distributed model parallel library makes it easy to implement model parallel distributed training, for optimal training results consider the following best practices:

- **Using manual versus auto-partitioning**: You can partition the model onto multiple nodes (or devices) using either manual or auto-partitioning. While both of the options are supported, you should choose auto-partitioning over the manual approach. With auto-partitioning, training operations and modules that share the same parameters will automatically be placed on the same device for correctness. With a manual approach, you will have to take care of the details on how to split up the model parts, and which part should be placed on which device. This is a time-consuming and error-prone process.

- **Choosing the batch size**: The model parallel library is most efficient with large batch sizes. In case you start with a smaller batch size to fit the model into a single node, then decide to implement model parallelism across multiple nodes, you should increase the batch size accordingly. Model parallelism saves memory for large models, allowing training with large batch sizes.

- **Choosing the number and size of micro-batches**: The model parallel library executes each micro-batch sequentially in each node or device. So, the micro-batch size should be large enough to fully utilize each GPU. At the same time, pipeline efficiency increases with the number of micro-batches, so balancing the two is important.

It is best practice to start with two or four micro-batches and increase the batch size according to the available memory of the node/device. Then experiment with larger batch sizes and increase the number of micro-batches. As the number of micro-batches is increased, larger batch sizes might become feasible if an interleaved pipeline is used.

Incremental training

When huge volumes of data are available upfront before training your model, distributed training strategies should be used. But what happens when a trained model is deployed and then you collect new data that might improve the model predictions? In this situation, you can incrementally train a new model starting with artifacts from an existing model and using an expanded dataset.

Incremental training can save training time, resources, and costs in the following situations:

- An existing model is under-performing and new data becomes available that can potentially improve model performance.

- You want to use publicly available models as a starting point for your model without having to train from scratch.
- You want to train multiple versions of a model, with either different hyperparameters or using different datasets.
- You want to restart a previously stopped training job, without having to start from scratch again.

Additionally, to complement or substitute for loading existing model weights and incrementally training, you can retrain on a sliding window on the most recent data.

In this section, you learned how to use SageMaker capabilities to train with large volumes of data and complex model architectures. Besides the training data and model architecture, a critical part of ML training is tuning hyperparameters of the ML algorithm. In the next section, you will learn the best practices for using SageMaker to handle model tuning at scale.

Automated model tuning with SageMaker hyperparameter tuning

Hyperparameter tuning (HPT) helps you find the right parameters to use with your ML algorithm or the neural network to find an optimal version of the model. Amazon SageMaker supports managed hyperparameter tuning, also called **automatic model tuning**. In this section, we discuss the best practices to consider while configuring hyperparameter jobs on Amazon SageMaker.

To execute a SageMaker hyperparameter tuning job, you specify a set of hyperparameters, a range of values to explore for each hyperparameter, and an objective metric to measure the model's performance. Automatic tuning executes multiple training jobs on your training dataset with the ML algorithm and the hyperparameter values to find the best-performing model as measured by the objective metric.

In the following code blocks, we will see how to create an HPT job on SageMaker:

1. First, initialize the hyperparameter names and range of values for each hyperparameter you want to explore:

```
from sagemaker.tuner import (
    IntegerParameter,
    CategoricalParameter,
    ContinuousParameter,
```

```
    HyperparameterTuner,
)
hyperparameter_ranges = {
  "eta": ContinuousParameter(0, 1),
  "min_child_weight": ContinuousParameter(1, 10),
  "alpha": ContinuousParameter(0, 2),
  "max_depth": IntegerParameter(1, 10)
}
```

2. Next, configure the SageMaker `estimator` object:

```
estimator_hpo = \ sagemaker.estimator.Estimator(
  image_uri=xgboost_container,
  hyperparameters=hyperparameters,
  role=sagemaker.get_execution_role(),
  instance_count=1,
  instance_type='ml.m5.12xlarge',
  volume_size=200, # 5 GB
  output_path=output_path
)
```

3. Next, configure the `HyperparameterTuner` object:

```
tuner = HyperparameterTuner(
          estimator_hpo,
     objective_metric_name,
     hyperparameter_ranges,
     max_jobs=10,
     max_parallel_jobs=2,
     objective_type = 'Minimize'
)
```

4. Finally, call the `fit()` method on the `tuner` object:

```
tuner.fit({'train': train_input,
          'validation': validation_input})
```

Once the hyperparameter job is completed, you can view the different training jobs executed by SageMaker, along with the objective metric for each job, in *Figure 6.4*:

Name	Status	Objective metric value	Creation time	Training Duration
○ sagemaker-xgboost-210617-2118-010-e02d63a9	⊘ Completed	0.00009000000136438757	Jun 17, 2021 21:34 UTC	1 minute(s)
○ sagemaker-xgboost-210617-2118-009-8e669977	⊘ Completed	0.0002899999963119626	Jun 17, 2021 21:34 UTC	1 minute(s)
○ sagemaker-xgboost-210617-2118-008-a61aa0e4	⊘ Completed	0.0002899999963119626	Jun 17, 2021 21:30 UTC	1 minute(s)
○ sagemaker-xgboost-210617-2118-007-68af19a1	⊘ Completed	0.00009000000136438757	Jun 17, 2021 21:30 UTC	1 minute(s)
○ sagemaker-xgboost-210617-2118-006-a039f074	⊘ Completed	0.02621999941766262	Jun 17, 2021 21:26 UTC	1 minute(s)
○ sagemaker-xgboost-210617-2118-005-f34d17ee	⊘ Completed	-	Jun 17, 2021 21:26 UTC	1 minute(s)
○ sagemaker-xgboost-210617-2118-004-8f52ea43	⊘ Completed	-	Jun 17, 2021 21:22 UTC	1 minute(s)
○ sagemaker-xgboost-210617-2118-003-5a51ce5a	⊘ Completed	0.3014200031757355	Jun 17, 2021 21:22 UTC	1 minute(s)
○ sagemaker-xgboost-210617-2118-002-f804d00b	⊘ Completed	0.00860000029206276	Jun 17, 2021 21:18 UTC	1 minute(s)
○ sagemaker-xgboost-210617-2118-001-e86a5d43	⊘ Completed	0.005489999894052744	Jun 17, 2021 21:18 UTC	1 minute(s)

Training jobs — View logs · View instance metrics · Stop · Create model
Sorting by objective metric value will display only jobs that have metric values.

Figure 6.4 – SageMaker HPT results

You can dive further into each of the training jobs to view the exact values of the hyperparameters used, as shown in *Figure 6.5*:

Hyperparameters

Key	Value
_tuning_objective_metric	validation:rmse
alpha	1.8186663758933634
eta	0.09619456240796877
gamma	4
max_depth	8
min_child_weight	3.695403499385228
num_round	5
objective	reg:squarederror
subsample	0.7

Figure 6.5 – Hyperparameter values for a specific training job

> **Important Note**
>
> An example notebook that provides a complete walk-through of using SageMaker HPT, along with analysis of results, is provided in the GitHub repository: `https://gitlab.com/randydefauw/packt_book/-/blob/main/CH05/HPO.ipynb`.

Now that you know the basics, let's discuss some of the best practices to consider while configuring hyperparameter jobs on Amazon SageMaker:

- **Selecting a small number of hyperparameters**: HPT is a computationally intensive task, the computational complexity being proportional to the number of hyperparameters you want to tune. SageMaker allows you to specify up to 20 hyperparameters to optimize for a tuning job but limiting your search to a smaller number is likely to give you better results.

- **Selecting a small range for hyperparameters**: Along the same lines, the range of values for hyperparameters can significantly affect the success of hyperparameter optimization. Intuitively, you may want to specify a very large range to explore all possible values for a hyperparameter, but you will in fact get better results by limiting your search to a small range of values.

- **Specifying hyperparameter type**: For the hyperparameters you want to explore, select the right type from the three types supported—categorical, integer, and continuous. Use the categorical type to test different categorical values for a hyperparameter, such as different optimizers for a neural network. Additionally, you can also use the categorical type when you want to test specific values.

  For example, for the `train_batch_size` hyperparameter, instead of exploring a range in a linear fashion, you might want only to evaluate the two values–128 and 256. In this case, you treat the parameter as a categorical value. In contrast, if you want to explore the values for the `train_batch_size` hyperparameter in a range from a minimum threshold value of 128 to a maximum threshold value of 256, you will use the `Integer` type. The `Integer` type allows for greater exploration of the range.

  If you search a range that spans several orders of magnitude, you can optimize the search by choosing a logarithmic scale for `Integer` hyperparameters. Finally, choose a continuous parameter if the range of all values to explore, from the lowest to the highest, is relatively small. For example, exploring the `learning_rate` hyperparameter in the range of `0.0001` and `0.0005` at a linear scale.

- **Enabling warm start**: SageMaker HPT supports warm start, which reuses results from one or more prior tuning jobs as a starting point. Configure your HPT job to use warm start to limit the combinations of hyperparameters to search over in the new tuning job. This results in a faster tuning job. Warm start is particularly useful when you want to change the HPT ranges from the previous job or add new hyperparameters.

- **Enabling early stop to save tuning time and costs**: With early stop enabled, the individual training jobs launched by the HPT job will terminate early when the objective metric is not improving significantly. After each epoch of training, a running average of the objective metric for all the previous training jobs up to the same epoch is determined and the median of running averages is calculated. If the value of the objective metric for the current training job is worse than the median value, SageMaker stops the current training job.

  Stopping jobs early reduces the overall compute time and thereby the cost of the job. An additional benefit is that early stopping helps prevent overfitting.

- **Selecting a small number of concurrent training jobs**: SageMaker allows you to execute multiple training jobs concurrently as part of the overall tuning job using the `MaxParallelTrainingJobs` parameter. On one hand, running more HPT jobs concurrently completes the tuning job quickly. On the other, a tuning job can only find better combinations of hyperparameters through successive rounds of experiments. In the long run, executing a single training job at a time gives the best results with minimum computation time.

  This is the case when the default **Bayesian** optimization tuning strategy is used by SageMaker HPO. However, if you have experience with your algorithm and dataset, you can also use the random search strategy natively supported by SageMaker, since it enables concurrency but doesn't require serial rounds of experiments.

While in this section we focused on a single algorithm for best practice. The `CreateHyperParameterTuningJob` API can also be used to tune multiple algorithms by providing multiple training job definitions pointing to the different algorithms. For a detailed explanation of this API, see the following article: `https://docs.aws.amazon.com/sagemaker/latest/APIReference/API_CreateHyperParameterTuningJob.html`.

In the next section, you will learn how to keep track of all your ML experiments related to solving a specific problem.

Organizing and tracking training jobs with SageMaker Experiments

A key challenge ML practitioners face is keeping track of the myriad ML experiments that need to be executed before a model achieves desired results. For a single ML project, it is not uncommon for data scientists to routinely train several different models looking for improved accuracy. HPT adds more training jobs to these experiments. Typically, there are many details to track for experiments such as hyperparameters, model architectures, training algorithms, custom scripts, metrics, result artifacts, and more.

In this section, we will discuss **Amazon SageMaker Experiments**, which allows you to organize, track, visualize, and compare ML models across all phases of the ML lifecycle, including feature engineering, model training, model tuning, and model deploying. SageMaker Experiments' capability tracks model lineage, allowing you to troubleshoot production issues and audit your models to meet compliance requirements.

Basic components that make up Amazon SageMaker Experiments include an experiment, a trial, a trial component, and a tracker, as shown in *Figure 6.6*:

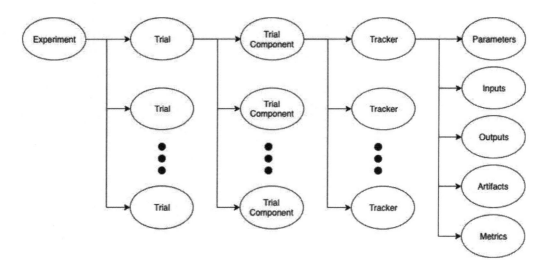

Figure 6.6 – Amazon SageMaker Experiments overview

Let's look at each component:

- **Experiment**: An experiment encapsulates all related components that represent the ML problem you are attempting to solve. Each experiment is a collection of trials, with the goal of determining the trial that produces the best model.

- **Trial**: A trial represents a single attempt at solving the ML problem that captures the end-to-end ML process within an experiment. Each trial is a collection consisting of several trial components.

- **Trial Component**: A trial component represents a specific step within a given trial. For example, the data preprocessing step could be one trial component, and model training could be another trial component.

- **Tracker**: A tracker is used to track metadata of individual trial components, including all parameters, inputs, outputs, artifacts, and metrics. Since this metadata is tracked and persisted, you can link the final model artifact to its origin.

In the following code blocks, we will see how to create a SageMaker experiment:

1. First, create an experiment:

```
weather_experiment = Experiment.create(
    experiment_name=f"weather-experiment-{int(time.
time())}",
    description="Weather Data Prediction",
    sagemaker_boto_client=sm)
```

2. Next, create a `Tracker` instance to track the `Training` stage:

```
with Tracker.create(display_name="Training", sagemaker_
boto_client=sm) as tracker:

    # Log the location of the training dataset
    tracker.log_input(name="weather-training-dataset",
    media_type="s3/uri",
    value="s3://{}/{}/{}/".format(s3_bucket, s3_prefix,
'train'))
```

Next, define experiment variables to define what you want to change to see how your objective is affected. In this example, we will experiment with several values for the number of the `max_depth` hyperparameter of `XGBoost model`. We will create a trial to track each training job run.

We will also create a `TrialComponent` instance from the `Tracker` instance we created earlier and add this to the `Trial` instance. This will allow you to capture metrics from the training step as follows:

```
for i, max_depth in enumerate([2, 5]):
```

```
    # create trial
    trial_name = f"xgboost-training-job-trial-{max_
depth}-max-depth-{int(time.time())}"
    xgboost_trial = Trial.create(
        trial_name=trial_name,
        experiment_name=weather_experiment.experiment_
name,
        sagemaker_boto_client=sm,
    )
    max_depth_trial_name_map[max_depth] = trial_name

    xgboost_training_job_name = "xgboost-training-
job-{}".format(int(time.time()))
```

3. When running the training job with the `fit()` method, associate `estimator` with the experiment and trial:

```
    # Now associate the estimator with the Experiment and
    Trial
    estimator.fit(
        inputs={'training': train_input},
        job_name=xgboost_training_job_name,
        experiment_config={
            "TrialName": xgboost_trial.trial_name,
            "TrialComponentDisplayName": "Training",
        },
        wait=False,
    )
```

4. Finally, after the experiment is completed, let's analyze the experiment results:

```
trial_component_analytics = \
ExperimentAnalytics(sagemaker_session=sagemaker_session,
experiment_name=experiment_name )

trial_component_analytics.dataframe()
```

Figure 6.7 shows a list of all the trial components that were created as part of the experiment:

	TrialComponentName	DisplayName	SourceArn	dropout	epochs	hidden_channels	optimizer
0	cnn-training-job-1617571415-aws-training-job	Training	arn:aws:sagemaker:us-west-2:210766871901:train...	0.2	2.0	20.0	"sgd"
1	cnn-training-job-1617570651-aws-training-job	Training	arn:aws:sagemaker:us-west-2:210766871901:train...	0.2	2.0	2.0	"sgd"
2	cnn-training-job-1617571701-aws-training-job	Training	arn:aws:sagemaker:us-west-2:210766871901:train...	0.2	2.0	32.0	"sgd"
3	cnn-training-job-1617571161-aws-training-job	Training	arn:aws:sagemaker:us-west-2:210766871901:train...	0.2	2.0	10.0	"sgd"
4	cnn-training-job-1617570905-aws-training-job	Training	arn:aws:sagemaker:us-west-2:210766871901:train...	0.2	2.0	5.0	"sgd"

Figure 6.7 – Trial components from the experiment

As you can see from this section, a SageMaker experiment gives you a way to organize your efforts toward an ML goal and allows visibility into several important aspects of those efforts. A best practice we recommend is that any time you launch a training or tuning job, wrap it in an experiment. This allows you to gain visibility into the training and tuning jobs without any additional cost.

> **Important note**
>
> An example notebook that provides a complete walk-through of using SageMaker Experiments is provided in the GitHub repository: `https://gitlab.com/randydefauw/packt_book/-/blob/main/CH05/Experiments.ipynb`.

Summary

In this chapter, you learned the advanced techniques required to train models at scale using different distribution strategies. You further reviewed best practices for hyperparameter tuning to find the best version of the model to meet your objectives. You learned how to organize and track multiple experiments conducted in a typical ML workflow and create comparison reports.

Using the SageMaker capabilities and best practices discussed in this chapter, you can tackle ML at scale, allowing your organization to move out of the experimentation phase. You can take advantage of large datasets collected over years, and move toward realizing the full benefits of ML. In the next chapter, you will continue to enhance ML training by profiling training jobs using **Amazon SageMaker Debugger**.

References

For additional reading material, please review these references:

- *Learn Amazon SageMaker: A guide to building, training, and deploying ML models for developers and data scientists*:

  ```
  https://www.amazon.com/Learn-Amazon-SageMaker-developers-
  scientists/dp/180020891X/ref=sr_1_1?dchild=1&keywords
  =Learn+Amazon+SageMaker+%3A+A+guide+to+building%
  2C+training%2C+and+deploying+machine+learning+models+for
  +developers+and+data+scientists&qid=1624801601&sr=8-1
  ```

- *Multi-GPU and distributed training using Horovod in Amazon SageMaker Pipe mode*:

  ```
  https://aws.amazon.com/blogs/machine-learning/multi-
  gpu-and-distributed-training-using-horovod-in-amazon-
  sagemaker-pipe-mode/
  ```

- *Streamline modeling with Amazon SageMaker Studio and the Amazon Experiments SDK*:

  ```
  https://aws.amazon.com/blogs/machine-learning/streamline-
  modeling-with-amazon-sagemaker-studio-and-amazon-
  experiments-sdk
  ```

7

Profile Training Jobs with Amazon SageMaker Debugger

Training **machine learning** (**ML**) models involves experimenting with multiple algorithms, with their hyperparameters typically crunching through large volumes of data. Training a model that yields optimal results is both a time- and compute-intensive task. Improved training time yields improved productivity and reduces overall training costs.

Distributed training, as we discussed in *Chapter 6, Training and Tuning at Scale*, goes a long way in achieving improved training times by using a scalable compute cluster. However, monitoring training infrastructure to identify and debug resource bottlenecks is not trivial. Once a training job has been launched, the process becomes non-transparent, and you don't have much visibility into the model training process. Equally non-trivial is real-time monitoring to detect sub-optimal training jobs and stop them early to avoid wasting training time and resources.

Amazon SageMaker Debugger provides visibility into training jobs and the infrastructure a training job is executing on. Real-time training metrics such as **learning gradients** and **network weights** captured by SageMaker Debugger provide visibility into a training job in progress, so you can act on conditions such as **vanishing gradients** and **overfitting**.

Debugger also monitors and provides reports about the system's resources such as CPU, GPU, and memory, providing you with insights into resource utilization and bottlenecks. Additionally, if you use TensorFlow or PyTorch for your deep learning training jobs, Debugger provides you with a view into framework metrics that can be used to speed up your training jobs.

By the end of this chapter, you will be able to use the capabilities of Amazon SageMaker Debugger and apply best practices to address challenges typical to debugging ML training. These challenges include identifying and reacting to sub-optimal training, gaining visibility into the resource utilization of the training infrastructure, and optimizing training framework parameters. You will also learn how to improve the training time and costs by applying detailed recommendations provided by SageMaker Debugger.

In this chapter, we are going to cover the following main topics:

- Amazon SageMaker Debugger essentials
- Real-time monitoring of training jobs using built-in and custom rules
- Gain insight into the training infrastructure and training framework

Technical requirements

You will need an AWS account to run the examples included in this chapter. If you have not set up the data science environment for this book yet, please refer to *Chapter 2, Data Science Environments*, which will walk you through the setup process.

The code examples included in this book are available on GitHub at `https://github.com/PacktPublishing/Amazon-SageMaker-Best-Practices/tree/main/Chapter07`. You will need to install a Git client to access them (`https://git-scm.com/`).

Amazon SageMaker Debugger essentials

In this section, you will learn about the basic terminology and capabilities of Amazon SageMaker Debugger. Using Debugger with your training jobs involves three high-level steps:

1. *Configuring* the training job to use SageMaker Debugger.
2. *Analyzing* the collected tensors and metrics.
3. *Taking* action.

The preceding points are illustrated in the following diagram:

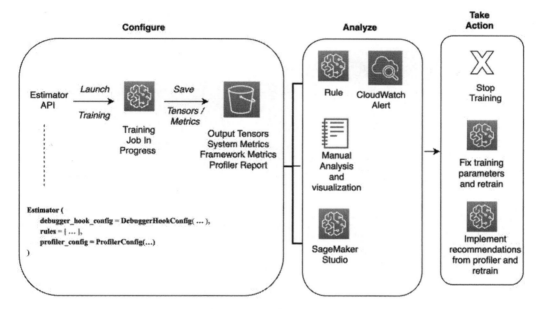

Figure 7.1 – Amazon SageMaker Debugger overview

As we dive into each one of these steps, we will introduce the necessary terminology.

Configuring a training job to use SageMaker Debugger

The first step is to configure training jobs to use Amazon SageMaker Debugger. By now, you are familiar with using the `Estimator` object from SageMaker SDK to launch training jobs. To use Amazon SageMaker Debugger, you must enhance `Estimator` with three additional configuration parameters: `DebuggerHookConfig`, `Rules`, and `ProfilerConfig`.

With `DebuggerHookConfig`, you can specify which debugging metrics to collect and where to store them, as shown in the following code block:

```
Estimator(
    ...

    debugger_hook_config=DebuggerHookConfig(
        s3_output_path=bucket_path,   # Where the debug data is
stored.
        collection_configs=[ # Organize data to collect into
collections.
            CollectionConfig(
                name="metrics",
                parameters={
                    "save_interval": str(save_interval)
                }
            )
        ],
    ),
    ...
)
```

`s3_output_path` is the location where all the collected data is persisted. If this location is not specified, Debugger uses the default path, `s3://<output_path>/debug-output/`, where `<output_path>` is the output path of the SageMaker training job. The `CollectionConfig` list allows you to organize the debug data or tensors into collections for easier analysis. A tensor represents the state of a training network at a specific time during the training process. Data is collected at intervals, as specified by `save_interval`, which is the number of steps in a training run.

How do you know which tensors to collect? SageMaker Debugger comes with a set of built-in collections to capture common training metrics such as `weights`, `layers`, and `outputs`. You can choose to collect all of the available tensors or a subset of them. In the preceding code sample, Debugger is gathering the `metrics` collection.

> **Note**
>
> For a complete list of built-in collections, refer to `https://github.com/awslabs/sagemaker-debugger/blob/master/docs/api.md#collection`.

You can also create a custom collection of metrics to collect. In the following code block, Debugger captures all the metrics with `relu`, `tanh`, or `weight` in their names:

```
# Use Debugger CollectionConfig to create a custom collection
collection_configs=[
        CollectionConfig(
            name="custom_collection",
            parameters={
                "include_regex": ".*relu |.*tanh | *weight ",

        })
]
```

> **Note**
>
> While it may be tempting to collect all the tensors, this leads to collecting a lot of data, which increases training time, training costs, and storage costs. In this case, using a `ReductionConfig` allows you to save reduced tensors instead of saving the full tensor (`https://github.com/awslabs/sagemaker-debugger/blob/master/docs/api.md#collection`).

While `DebuggerHookConfig` allows you to configure and save tensors, a rule analyzes the tensors that are captured during the training for specific conditions such as **loss not decreasing**. SageMaker Debugger supports two different types of rules: **built-in** and **custom**. SageMaker Debugger comes with a set of built-in rules in Python that can detect and report common training problems such as overfitting, underfitting, and vanishing gradients. With custom rules, you write your own rules in Python for SageMaker Debugger to evaluate against the collected tensors.

For example, in the following code block, Debugger collects tensors related to the `metrics` collection and evaluates the tensors to detect whether the training loss is reduced throughout the training process:

```
Estimator(
    ...

    rules=[
        Rule.sagemaker(
            rule_configs.loss_not_decreasing(),
            rule_parameters={
                "collection_names": "metrics",
                "num_steps": str(save_interval * 2),
            },
        ),
    ],
)
```

Finally, `ProfilerConfig` allows you to collect system metrics such as CPU, GPU, Memory, I/O, and framework metrics specific to the framework being used in your training job. For the system metrics, you must specify the time interval for which you want to collect metrics, while for framework metrics, you specify the starting step and the number of steps, as shown in the following code block:

```
Estimator(
    ...

    profiler_config = ProfilerConfig(
        ## Monitoring interval in milliseconds

        system_monitor_interval_millis=500,        ## Start
collecting metrics from step 2 and collect from the next 7
steps.
        framework_profile_params=FrameworkProfile(
    start_step=2,
    num_steps=7
)    )
```

The following table summarizes the tensors and metrics that are collected by SageMaker. It shows the different types of metrics, examples of each type, and how to collect and use them:

Type	Description	Metrics	Debugger Configuration Parameters to Use
Output Tensors	Collections of model parameters that are updated while optimizing the training process or back propagating deep learning models.	Scalar values (accuracy and loss) and matrices (weights, gradients, input layers, and output layers).	Use `DebuggerHook` and `CollectionConfigs`
System Metrics	Hardware resource utilization data.	CPU, GPU, CPU. and GPU memory, network, and data input and output (I/O).	`ProfilerConfig`
Framework Metrics	Details of the underlying learning frameworks, such as TensorFlow and PyTorch.	Metrics such as time spent on convolutional operations in the forward pass, batch normalization operations in the backward pass, data loader processes between steps, and gradient descent algorithm operations to calculate and update the loss function.	`ProfilerConfig`

Figure 7.2 – Tensors and metrics collected by SageMaker Debugger

Using these configuration parameters, SageMaker Debugger collects quite a lot of information about your training jobs. But how do you ensure that the data that's been collected is secure?

A best practice is to encrypt all the data in an S3 bucket, either with a key provided by AWS or your own key with **customer-managed key** (**CMK**). Additionally, the rules that have been configured are executed on isolated Debugger rule containers. The rule containers also execute in the same VPC as the training job and use the IAM role that's used by the training job.

Once you are satisfied with your Debugger configuration, kick off training using `estimator.fit()`. Next, we will analyze the information that's collected by the Debugger during the training job.

Analyzing the collected tensors and metrics

All tensors and metrics that are collected during training are persisted in S3. SageMaker Debugger uses a `trial` object to represent a single training run. A trial object consists of multiple steps, where each step represents a single batch of training data. At each step, a collected tensor has a specific value.

To access the tensor values, you get the path to the tensors from the estimator, create a trial, get the list of tensors, find out the steps where you have data for a specific tensor you are interested in, and view the values of the tensor.

By following this path from the trial to the individual tensor values, you can manually query the tensor values, as shown in the following code block:

```
tensors_path = estimator.latest_job_debugger_artifacts_path()
print('S3 location of tensors is: ', tensors_path)
trial.tensor_names()
trial.tensor("feature_importance/cover/f1").values()
```

You can visualize the tensor values that have been collected even further by using custom plot code in the notebook. The following diagram shows a visualization of the **train-rmse** and **validation-rmse** training metrics, which were collected during training:

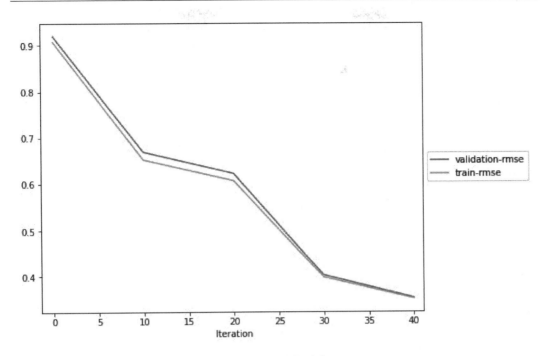

Figure 7.3 – Training and validation errors

Note that you can also view the visualizations in SageMaker Studio. Additionally, if you have rules configured, Debugger automatically analyses the tensors to evaluate training conditions and trigger cloud watch alerts. Similarly, when you set the `ProfileConfig` parameter, a detailed profiler report is generated and saved in S3. Next, let's take a look at how to act on the rule results.

Taking action

Rules evaluate the collected tensor data. As the rule evaluation's status changes during training, a CloudWatch Event is triggered. You can configure a CloudWatch rule to be triggered for the CloudWatch Event to automate actions in response to the issues found by the rules.

Additionally, you can use Debugger's built-in actions to automate the responses. The following code block shows how to use a combination of Debugger's built-in rules and actions to stop a training job if the loss is not continuously reduced during the training process:

```
built_rules=[
        #Check for loss not decreasing during training and stop
the training job.
        Rule.sagemaker(
            rule_configs.loss_not_decreasing(),
            actions = (rule_configs.StopTraining())
        )
]
```

On the other hand, when you have the `ProfilerConfig` parameter configured, a profiler report with a detailed analysis of system metrics and framework metrics is generated and persisted in S3. You can download, review, and apply recommendations to the profiler report.

In the next two sections, you will learn how to automate responses to rule evaluations and implement recommendations from the profiler report.

Real-time monitoring of training jobs using built-in and custom rules

In this section, you will use Debugger capabilities to monitor a job with built-in and custom rules to detect sub-optimal training conditions such as `LossNotDecreasing` and `ExplodingGradients`.

SageMaker provides a set of built-in rules to identify common training issues such as `class_imbalance`, `loss_no_decreasing`, and `overfitting`.

> **Note**
> The complete list of SageMaker built-in rules can be accessed here: `https://docs.aws.amazon.com/sagemaker/latest/dg/debugger-built-in-rules.html`.

The following code sample shows how to configure `built_in` rules with SageMaker Debugger:

```
#Specify the rules you want to run
built_in_rules=[
        #Check for loss not decreasing during training and stop
the training job.
        Rule.sagemaker(
            rule_configs.loss_not_decreasing(),

            actions = (rule_configs.StopTraining())
        ),
        #Check for overfit, overtraining and stalled training
        Rule.sagemaker(rule_configs.overfit()),
    Rule.sagemaker(rule_configs.overtraining()),
    Rule.sagemaker(rule_configs.stalled_training_rule())
]

#Create an estimator and pass in the built_in rules.
pt_estimator = PyTorch(
    ...

    rules = built_in_rules
)
```

After calling fit, SageMaker starts one training job and one processing job for each configured built-in rule. The rule evaluation status is visible in the training logs in CloudWatch at regular intervals. You can also view the results of the rule execution programmatically using the following command:

```
pt_estimator.latest_training_job.rule_job_summary()
```

The results from the built-in rules that have been configured should be similar to the following:

```
[{'RuleConfigurationName': 'LossNotDecreasing',
  'RuleEvaluationJobArn': 'arn:aws:sagemaker:us-west-2:        ':processing-job/pytorch-training-2021-07-1-lossnot
decreasing-13bdb0ae',
  'RuleEvaluationStatus': 'IssuesFound',
  'StatusDetails': 'RuleEvaluationConditionMet: Evaluation of the rule LossNotDecreasing at step 4000 resulted in the
condition being met\n',
  'LastModifiedTime': datetime.datetime(2021, 7, 10, 4, 4, 38, 629000, tzinfo=tzlocal())},
 {'RuleConfigurationName': 'Overfit',
  'RuleEvaluationJobArn': 'arn:aws:sagemaker:us-west-2:                 :processing-job/pytorch-training-2021-07-1-overfit
-757f5c9a',
  'RuleEvaluationStatus': 'NoIssuesFound',
  'LastModifiedTime': datetime.datetime(2021, 7, 10, 4, 4, 38, 629000, tzinfo=tzlocal())},
 {'RuleConfigurationName': 'Overtraining',
  'RuleEvaluationJobArn': 'arn:aws:sagemaker:us-west-2:                 :processing-job/pytorch-training-2021-07-1-overtra
ining-bee8cdc5',
  'RuleEvaluationStatus': 'NoIssuesFound',
  'LastModifiedTime': datetime.datetime(2021, 7, 10, 4, 4, 38, 629000, tzinfo=tzlocal())},
 {'RuleConfigurationName': 'StalledTrainingRule',
  'RuleEvaluationJobArn': 'arn:aws:sagemaker:us-west-2:                 :processing-job/pytorch-training-2021-07-1-stalled
trainingrule-16739dd4',
  'RuleEvaluationStatus': 'NoIssuesFound',
  'LastModifiedTime': datetime.datetime(2021, 7, 10, 4, 4, 38, 629000, tzinfo=tzlocal())},
 {'RuleConfigurationName': 'ProfilerReport-1625888884',
  'RuleEvaluationJobArn': 'arn:aws:sagemaker:us-west-2:                 :processing-job/pytorch-training-2021-07-1-profile
rreport-1625888884-61739bce',
  'RuleEvaluationStatus': 'Stopping',
  'LastModifiedTime': datetime.datetime(2021, 7, 10, 4, 4, 37, 403000, tzinfo=tzlocal())}]
```

Figure 7.4 – Summary of built-in rule execution

By analyzing the rule summary, you can see that the LossNotDecreasing rule is triggered, as indicated by RuleEvaluationStatus – IssuesFound. Since the action that's been configured is used to stop the training job, you will notice that the training job is stopped before all epochs are executed. You can also see that the other built-in rules – Overfit, Overtraining, and StalledTrainingRule – were not triggered during training.

Built-in rules are managed by AWS, freeing you from having to manage updates to rules. You simply plug them into the estimator. However, you may want to monitor a metric that is not included in the built-in rules, in which case you must configure a custom rule. A bit more work is involved with custom rules. For example, let's say you want to track if the gradients are becoming too large during training. To create a custom rule for this, you must extend the Rule interface provided by SageMaker Debugger.

> **Note**
> SageMaker provides two sets of Docker images for rules: one set for evaluating built-in rules and one set for evaluating custom rules. The **Elastic container registry (ECR)** URLs for these Docker images are available at https://docs.aws.amazon.com/sagemaker/latest/dg/debugger-docker-images-rules.html.

In the following example, the custom rule will work with the tensors that were collected using the gradients collection. The invoke_at_step method provides the logic to be executed. At each step, the mean value of the gradient is compared against a threshold. If the gradient value is greater than the threshold, the rule is triggered, as shown in the following code:

```
class CustomGradientRule(Rule):
    def __init__(self, base_trial, threshold=10.0):
        super().__init__(base_trial)
        self.threshold = float(threshold)

    def invoke_at_step(self, step):
        for tname in self.base_trial.tensor_
names(collection="gradients"):
            t = self.base_trial.tensor(tname)
            abs_mean = t.reduction_value(step, "mean",
abs=True)
            if abs_mean > self.threshold:
                return True
        return False
```

Next, define the custom rule, as follows:

```
custom_rule = Rule.custom(
    name='CustomRule', # used to identify the rule
    # rule evaluator container image

image_uri='759209512951.dkr.ecr.us-west-2.amazonaws.com/
sagemaker-debugger-rule-evaluator:latest',        instance_
type='ml.t3.medium',        source='rules/my_custom_rule.py', #
path to the rule source file
    rule_to_invoke='CustomGradientRule', # name of the class to
invoke in the rule source file
    volume_size_in_gb=30, # EBS volume size required to be
attached to the rule evaluation instance
    collections_to_save=[CollectionConfig("gradients")],
    # collections to be analyzed by the rule. since this is a
first party collection we fetch it as above
    rule_parameters={
```

```
       #Threshold to compare the gradient value against
       "threshold": "20.0"        }
)
```

Configure the custom rule in the estimator and call the `fit` method, as follows:

```
pt_estimator_custom = PyTorch(
    ...
    ## New parameter
    rules = [custom_rule]
)
estimator.fit(wait = False)
```

After calling `fit`, Amazon SageMaker starts one training job and one processing job for each configured customer rule. The rule evaluation status is visible in the training logs in CloudWatch at regular intervals. Similar to the rule summary for `built_in` rules, you can view the custom rule summary using the following code:

```
pt_estimator.latest_training_job.rule_job_summary()
```

Using a combination of built-in and custom rules, you can gain insight into the training process and proactively stop the training jobs, without having to run an ineffective training job to completion.

> **Important note**
>
> An example notebook that provides a complete walkthrough of using SageMaker Debugger's built-in and custom rules is provided in the following GitHub repository: `https://gitlab.com/randydefauw/packt_book/-/blob/master/CH06/debugger/weather-prediction-debugger-rules.ipynb`.

In this section, you got an inside look at the training process and improved the training job based on issues that have been detected by built-in and custom rules. In the next section, you will learn how to gain insight into the infrastructure and framework that's used for training jobs.

Gaining insight into the training infrastructure and training framework

In this section, you will learn how to gain visibility into the resource utilization of the training infrastructure and the training framework. You will also learn how to analyze and implement recommendations provided by the deep profiler capability of SageMaker Debugger.

Debugger profiler provides you with visibility into the utilization of the infrastructure running ML training jobs on SageMaker. Debugger automatically monitors system resources such as CPU, GPU, network, I/O, and memory. Additionally, Debugger collects metrics specific to the training framework such as step duration, data loading, preprocessing, and operator runtime on CPU and GPU. You can decide to profile the training job in its entirety or just portions of it to collect the necessary framework metrics.

In addition to collecting the system and framework metrics, behind the scenes, Debugger correlates these metrics automatically, which makes it easy for you to identify possible resource bottlenecks and perform root cause analysis.

Let's explore this in detail with our example use case – predicting weather using PyTorch. Here, we will explore the system metrics, the framework metrics that are generated by the profiler, and look at implementing recommendations made by the profiler. This kind of deep profiling of training jobs includes the following high-level steps:

1. Training a PyTorch model for weather prediction with Debugger enabled.
2. Analyzing and visualizing the system and framework metrics generated by the profiler.
3. Analyzing the profiler report generated by SageMaker Debugger.
4. Reviewing and implementing recommendations from the profiler report.
5. Comparing the training jobs.

Let's look at each of these steps in detail.

Training a PyTorch model for weather prediction

First, we will train a deep learning model using the PyTorch framework. Because of the large volumes of data and the deep learning framework, we'll train on GPU instances. We will train on two `ml.p3.2xlarge` instances. Our infrastructure configuration will look as follows:

```
...
train_instance_type = "ml.p3.2xlarge"
instance_count = 2
```

Next, let's define `ProfilerConfig` so that it can collect system and framework metrics:

```
profiler_config = ProfilerConfig(
    system_monitor_interval_millis=500,
    framework_profile_params=FrameworkProfile(start_step=2,
num_steps=7)
)
```

Now, we must configure the PyTorch estimator by using the infrastructure and profiler configuration as parameters:

```
pt_estimator = PyTorch(
    entry_point="train_pytorch.py",
    source_dir="code",
    role=sagemaker.get_execution_role(),
    instance_count=instance_count,
    instance_type=train_instance_type,
    framework_version="1.6",
    py_version="py3",
    volume_size=1024,
    # Debugger-specific parameters
    profiler_config=profiler_config,
)
```

Now, let's start the training job with the `fit()` method:

```
estimator.fit(inputs, wait= False)
```

In the next section, you will analyze and visualize the metrics generated by Debugger.

Analyzing and visualizing the system and framework metrics generated by the profiler

Once the training job starts, Debugger starts collecting system and framework metrics. In this section, you will learn how to query, analyze, and visualize the collected metrics.

First, let's look at how to analyze the collected metrics manually. The following code block shows how to query for system metrics:

```
#All collected metrics are persisted in S3.  Define path to the
profiler artifacts
path = estimator.latest_job_profiler_artifacts_path()
#Create a reader for the system metrics
system_metrics_reader = S3SystemMetricsReader(path)
#Get the latest event
last_timestamp = system_metrics_reader.get_timestamp_of_latest_
available_file()
events = system_metrics_reader.get_events(0, last_timestamp *
1000000)   # UTC time in microseconds
#Show the first system metric event collected
print(
    "Event name:",  events[0].name,
    "\nTimestamp:",  timestamp_to_utc(events[0].timestamp),
    "\nValue:", events[0].value,
)
```

The preceding code block results in the following output, which shows the GPU of one of the training instances at a particular time:

```
Event name: gpu2
Timestamp: 2021-07-02 18:44:20
Value: 0.0
```

The value of 0.0 indicates that this GPU is not being utilized.

Similar to the system metrics, you can review framework metrics as well. The following code block shows how to query for framework metrics:

```
#Create a reader for the system metrics
framework_metrics_reader = S3AlgorithmMetricsReader(path)
framework_metrics_reader.refresh_event_file_list()
```

```
last_timestamp = framework_metrics_reader.get_timestamp_of_
latest_available_file()
```

```
events = framework_metrics_reader.get_events(0, last_timestamp)
```

```
#We can inspect one of the recorded events to get the
following:
```

```
print("Event name:", events[0].event_name,
      "\nStart time:", timestamp_to_utc(events[0].start_
time/1000000000),
      "\nEnd time:", timestamp_to_utc(events[0].end_
time/1000000000),
      "\nDuration:", events[0].duration, "nanosecond")
```

The preceding code block results in the following, showing one of the framework metrics at a particular time:

```
Event name: embeddings.0
Start time: 1970-01-19 19:27:42
End time: 1970-01-19 19:27:42
Duration: 141298 nanosecond
```

Once the metrics have been collected, you can visualize them using a heat map or custom plots in the notebook.

> **Important note**
>
> For a more colorful visualization of the heat map and a more in-depth analysis of system and framework metrics, take a look at the following notebook: `https://gitlab.com/randydefauw/packt_book/-/blob/master/CH06/weather-prediction-debugger-profiler.ipynb`.

Analyzing the profiler report generated by SageMaker Debugger

In this section, we will download and review the profiler report that was generated by Debugger. SageMaker Debugger creates a detailed profiler report and saves it in an S3 bucket at s3://<your bucket> /<job-name>/profiler-output/. You can download the report directly from S3. In the following list, we will review a few sections of the downloaded report:

- **Training job summary**

  This section of the report provides a detailed summary of the training job, including the start and end time of the job and the time that was spent on various phases of training. The following screenshot shows a sample of the training job's summary:

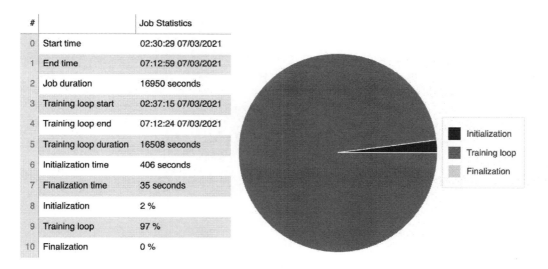

#		Job Statistics
0	Start time	02:30:29 07/03/2021
1	End time	07:12:59 07/03/2021
2	Job duration	16950 seconds
3	Training loop start	02:37:15 07/03/2021
4	Training loop end	07:12:24 07/03/2021
5	Training loop duration	16508 seconds
6	Initialization time	406 seconds
7	Finalization time	35 seconds
8	Initialization	2 %
9	Training loop	97 %
10	Finalization	0 %

Figure 7.5 – Training job summary of the profiler report

- **System metrics summary**

  This section of the report shows the resource utilization of the training nodes. The following screenshot shows CPU, GPU, memory utilization, I/O wait time, and the amount of data that was sent and received:

#	node	metric	unit	max	p99	p95	p50	min
0	algo-1	Network	bytes	31516.36	0	0	0	0
1	algo-2	Network	bytes	4159.83	0	0	0	0
2	algo-1	GPU	percentage	33	8	8	8	0
3	algo-2	GPU	percentage	30	9	8	7	0
4	algo-1	CPU	percentage	98.2	33.97	24.1	13.29	0
5	algo-2	CPU	percentage	100	37.37	27.49	13.86	0.75
6	algo-1	CPU memory	percentage	40.32	40.29	40.28	40.25	2.38
7	algo-2	CPU memory	percentage	44.35	44.25	44.23	44.21	2.35
8	algo-1	GPU memory	percentage	2	2	2	1	0
9	algo-2	GPU memory	percentage	2	2	2	1	0
10	algo-1	I/O	percentage	78.76	2.95	0.5	0	0
11	algo-2	I/O	percentage	99.48	1.7	0.52	0	0

  Figure 7.6 – System metrics summary of the profiler report

- **Framework metrics summary**

  This section of the report starts by showing how much time the training job spent in the training and validation phases, as well as the time it spent waiting:

The ratio between the time spent on the TRAIN/EVAL phase and others

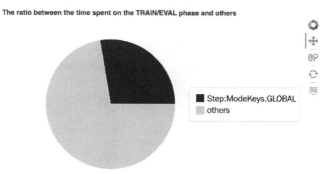

The following piechart shows a breakdown of the CPU/GPU operators. It shows that 49% of training time was spent on executing the "gpu_functions-dev:0" operator.

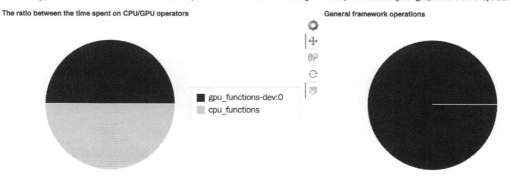

Figure 7.7 – Framework metrics summary of the profiler report

- **Rules summary**

  As the training job is running, Debugger executes a set of rules to profile the training process. This section of the profiler report summarizes all the debugger rules that have been evaluated, the description of the rule, the number of times each rule was triggered during training, the analysis, and recommendations for improving the training job. The following screenshot shows the rule summary in table format:

Rules summary

The following table shows a profiling summary of the Debugger built-in rules. The table is sorted by the rules that triggered the most frequently. During your training job, the LowGPUUtilization rule was the most frequently triggered. It processed 36420 datapoints and was triggered 592 times.

	Description	Recommendation	Number of times rule triggered	Number of datapoints	Rule parameters
LowGPUUtilization	Checks if the GPU utilization is low or fluctuating. This can happen due to bottlenecks, blocking calls for synchronizations, or a small batch size.	Check if there are bottlenecks, minimize blocking calls, change distributed training strategy, or increase the batch size.	592	36420	threshold_p95:70 threshold_p5:10 window:500 patience:1000
BatchSize	Checks if GPUs are underutilized because the batch size is too small. To detect this problem, the rule analyzes the average GPU memory footprint, the CPU and the GPU utilization.	The batch size is too small, and GPUs are underutilized. Consider running on a smaller instance type or increasing the batch size.	592	36419	cpu_threshold_p95:70 gpu_threshold_p95:70 gpu_memory_threshold_p95:70 patience:1000 window:500
StepOutlier	Detects outliers in step duration. The step duration for forward and backward pass should be roughly the same throughout the training. If there are significant outliers, it may indicate a system stall or bottleneck issues.	Check if there are any bottlenecks (CPU, I/O) correlated to the step outliers.	368	464225	threshold:3 mode:None n_outliers:10 stddev:3
CPUBottleneck	Checks if the CPU utilization is high and the GPU utilization is low. It might indicate CPU bottlenecks, where the GPUs are waiting for data to arrive from the CPUs. The rule evaluates the CPU and GPU utilization rates, and triggers the issue if the time spent on the CPU bottlenecks exceeds a threshold percent of the total training time. The default threshold is 50 percent.	Consider increasing the number of data loaders or applying data pre-fetching.	300	72913	threshold:50 cpu_threshold:90 gpu_threshold:10 patience:1000

Figure 7.8 – Rules summary of the profiler report

In addition to directly querying and visualizing the metrics, as well as downloading the profiler report in your notebook, you can use SageMaker Studio, which provides built-in visualizations for analyzing profiling insights.

To access Debugger in Studio, follow these steps:

1. On the navigation pane, choose **Components and registries**.
2. Choose **Experiments and trails**.
3. Choose your training job (right-click).
4. Choose **Debugger Insights** from the Debugger tab that opens.

In the **Debugger** tab, you will see multiple sections. One of these sections is called **Training job summary**, as shown in the following screenshot. This built-in visualization shows training job details, such as the start time, end time, duration, and time spent in individual phases of training. The pie chart visualization shows the relative time spent by the training job in the initialization, training, and finalization phases:

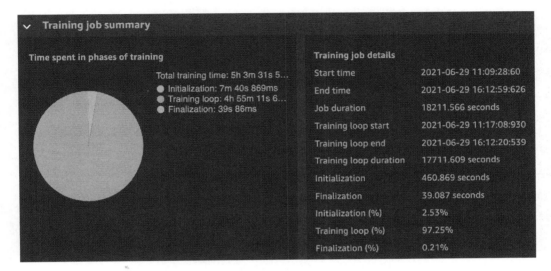

Figure 7.9 – Debugger visualization in SageMaker Studio

In this section, we reviewed a few sections of the downloaded profiler report at a high level. To explore the profiler report in more detail, please run through the notebook in our Git repository.

Analyzing and implementing recommendations from the profiler report

Now that we have recommendations from the profiler, let's analyze and implement a recommendation to see if it leads to an improved training job.

From the rules summary table in the preceding section, we can see that the rule triggered a maximum number of times during our training is LowGPUUtilization. This rule indicates that there is a possibility of bottlenecks occurring due to blocking calls and recommends changing the distributed training strategy or increasing the batch size. The next rule that was triggered the most times was BatchSize, which indicates that the GPU utilization could be low because of the smaller batch size.

The recommendation from the profiler, based on this rule's execution, is to consider running on a smaller instance type and to increase the batch size. Let's combine the profiler recommendations from these two most triggered rules, run two new training jobs with different settings, and check the profiler reports for the new training jobs to see if there is any improvement.

We will run the first training job with the same infrastructure, ( ), but with an increased batch size, as shown in the following code block:

```
train_instance_type='ml.p3.2xlarge'
instance_count = 2
hyperparameters = {"batch_size": 1024}
```

For the next training job, we will use smaller training instances, ( ), and increase the batch size:

```
training_job_name=
train_instance_type='ml.p2.8xlarge'
instance_count = 2
hyperparameters = {"batch_size": 1024}
```

Using these two different configurations, run two different training jobs using `estimator.fit()`. Once the training jobs are complete, download and analyze the two profiler reports.

Comparing the two training jobs

At this point, we have a total of three completed training jobs with different configurations. In this section, we'll compare the original training job to the two new training jobs we configured based on the recommendations from the profiler. When comparing these jobs, we will focus on the training time and the resulting training costs. The following table shows the initial and revised training job configurations, along with the training time, resource utilization, and cost comparisons:

Original Training Configuration		Revised Training Configuration1 (batch_size updated)	Revised Training Configuration2 (batch_size and instance_type updated)
Instance Type	p3.2xlarge	p3.2xlarge	p2.8xlarge
Instance Count	2	2	2
Batch Size	64	1024	1024
Training Time (in seconds)	18262	895	1054
Cost (in $)	2328.405	114.11	39.5

Figure 7.10 – Comparison of training jobs

First, let's compare the original training job with the training job that uses the first revised training configuration. In the revised training configuration, the batch size is increased from 64 to 1024. This configuration change decreased the training time by 17637 seconds; that is, from 18262 seconds to 895 seconds. Assuming that the training jobs were run in the us-west-2 region, the cost of p3.2xlarge is $3.825 at the time of writing. This leads to a cost saving of 26.67%.

Similarly, if you compare the second revised training configuration, where we updated both the batch size and instance type to the original, the training time increased but the overall training cost improved by 65.36%. If you can tolerate a slight increase in the training time, you can save on training costs by implementing recommendations from the profiler.

> **Important note**
>
> An example notebook that provides a complete walkthrough of using the SageMaker Debugger profiler is provided in the following GitHub repository: https://gitlab.com/randydefauw/packt_book/-/blob/master/CH06/weather-prediction-debugger-profiler.ipynb.
>
> The results that were discussed in this section are from using the full dataset for PyTorch training. In the notebook, you will have the chance to explore the same functionality but with a smaller dataset.

In this section, we implemented a couple of recommendations from the profiler and saw considerable training improvements. There are still more recommendations that you can experiment with.

Additionally, in this section, we focused on how to kick off an estimator with Debugger enabled. You can also attach a profiler to a running training job using `estimator.enable_default_profiling()`. Similarly, to enable Debugger's built-in rules, system monitoring, and framework profiling with customizable configuration parameters, use `estimator.update_profiler()`.

Summary

In this chapter, you learned how to use the capabilities of Amazon SageMaker Debugger to gain visibility of the training process, training infrastructure, and training framework. This visibility allows you to react to typical training issues such as overfitting, training loss, and stopping the training jobs from running to completion, only to result in sub-optimal models. Using recommendations from the deep profiler capabilities of Amazon SageMaker, you learned how to improve training jobs with respect to training time and costs.

Using the debugger capabilities discussed in this chapter, you can continuously improve your training jobs by tweaking the underlying ML framework parameters and the training infrastructure configurations for faster and cost-effective ML training. In the next chapter, you will learn how to manage trained models at scale.

Further reading

For additional reading material, please review these references:

- Identify bottlenecks, improve resource utilization, and reduce ML training costs with the deep profiling feature in Amazon SageMaker Debugger:

  `https://aws.amazon.com/blogs/machine-learning/identify-bottlenecks-improve-resource-utilization-and-reduce-ml-training-costs-with-the-new-profiling-feature-in-amazon-sagemaker-debugger/`

- ML Explainability with Amazon SageMaker Debugger:

  `https://aws.amazon.com/blogs/machine-learning/ml-explainability-with-amazon-sagemaker-debugger/`

Section 3:
Manage and
Monitor Models

This section addresses the challenges of managing and monitoring a large number of models, updating models in production with minimal downtime, and choosing an appropriate deployment strategy for a cost-optimized way to satisfy business goals.

This section comprises the following chapters:

- *Chapter 8, Managing Models at Scale Using a Model Registry*
- *Chapter 9, Updating Production Models Using Amazon SageMaker Endpoint Production Variants*
- *Chapter 10, Optimizing Model Hosting and Inference Costs*
- *Chapter 11, Monitoring Production Models with Amazon SageMaker Model Monitor and Clarify*

8

Managing Models at Scale Using a Model Registry

As you begin to deploy multiple models and manage multiple model versions, ensuring core architectural practices such as governance, traceability, and recoverability are followed is challenging without using a model registry. A model registry is a central store containing metadata specific to a model version. It includes information on how the model was built, the performance of that model, as well as where and how the model is deployed. Model registry services or solutions often include additional capabilities, such as approval workflows and notifications.

In this chapter, we'll cover the concept of a model registry and why a model registry is important for managing multiple models at scale. We'll also outline considerations you need to make when choosing a model registry implementation, in order to best meet the needs of your environment and operational requirements. For this, we'll examine two example implementations of a model registry. These will be a custom-built model registry using AWS services, as well as SageMaker's implementation (called the SageMaker model registry).

Amazon SageMaker provides a built-in model registry. This is a fully managed model registry, optimized for use within Amazon SageMaker. However, if the Amazon SageMaker model registry does not meet your needs, there are several common patterns utilizing either a custom-built model registry or a third-party solution that also work well with Amazon SageMaker. Although there are many third-party model registries available that can be used for SageMaker-trained models, we do not cover them specifically in this chapter.

In this chapter, we're going to cover the following main topics:

- Using a model registry
- Choosing a model registry solution
- Managing models using the Amazon SageMaker model registry

Technical requirements

You will need an AWS account to run the examples included in this chapter. If you have not set up the data science environment yet, please refer to *Chapter 2, Data Science Environments*. This provides a walk-through of the setup process.

Code examples included in the book are available on GitHub at the following URL: `https://github.com/PacktPublishing/Amazon-SageMaker-Best-Practices/tree/main/Chapter08`. You will need to install a Git client to access them (`https://git-scm.com/`).

The code for this chapter is in the `CH08` folder of the GitHub repository.

Using a model registry

A model registry allows you to centrally track key metadata for each model version. The granularity of metadata tracked is often dependent on the chosen implementation (Amazon SageMaker's model registry, a custom solution, or a third-party solution).

Regardless of the implementation, the key metadata to consider includes model version identifiers, and the following information about each model version registered:

- **Model inputs**: These include metadata related to the inputs and versions of those inputs used to train the model. This can include inputs such as the name of the Amazon S3 bucket storing the training data, training hyperparameters, and the **Amazon Elastic Container Registry** (**ECR**) repository or container image used for training.

- **Model performance**: This includes model evaluation data such as training and validation metrics.

- **Model artifact**: This includes metadata about the training model artifact. At a minimum, this includes the name of the Amazon S3 bucket storing the model artifact, as well as the name of the object (for example, `model.tar.gz`).

- **Model deployment**: This includes metadata relating to the deployment of a model. This includes information such as the environment(s) a model version is deployed to, or the inference code that can be used for the registered model.

Amazon SageMaker offers multiple options for training models including built-in algorithms, built-in frameworks (that is, script mode), and a bring-your-own container. Depending on the option chosen, the number of inputs required to train a model can vary. This could impact the metadata you choose to track. As a result, it's important to determine the minimum requirements of metadata that you need to track in order to meet any regulatory or internal traceability requirements you may have.

When evaluating levels of granularity, you need to track your use case. Keep in mind the way your teams are using Amazon SageMaker to build models. *Figure 8.1* illustrates an example of the inputs, metrics, and artifacts to consider for tracking across the SageMaker options for training models:

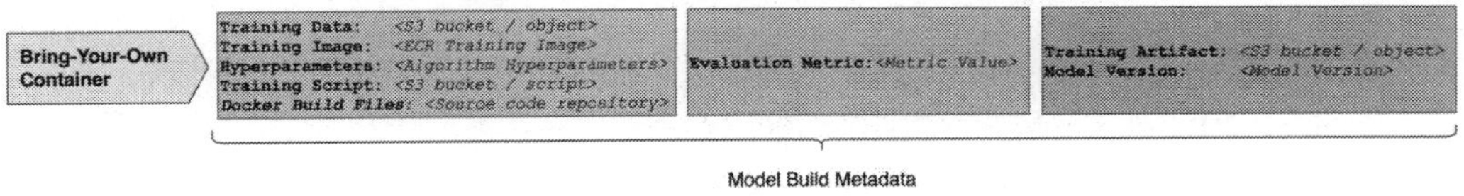

Figure 8.1 – Model build metadata across training options

Similar considerations exist for tracking and storing model deployment data. The metadata tracked for model deployments should provide enough information to package the model for deployment using Amazon SageMaker, to a real-time endpoint, or using batch transform. This should also allow someone to easily identify where a given model version is deployed, as well as how it is packaged for deployment and consumption. *Figure 8.2* illustrates an example of the inputs, deployment stages, and artifacts to consider for tracking across the SageMaker options for deploying models:

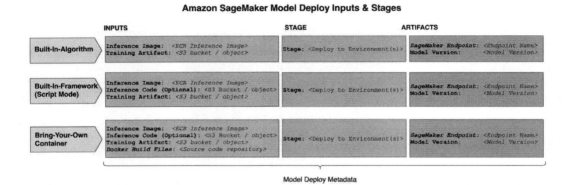

Figure 8.2 – Model deploy metadata across deployment options

If you had a couple of models to manage, you could potentially track the previous information using a simple method, such as a spreadsheet. However, as you begin to scale to 20, 100, or thousands of models, that mechanism for tracking model metadata no longer scales. Centrally storing and tracking the information (shown in *Figures 8.1* and *8.2*) for each model version provides the following benefits:

- **Operational efficiencies**: A model registry provides tracking and visibility into key inputs used to build a specific model version, output artifacts, and information about the deployment stages aligned to that version. Having this metadata allows for the ability to quickly understand how a model was built, how the model performed, information about the trained model artifact, and also provides the ability to track the environment(s) a specific version is deployed to.

- **Recoverability**: To be able to recover a deployed model or roll back to a previous version, you need to have visibility to the inputs and input versions used to create a deployable artifact or a deployed model. In the event of system or human error, you can recover to a specific point in time using the metadata stored in the model registry, combined with protected versioned inputs. As an example, if an administrator were to accidentally delete a model endpoint, it should be easy to identify the artifacts needed to recreate that endpoint. This can be identified using metadata stored in the model registry that points to the location of the versioned model artifact, in combination with the versioned inference container image.

- **Pipeline sources and triggers**: Often there is a need to bridge the model build and model deployment environments. This is typical in large enterprises that have central deployment teams, or in organizations that separate model build and model deployment roles. A model registry provides a mechanism to capture the minimum metadata needed for visibility into how a model is built. However, it can also be used to trigger approval workflows and downstream deployments.

In the next section, we'll cover three patterns for creating a model registry to centrally track and manage machine learning models at scale. The considerations and high-level architectures of each will be outlined in order to guide you to the right fit for your specific use case.

Choosing a model registry solution

There are multiple options available for implementing a model registry. While each implementation offers different features or capabilities, the concept of providing a central repository to track key metadata largely remains the same across implementations. In this section, we'll cover a few common patterns for creating a model registry, as well as discuss the considerations for each. The patterns covered in this section include the following:

- Amazon SageMaker model registry

- Building a custom model registry

- Utilizing a third-party or **open source software** (**OSS**) model registry

Amazon SageMaker model registry

The Amazon SageMaker model registry is a managed service that allows you to centrally catalog models, manage model versions, associate metadata with your model versions, and manage the approval status of a model version. The service is continuously evolving with new features, so the information contained in this section is current as of the publication date. It's always recommended to validate the current features and capabilities with the official documentation for the *Amazon SageMaker model registry* (`https://docs.aws.amazon.com/sagemaker/latest/dg/model-registry.html`). The SageMaker model registry is optimized for use in conjunction with Amazon SageMaker Pipelines and projects; however, it can also be used independently as well.

You can interact with the SageMaker's model registry programmatically, as well as within Amazon SageMaker Studio. Studio provides a visual interface and experience for version management. The Studio interface also provides additional search capabilities. These can be seen in the following screenshot:

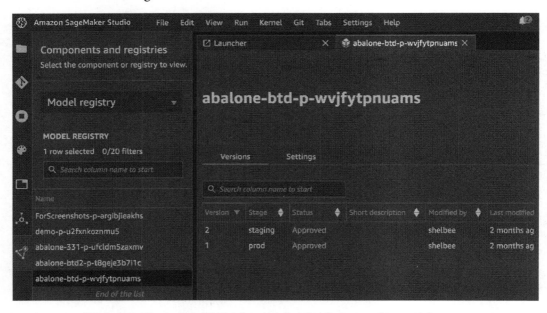

Figure 8.3 – The SageMaker Studio interface for the SageMaker model registry

The SageMaker model registry also includes an approval status that can be modified when a model is approved for production. This could be after a peer or designated deployment approver reviews the model metadata and metrics as a final quality gate for deployment. In the following screenshot, you can see how the approval status field integrates natively with MLOps projects in Amazon SageMaker Pipelines to create automatic triggers based on a change in model status:

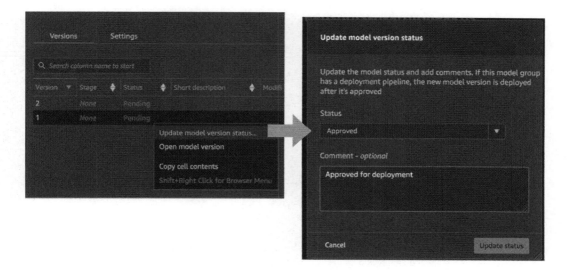

Figure 8.4 – SageMaker model registry – approval status

The main components of the SageMaker model registry include the following:

- **Model registry**: This is the central store containing model groups and it exists at the AWS account and AWS region levels. Cross-account privileges can be set up to interact with the model registry from other AWS accounts.

- **Model groups**: Model groups are a logical grouping. They allow you to track different model versions that are related to, or grouped by, the same machine learning problem.

- **Model packages**: Model packages are registered models or specific versions of a model.

Figure 8.5 illustrates the main components, where each model version is a model package contained in a model group inside the model registry:

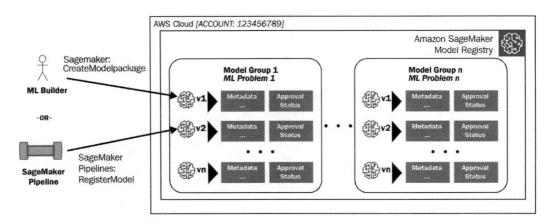

Figure 8.5 – Amazon SageMaker model registry components and usage

When registering a new model version within a model group, you can use either the AWS SDK for Python (`boto3`) with the `create_model_package` method (`https://boto3.amazonaws.com/v1/documentation/api/latest/reference/services/sagemaker.html#SageMaker.Client.create_model_package`), or create a step within a model build pipeline, using the `RegisterModel` step (`https://sagemaker.readthedocs.io/en/stable/workflows/pipelines/sagemaker.workflow.pipelines.html#pipeline`) within Amazon SageMaker Pipelines. Understanding the ways you can register a model is important for understanding how you can use the SageMaker model registry outside of SageMaker Pipelines. It is also important for understanding how you can integrate the SageMaker model registry into other workflow tooling options you may already be using.

It's possible to register a model as either **versioned** or **unversioned**. Model packages that are versioned are part of a model group, and unversioned model packages are not part of a model group. The benefit of using a model group, or a versioned model, is the ability to logically group and manage models that are related, as well as provide the ability to automatically version models related to a specific **machine learning** (**ML**) problem. It's recommended to register your models using model groups with registered models that are versioned. This is the default setting.

A registered model has specific metadata that can be associated with that version. The metadata is defined and configured by the API request parameters. At high-level, the API accepts and associates the following key metadata as input:

- **Inference specification**: A series of parameters that provide detailed information and guidance on hosting the model for inference. Information passed includes data such as the Amazon ECR data. This contains the inference code image, the Amazon S3 bucket containing the trained model artifact, and the supported instance types when hosting the model for either real-time inference or for batch inference. For example, if a model requires GPU for inference, that can be captured in the registry.

- **Model metrics**: Model evaluation metrics across evaluated categories, such as statistical bias in a model, or model quality.

- **Validation specification**: Information about the SageMaker batch transform job(s) that were used to validate the model package (if applicable).

- **Algorithm specification**: Details about the algorithm(s) used to create the model, as well as the Amazon S3 bucket containing the trained model artifact.

- **Metadata properties**: These properties contain metadata for the `CodeCommit` commit ID, author of the source, the SageMaker Pipelines project ID, and the name of the `CodeCommit` repository. While they are not restricted for use outside Amazon SageMaker Pipelines, they are direct pointers to SageMaker Pipelines project resources.

- **Model approval status**: This parameter is used to indicate whether a model is approved for deployment. This parameter can be used to manage workflows. In the case of SageMaker Pipelines projects, the automated workflow triggers are automatically set up based on the status of this field. If a model status is changed to **approved**, a downstream deployment workflow can be triggered.

Amazon SageMaker's model registry is fully managed, meaning there are no servers to manage. It also natively integrates into SageMaker Pipelines, providing the ability to integrate directly with the model registry as a native step in your model build pipeline. It does this using the `RegisterModel` step.

For example, if you build a model build pipeline that contains the automated steps for data processing, training, and model evaluation, you can add a conditional step to validate the evaluation metric. If the evaluation metric is above a specified threshold (for example, accuracy > 90%), the pipeline can then be configured to automatically register your model.

SageMaker's model registry also integrates natively with SageMaker Pipelines projects. Projects allow you to automatically provision MLOps pipelines and provision patterns that take advantage of the model registry. SageMaker projects can be used to automatically set up the model package group, as well as the approval workflows that can be used to trigger the pre-configured downstream deployment pipeline.

> **Important note**
> Amazon SageMaker Pipelines is covered in more detail in *Chapter 12, Machine Learning Automated Workflows*. The model registry is a component within SageMaker Pipelines but can be used independently of SageMaker Pipelines.

Many of the parameters passed as input to the `CreateModelPackage` API are tailored for Amazon SageMaker use and integrations with other Amazon SageMaker features. For example, data that can be associated with model metrics has a direct correlation with metrics produced with features such as Amazon SageMaker Clarify, model statistical bias metrics, Amazon SageMaker Model Monitor, and data quality constraint metrics. In another example, the validation specification relates specifically to a SageMaker batch transform job run to evaluate the SageMaker model package.

In this section, we reviewed the high-level architecture and usage of the Amazon SageMaker model registry to provide a basis for comparison against other options that will be covered in the next sections. Multiple options are being covered in this chapter. This is in order to support a variety of use cases and to help you choose the right option for your specific use case.

Building a custom model registry

A model registry can also be built using AWS services. Building a custom registry requires more effort to build the solution, set up the integrations between AWS services, set up the ML pipeline integrations, and then manage the solution. However, a custom registry also offers the ability to completely customize a registry to meet the needs specific to your use case. This could include requirements specific to tracking more granular metadata, or requirements to support multiple ML services/platforms. In this section, we'll review one pattern for creating a custom model registry using AWS services.

The pattern shown in *Figure 8.6* illustrates a simple model registry built using Amazon DynamoDB. DynamoDB can be used to store model metadata using a design pattern that separates groups of models by partition key. You could also consider a design pattern establishing a new table for different teams or business units if table-level isolation is preferred. Controls should also be set up using **AWS Identity and Access Management (IAM)** to control access to DynamoDB for specific tables, as well as specific primary keys to set up controls on who can access specific model groupings:

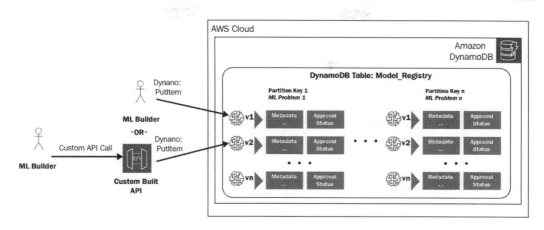

Figure 8.6 – Custom-built model registry using AWS services

The schema for a model registry based on DynamoDB provides flexibility in the metadata that can be stored for each model version. As an example, you may want to track data versions that correspond to the object(s) in an Amazon S3 bucket. A custom-built model registry provides the flexibility to define and adjust the schema to meet your individual requirements for traceability or for more granular metadata tracking.

Interacting with a custom-built model registry can be done through the Amazon DynamoDB API (**PutItem**) or through a custom-built API. Using a simple **PutItem**, API can often work for smaller teams or teams that perform end-to-end tasks, such as model building, model deployment, and operating in a production environment. However, in many cases, a model registry is built as part of a shared service (or ML platform component) that serves multiple teams and use cases. In this case, it's recommended to build an API that includes similar controls and validations that are seen in a managed service, such as SageMaker's model registry.

To extend a custom-built model registry to include workflow tasks, such as triggering a model deployment pipeline based on a changed attribute, the solution needs to be extended to set up the trigger to detect a change and then execute any downstream processes you want to invoke. To do this, you can enable DynamoDB Streams and AWS Lambda triggers.

In this section, we covered a high-level implementation pattern for creating a custom model registry using AWS services. This example provides complete flexibility in the registry schema, data points collected, and in defining the intended usage.

As an example, you may have some teams that utilize Amazon SageMaker features, but other teams that are utilizing other services or even building models on-premises. Building a custom registry also allows the flexibility to place the model registry in the AWS account you choose, based on your existing multi-account strategy, and adjust the schema based on usage.

The pattern discussed also utilizes AWS-managed services, DynamoDB and API Gateway, meaning there are still no servers to manage. However, this is not a packaged solution. Therefore, the services need to be set up and configured. Interfacing code may need to be written, integrations between services need to be set up, and the solution needs to be managed.

Utilizing a third-party or OSS model registry

Next, we'll briefly cover using a third-party or OSS implementation of a model registry. Because there are a lot of options available, this section will focus on high-level considerations, rather than diving deep into any specific implementation. Common implementations, such as MLflow, have existing documentation provided for integrating with Amazon SageMaker. Those resources should be utilized when implementing a third-party/OSS implementation and integrating with Amazon SageMaker.

When considering a third-party or OSS implementation, there are a few questions to consider when evaluating your options:

- Does the implementation require you to manage the underlying servers, meaning you need to incur some additional operational overhead to ensure servers are patched, monitored, scaled, and set up using a readily available architecture?

- Does the implementation offer native integrations that make it easy to integrate with Amazon SageMaker?

- What additional credentials do you need to set up and manage in order to integrate with Amazon SageMaker?

Using a third-party or OSS option can add some additional overheads in terms of setup, integration, and ongoing management. However, many of these implementations offer robust capabilities, interfaces, and extensibility that may be preferred depending on your ML environments and use cases.

In this section, we discussed three common patterns for model registry implementations for use with Amazon SageMaker models. Each pattern can be a valid choice depending on your requirements. As a result, key considerations for each were discussed to provide general guidance in order to choose the best implementation.

In general, it is recommended to choose the option that provides the capabilities you need based on your own requirements, combined with the option that offers the lowest development and operational overhead. In the next section, we'll narrow the focus to a technical deep dive into the Amazon SageMaker model registry.

Managing models using the Amazon SageMaker model registry

An introduction to the Amazon SageMaker model registry was included in the section titled *Amazon SageMaker model registry*. This was done in order to explain the high-level architecture and features that are important to consider when choosing a model registry implementation. In this section, we'll dive deeper into the Amazon SageMaker model registry by covering the process and best practice guidance when setting up and using SageMaker's model registry.

SageMaker's model registry includes the model registry, as well as model groups and model packages. Each model group contains model versions, or model packages, related to the same ML problem. Each model package represents a specific version of a model and includes metadata associated with that version. The SageMaker model registry APIs are used when interacting with the SageMaker model registry, and those APIs can also be called through any of the following:

- **AWS Command Line Interface (CLI)**: This uses commands to interact with the model registry, such as `create-model-package-group` or `create-model-package` commands.

- **AWS Python SDK** (`boto3`): This uses methods to interact with the model registry, such as the `create_model_package_group` or `create_model_package` methods.

- **Amazon SageMaker Studio**: This uses the click-through interface in SageMaker Studio (as shown in *Figure 8.7*) to create a model package group.

- **Amazon SageMaker Pipelines**: This uses the built-in `RegisterModelstep`.

Figure 8.7 illustrates creating a model package group using the Studio UI:

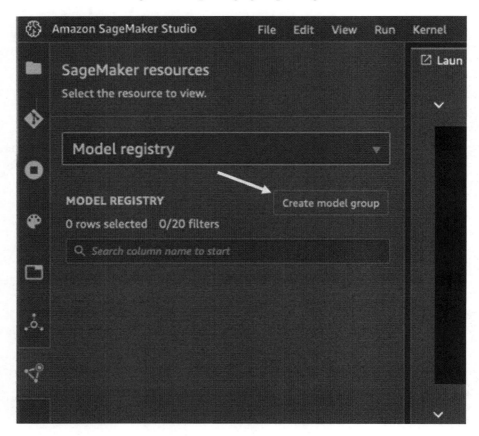

Figure 8.7 – Using SageMaker Studio to create a new model group

Although you can interact with the model registry using any of the methods listed, in this chapter we'll cover interacting with the model registry using the AWS Python SDK (boto3), to showcase a lower level of abstraction that is not dependent on Amazon SageMaker Studio or Amazon SageMaker Pipelines.

In this section, you learned more about the primary components of the SageMaker model registry, as well as the different ways you can interact with the model registry either programmatically or via the Studio UI.

Creating a model package group

A model package group contains a collection of model packages or model versions. A model package group is not required for registering a model package; however, it is recommended for the manageability of your model versions across ML use cases. A model package group can contain one or more model packages.

Creating a model package group involves a method that accepts only a few parameters on input to configure, as follows:

```
import time
model_package_group_name = "air-quality-" + str(round(time.
time()))
model_package_group_input_dict = {
"ModelPackageGroupName" : model_package_group_name,
"ModelPackageGroupDescription" : "model package group for air
quality models",
"Tags": [
            {
            "Key": "MLProject",
            "Value": "weather"
            }
]
}
create_model_pacakge_group_response = sm_client.create_model_
package_group(**model_package_group_input_dict)
print('ModelPackageGroup Arn : {}'.format(create_model_pacakge_
group_response['ModelPackageGroupArn']))
```

The preceding code is used to create a model package group that can then be used by ML builders, as well as with ML pipelines to register model packages (versions) for deployment. Configuration for a model package group requires only a model package group name and optionally a description and any tags you want to associate with the model group.

Recommendations when creating model package groups include the following:

- **Establishing naming standards for model package groups**: As the number of model package groups grows, having clear naming standards can help with easily identifying and searching for related model package groups. Some considerations may include a team identifier and/or project identifier. Because it's common to have more than one team working on models, a team identifier can help easily sort and search for models specific to a given team. It's also common to have more than one model used in an overall solution. In this case, it is valuable to have a way to group models related to a specific project or solution. This can be done through established naming conventions, as well as tagging.

- **Utilizing tags for fine-grained access**: In the preceding example, a tag of `MLProject` is created with the value of `weather`. In this case, let's assume a weather team is responsible for building weather-related models and only team members belonging to the weather team should be able to view model package groups with this tag. Resource tags can be used to establish conditional policies for access.

Creating a model package

A model package is a model version that can exist outside of a model package group, referred to as *unversioned*, or inside a model package group, referred to as *versioned*. A model package outside of a model package group is referred to as unversioned because it's not using the versioning capabilities of a model package group. It's recommended to register model packages using model package groups for automatic management of model versions, and for added manageability as the number of model versions increases.

> **Important note**
>
> Amazon SageMaker has two concepts called **model package**. The two are independent of each other. The first example is a model package that is created to package a model for deployment using the `CreateModel` API. This is required to deploy your model using Amazon SageMaker and is discussed in the *Amazon SageMaker documentation* (`https://docs.aws.amazon.com/sagemaker/latest/dg/sagemaker-mkt-model-pkg-model.html`). The second example, and the one we refer to in this chapter, is a model package specifically for Amazon SageMaker's model registry that is created using the `CreateModelPackage` API.

The `CreateModelPackage` API accepts several parameters on input. The high-level parameter categories were already covered in the section titled *Amazon SageMaker model registry*, so in this section, we'll include an example that uses those parameters to then register a model using our sample use case. In *Chapter 12, Machine Learning Automated Workflows*, we'll again discuss the model registry in the context of an ML pipeline, to demonstrate how a model registry can be integrated into your automated workflows. For now, we'll focus on registering a model package as an indication that it has passed initial model validation outside of a pipeline workflow.

In this case, the model has been trained and we've evaluated the training metrics. Once our model reaches the minimum threshold identified for our evaluation metric, we are ready to register the model package. Using the AWS Python SDK (`boto3`), we'll register the model package, as shown in the following code:

```
modelpackage_inference_specification =  {
            "InferenceSpecification": {
            "Containers": [
            {
            "Image": xgboost_container,
            "ModelDataUrl": model_url
            }
            ],
            "SupportedContentTypes": [ "text/csv" ],
              "SupportedResponseMIMETypes": [ "text/csv" ],
   }
 }


create_model_package_input_dict = {
            "ModelPackageGroupName" : model_package_group_name,
            "ModelPackageDescription" : "Model to predict air
quality ratings using XGBoost",
            "ModelApprovalStatus" : "PendingManualApproval"
}
create_model_package_input_dict.update(modelpackage_inference_
specification)
create_mode_package_response = sm_client.create_model_
package(**create_model_package_input_dict)
model_package_arn = create_mode_package_
response["ModelPackageArn"]
```

```
print('ModelPackage Version ARN : {}'.format(model_package_
arn))
```

`ModelPackageGroupName` is required to associate the model package with a model package group. This allows you to take advantage of automatic versioning, as previously discussed.

The model packages can then be viewed using the `list_model_packages` method, as well as within Amazon SageMaker Studio. To list the model package, use the following code:

```
sm_client.list_model_packages(ModelPackageGroupName=model_
package_group_name)
```

Recommendations when creating model packages include the following:

- **Creating versioned packages**: Associate model packages with a model group by specifying the model package group when you create your model package. This allows for automatic versioning and grouping of use cases for easier management.

- **Using model approval status**: The optimal use of the model approval status field is to allow for peer reviews and trigger downstream deployment workflows using Amazon SageMaker projects. However, even without the use of Amazon SageMaker projects, the same field can be used to ensure data used to register a model passes a minimum set of criteria. For example, if there is a team standard to include explainability metrics for a registered model, then that `ApprovalStatus` can optionally be used after a peer review of the registered model to indicate minimum standards or criteria have been met for that model.

- **Protecting the inputs/artifacts referred to in the model registry**: Details contained in the model registry can be used to recreate or roll back deployed models; however, those resources need to be protected from unauthorized access or accidental deletion. For example, if an administrator accidentally deletes a SageMaker endpoint, it can still be easily recreated using the resources identified in the model registry. This would include the S3 object containing the model artifact, the S3 object with inference code (optional), and the ECR inference image. If any of those inputs are not available or cannot be guaranteed, then re-creating that endpoint may not be possible. Therefore, the metadata gives the information required, but there are still additional steps needed to protect inputs and artifacts.

- **Considering tags when additional metadata is needed**: The metadata within SageMaker's model registry is fixed to the input parameters that are defined in the API. However, tags can be used to supplement additional metadata. An example of the recommended use of tags here would be to capture the S3 version for resources such as the model artifact, in order to include more granularity on artifact tracking.

- **Utilizing tags for fine-grained access**: In the preceding example, a tag of `MLProject` is created with the value of `weather`. In this case, let's assume a weather team is responsible for building weather-related models and only team members from this team should be able to register new models to this model package group or other model package groups created with this tag. Resource tags can be used to establish conditional policies for access, in order to create model packages within specific model package groups. Resource tags can be used to establish conditional policies for access.

In this section, we detailed the steps necessary to create a model package group and register model packages to that model package group using the sample code provided for this chapter. We also outlined recommendations to consider when creating your own model package groups and model packages. *Chapter 12, Machine Learning Automated Workflows*, will expand on the information covered in this chapter to include integrating Amazon SageMaker's model registry into an MLOps pipeline.

Summary

In this chapter, we covered model registries and the benefits of utilizing a model registry to manage Amazon SageMaker models at scale. Common patterns for model registry implementations were covered, including Amazon SageMaker's model registry, building a custom model registry using AWS services, and utilizing a third-party or OSS model registry implementation. Each option is a valid choice depending on your use case and needs. However, we also highlighted some of the considerations when choosing the implementation that best fits your requirements.

Finally, we did a deep dive into Amazon SageMaker's model registry, covering detailed recommendations for creating model package groups, as well as registering models by creating model packages.

In the next chapter, we'll cover performing live tests and updates of production models using Amazon SageMaker endpoint production variants.

9

Updating Production Models Using Amazon SageMaker Endpoint Production Variants

A deployed production model needs to be updated for a variety of reasons, such as to gain access to new training data, to experiment with a new algorithm and hyperparameters, or to model predictive performance deteriorating over time. Any time you update a model with a new version in production, there is a risk of the model becoming unavailable during the update and the model's quality being worse than the previous version. Even after careful evaluation in the development and QA environments, new models need additional testing, validation, and monitoring to make sure they work properly in production.

When deploying new versions of models into production, you should carefully consider reducing deployment risks and minimizing downtime for the model consumers. It is also important to proactively plan for an unsuccessful model update and roll back to a previous working model. Replacing an existing model with a newer model should, ideally, not cause any service interruptions to the model's consumers. Model consumers may be applications that are internal to your organization or external, customer-facing applications.

This chapter will address the challenge of updating production models with minimal disruption for model consumers using **Amazon SageMaker Endpoint Production Variants**. You will learn how to use SageMaker Endpoint Production Variants to implement Standard deployment and advanced model deployment strategies such as **A/B testing**, **Blue/Green**, **Canary**, and **Shadow** deployments, which balance cost with model downtime and ease of rollbacks.

By the end of this chapter, you will be able to implement multiple deployment strategies for updating production machine learning models. You will learn when and how to use live production traffic to test new model versions. You will also learn about the best practices for balancing cost, availability, and reducing risk while choosing the right deployment strategy for your use case.

In this chapter, we are going to cover the following main topics:

- Basic concepts of Amazon SageMaker Endpoint Production Variants
- Deployment strategies for updating ML models with Amazon SageMaker Endpoint Production Variants
- Selecting an appropriate deployment strategy

Technical requirements

You will need an **AWS** account to run the examples included in this chapter. If you have not set up the data science environment yet, please refer to *Chapter 2, Data Science Environments*, which provides a walk-through of the setup process.

The code examples included in the book are available on GitHub at `https://github.com/PacktPublishing/Amazon-SageMaker-Best-Practices/tree/main/Chapter09`. You will need to install a Git client to access them (`https://git-scm.com/`).

Basic concepts of Amazon SageMaker Endpoint Production Variants

In this section, you will review the basics of deploying and updating ML models using SageMaker Endpoint Production Variants. There are two ways you can deploy a machine learning model using SageMaker: by using a real-time endpoint for low latency live predictions or a batch transform for making asynchronous predictions on large numbers of inference requests. Production Variants can be applied to real-time endpoints.

Deploying a real-time endpoint involves two steps:

1. **Creating an Endpoint Configuration**

   An endpoint configuration identifies one or more Production Variants. Each production variant indicates a model and infrastructure to deploy the model on.

2. **Creating an Endpoint Pointing to the Endpoint Configuration**

   Endpoint creation results in an HTTPS endpoint that the model consumers can use to invoke the model.

The following diagram shows two different endpoint configurations with Production Variants. **Endpoint 1** has a single model called `model_1` that's deployed on an `ml.m4.xlarge` instance; all inference traffic is served by this single model. **Endpoint 2** is deployed with two models called `model_1` and `model_2` on `ml.m4.xlarge` and `ml.m4.2xlarge`, respectively. Both models serve the inference requests equally because they have the same `initial_weight` configuration:

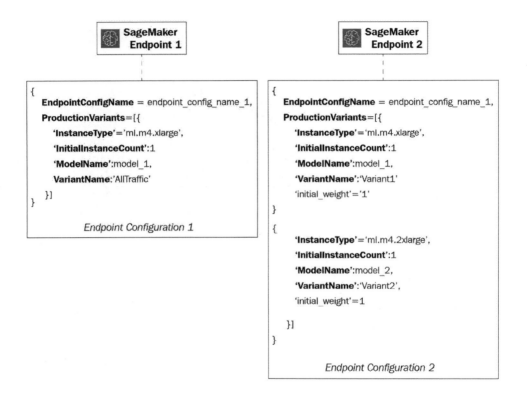

Figure 9.1 – Endpoint configurations with Production Variants

When an endpoint has been configured with multiple Production Variants, how do you know which model is serving the inference requests? There are two ways to determine this:

- First, the `initial_weight` parameter of the production variant determines the relative percentage of the requests served by the model specified by that variant.

- Second, the inference request may also include the model variant to invoke.

The following diagram shows these two ways of invoking the endpoint

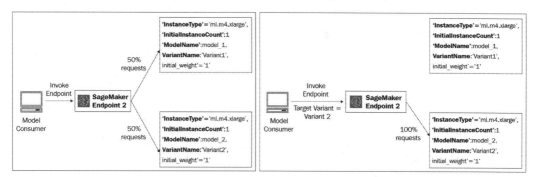

Figure 9.2 – Two ways to invoke SageMaker Endpoint

As the SageMaker Endpoints are serving inference traffic, they are monitored using **Amazon CloudWatch Metrics**. Use the `EndpointName` and `VariantName` dimensions to monitor metrics for each distinct production variant of the same endpoint. The `Invocations` metric captures the number of requests that are sent to a model, as indicated by the production variant. You can use this metric to monitor the number of requests that are served by different models and deployed with a single endpoint.

The following diagram shows a comparison of the `Invocations` metrics that have been captured for an endpoint that's been configured with two Production Variants. The first chart shows the number of invocations per production variant when the initial weights are set to 1 and 1. In this case, each variant serves a similar number of requests. The second chart shows the same metric with the initial weights of 2 and 1. As you can see, the number of requests that are served by variant 1 is double the number of requests that are served by variant 2:

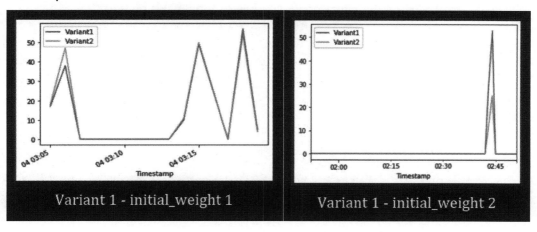

Figure 9.3 – Invocations of SageMaker Endpoint Production Variants

While the `Invocations` metric is intuitively easy to understand, there are other CloudWatch metrics such as `Latency` and `Overhead` that you can use to monitor, compare, and contrast multiple endpoints and multiple Production Variants of a single endpoint.

> **Note**
>
> For a full list of CloudWatch Metrics for Amazon SageMaker, please see `https://docs.aws.amazon.com/sagemaker/latest/dg/monitoring-cloudwatch.html#cloudwatch-metrics-endpoint-invocation`.

Similar to Production Variants, SageMaker **multi-model endpoints (MME)** also allow us to host multiple models on a single endpoint. If that is the case, how are Production Variants different from multi-model endpoints?

With an MME, all models are hosted on the same compute infrastructure. However, not all the models are loaded into the container memory when the endpoint is created. Instead, the model is loaded into memory when an inference request is made. Each inference request must specify the model to invoke. The invoked model is then loaded into memory from the **S3 bucket** if it is not already in memory. Depending on the invocation pattern, a model that hasn't been invoked recently may not be in memory. This could result in increased latency when serving the request. When you have a large number of similar ML models that are infrequently accessed and can tolerate slightly increased latency, then a single MME can serve inference traffic at significantly low costs.

On the other hand, with Production Variants, each model is hosted on a completely different compute infrastructure, and all the models are readily available without having to be loaded into container memory on demand. Each inference request may or may not specify the variant to invoke. If the variant to invoke is not specified, the number of inference requests that are served by each variant depends on the `initial_weight` parameter of the production variant. In the context of model deployment, use Production Variants to test different versions of ML models that have been trained using different datasets, algorithms, and ML frameworks or to test how a model performs on different instance types.

In the next section, you will learn how to use Production Variants in various deployment strategies. As we discuss these various deployment strategies, we will focus on what it takes to update an existing production model deployed as a real-time SageMaker endpoint using Production Variants.

Deployment strategies for updating ML models with SageMaker Endpoint Production Variants

In this section, we will dive into multiple deployment strategies you can adopt to update production models using SageMaker Endpoint Production Variants. While some deployment strategies are easy to implement and are cost-effective, others add complexity while lowering deployment risks. We will dive into five different strategies, including Standard, A/B, Blue/Green, Canary, and Shadow deployments, and discuss the various steps involved in each approach.

Standard deployment

This strategy is the most straightforward approach to deploying and updating models in production. In a Standard model deployment, there is always a single active SageMaker endpoint, and the endpoint is configured with a single production variant, which means only a single model is deployed behind the endpoint. All inference traffic is processed by a single model. The endpoint configuration is similar to **Endpoint Configuration 1** in *Figure 9.1* in the previous section. The following code block shows how to create a production variant. The production variant, `variant1`, hosts `model_name_1` on a single `ml.m5.xlarge` instance and serves all inference traffic, as indicated by `initial_weight=1`:

```
### Create production variant
from sagemaker.session import production_variant
variant1 = production_variant(model_name=model_name_1,
                              instance_type="ml.m5.xlarge",
                              initial_instance_count=1,
                              variant_name='VariantA',
                              initial_weight=1)
```

The following code block shows how to create an endpoint from the production variant. `endpoint_from_production_variants` automatically creates an `endpoint_configuration` with the same name as `endpoint_name`:

```
### Create the endpoint with a production variants
from sagemaker.session import Session
#Variable for endpoint name
endpoint_name=f"abtest-{datetime.now():%Y-%m-%d-%H-%M-%S}"
```

```
smsession = Session()
smsession.endpoint_from_production_variants(
        name=endpoint_name,
        production_variants=[variant1]
)
```

To update the endpoint with a newer version of the model, create a new endpoint configuration specifying the new model and infrastructure to deploy the model on. Then, update the endpoint with a new endpoint configuration. The following code block shows the code for updating the endpoint with the new model version:

```
#Create production variant 2
variant2 = production_variant(model_name=model_name_2,
                              instance_type="ml.m5.xlarge",
                              initial_instance_count=1,
                              variant_name='Variant2',
                              initial_weight=1)

#Create a new endpoint configuration
endpoint_config_new =f"abtest-b-config-{datetime.now():%Y-%m-%d-%H-%M-%S}"

smsession.create_endpoint_config_from_existing (
        existing_config_name=endpoint_name,
        new_config_name=endpoint_config_new,
        new_production_variants=[variant2]
)
##Update the endpoint to point to the new endpoint
configuration
smsession.update_endpoint(
  endpoint_name=endpoint_name, endpoint_config_name=endpoint_
config_new, wait=False)
```

SageMaker automatically creates and manages the infrastructure necessary for the new production variant and routes the traffic to the new model without any downtime. All inference traffic is now served by the new model. The following diagram shows the steps involved in updating a deployed model:

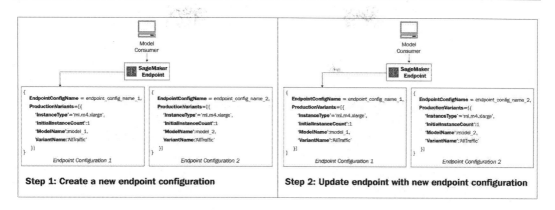

Figure 9.4 – Standard deployment with SageMaker Endpoint Production Variants

To roll back, simply update the endpoint with the original endpoint configuration, as represented by *Step 1*. As you can see, inference traffic is served by either the old version of the model or the new version at all times.

One benefit of this approach is that it is a simple, straightforward way to update an endpoint with a new model. When the endpoint is updated with the new endpoint configuration, SageMaker switches the inference requests to the new model while keeping the endpoint `InService`. This means that the model consumer does not experience any disruption to the service. This is also a cost-effective strategy for updating a real-time endpoint since you only pay for the infrastructure hosting a single model.

On the other hand, model evaluation and testing happen in non-production environments such as the QA or staging environments with test data. Since the new model is not tested in a production environment, it will face the production data volume and live traffic on the new infrastructure for the first time in production. This could lead to unforeseen complications, either with the model hosting the infrastructure or the model's quality.

> **Note**
>
> While evaluating the model in staging environments, it is recommended that you perform load testing to validate that the model can handle the traffic with acceptable latency before moving to production.
>
> Refer to `https://aws.amazon.com/blogs/machine-learning/load-test-and-optimize-an-amazon-sagemaker-endpoint-using-automatic-scaling/` to learn how to load test an endpoint using autoscaling and serverless-artillery.

Use Standard deployment if the model consumer is risk- and failure-tolerant, such as an internal application that can re-execute the predictions in case of failures. For example, an internal model that predicts employee turnover is a good candidate for Standard deployment.

Since only one model is serving inference requests at a time, this strategy is not suitable for comparing different models. If you are experimenting with different features, multiple algorithms, or hyperparameters, you want to be able to compare the models in production. The next deployment strategy helps with this need.

A/B deployment

In the Standard deployment, you have a single endpoint in the production environment with no scope for testing or evaluating the model in production. On the other hand, an A/B deployment strategy is focused on experimentation and exploration, such as comparing the performance of different versions of the same feature.

In this scenario, the endpoint configuration uses two Production Variants: one for model A and one for model B. For a fair comparison of the two models, initial_weight of the two production variants should be the same so that both models handle the same amount of inference traffic. Additionally, make sure the instance type and instance count are also the same. This initial setting is necessary so that neither version of the model is impacted by a difference in traffic patterns or a difference in the underlying compute capacity.

The following code blocks shows how to create and update an endpoint for A/B deployments.

First, create production variant A:

```
#Create production variant A
variantA = production_variant(model_name=model_name_1,
                              instance_type="ml.m5.xlarge",
                              initial_instance_count=1,
                              variant_name='VariantA',
                              initial_weight=1)
```

Then, create an endpoint with one production variant, which initially serves production traffic:

```
#Variable for endpoint name
endpoint_name=f"abtest-{datetime.now():%Y-%m-%d-%H-%M-%S}"
#Create an endpoint with a single production variant
```

```
smsession.endpoint_from_production_variants(
         name=endpoint_name,
         production_variants=[variantA]
)
```

When you are ready to test the next version of the model, create another production variant and update the endpoint so that it includes two Production Variants:

```
#Create production variant B
variantB = production_variant(model_name=model_name_2,
                               instance_type="ml.m5.xlarge",
                               initial_instance_count=1,
                               variant_name='VariantB',
                               initial_weight=1)


##Next update the endpoint to include both production variants
endpoint_config_new =f"abtest-new-config-{datetime.now():%Y-%m-
%d-%H-%M-%S}"


smsession.create_endpoint_config_from_existing (
         existing_config_name=endpoint_name,
         new_config_name=endpoint_config_new,
         new_production_variants=[variantA,variantB]   ## Two
production variants
)


##Update the endpoint
smsession.update_endpoint(endpoint_name=endpoint_name,
endpoint_config_name=endpoint_config_new, wait=False)
```

To invoke the endpoint, use the invoke_endpoint() API, as shown in the following code. The result of using the invoke_endpoint() API consists of the variant name that serves each specific request:

```
result = smrt.invoke_endpoint(EndpointName=endpoint_name,
                              ContentType="text/csv",
                              Body=test_string)
```

```
rbody = \ StreamingBody(raw_stream=result['Body'],content_
length=int(result['ResponseMetadata']['HTTPHeaders']['content-
length']))
```

```
print(f"Result from {result['InvokedProductionVariant']} =
{rbody.read().decode('utf-8')}")
```

The output from the endpoint should look similar to the following:

```
Result from VariantA = 0.17167794704437256
Result from VariantB = 0.14226064085960388
Result from VariantA = 0.10094326734542847
Result from VariantA = 0.17167794704437256
Result from VariantB = 0.050961822271347046
Result from VariantB = -0.2118145227432251
Result from VariantB = 0.16735368967056274
Result from VariantA = 0.17314249277114868
Result from VariantB = 0.16769883036613464
Result from VariantA = 0.17314249277114868
```

You can collect and examine results from VariantB. You can explore the CloudWatch metrics for VariantB even further as well, as explained in the *Basic concepts of Amazon SageMaker Endpoint Production Variants* section. Once you are happy with the performance of VariantB, gradually shift the balance toward the new model (40/60, 20/80) until your new model is processing all the live traffic. The following code block shows how to route 60% of live traffic to VariantB:

```
#Update the product variant weight to route 60% of traffic to
VariantB
sm.update_endpoint_weights_and_capacities(
        EndpointName=endpoint_name,
        DesiredWeightsAndCapacities=[
        {"DesiredWeight": 4, "VariantName":
variantA["VariantName"]},
        {"DesiredWeight": 6, "VariantName":
variantB["VariantName"]},
        ],
)
```

Alternatively, you can choose to update the endpoint to route all live traffic to `VariantB` in a single step, as shown in the following code block:

```
##Update the endpoint to point to VariantB
endpoint_config_new =f"abtest-b-config-{datetime.now():%Y-%m-%d-%H-%M-%S}"

smsession.create_endpoint_config_from_existing (
            existing_config_name=endpoint_name,
            new_config_name=endpoint_config_new,
            new_production_variants=[variantB]
)
##Update the endpoint
smsession.update_endpoint(endpoint_name=endpoint_name,
endpoint_config_name=endpoint_config_new, wait=False)
```

The following diagram shows the steps involved in updating a deployed model. To roll back, simply update the endpoint with the original endpoint configuration, as represented by Step 1:

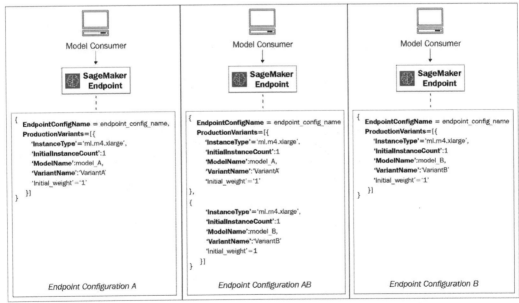

Figure 9.5 – A/B deployment with SageMaker Endpoint Production Variants

The benefits of this strategy are that it is well-understood and that SageMaker makes it simple to implement this strategy by managing traffic routing. Since the new model is evaluated in production with an increased percentage of live traffic on the new infrastructure, the risk of the model becoming unavailable to the model consumer during the update, or the model quality being worse than it was in the previous version, is reduced. This addresses the typical deployment issue of *the model worked perfectly in the dev/QA environment, so I'm not sure why it is failing in production*. However, since two Production Variants are active for a certain period, the cost increases as you are paying for two sets of infrastructure resources.

> **Note**
>
> A relatively recent type of A/B testing that's gaining popularity is **Multi-Arm Bandits (MAB)**. MAB is a machine learning-based approach that learns from the data that's collected during testing. Using a combination of exploration and exploitation, MAB dynamically shifts traffic to better-performing model variants much sooner than a traditional A/B test.
>
> Refer to `https://aws.amazon.com/blogs/machine-learning/power-contextual-bandits-using-continual-learning-with-amazon-sagemaker-rl/` to learn how to use Amazon SageMaker RL to implement MAB to recommend personalized content to users.

While the A/B strategy is helpful with experimentation and exploration, what about releasing major changes to your models? Is there a way to reduce the risk further? Blue/Green deployments can help with this.

Blue/Green deployment

The Blue/Green deployment strategy involves two identical production environments, one containing the current model and another containing the next version of the model that you want to update to. While one environment, say Blue, is serving live traffic, the next version of the model is tested in the Green environment. While model testing is happening in production, only test or synthetic data is used. The new model version should be tested against functional, business, and traffic load requirements.

Once you are satisfied with the test results over a certain period, update the live endpoint with the new (Green) endpoint configuration. Validate the tests again with the Green endpoint configuration using live inference traffic. If you find any issues during this testing period, route the traffic back to a Blue endpoint configuration. After a while, if there are no issues with the new model, go ahead and delete the Blue endpoint configuration.

The following diagram shows the steps involved in updating a deployed model:

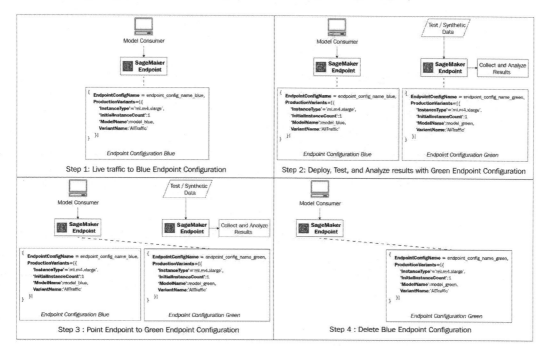

Figure 9.6 – Blue/Green deployment with SageMaker Endpoint Production Variants

The advantage of this approach is that before serving live traffic, the new model is evaluated in the production environment. Both the model itself and the infrastructure hosting the model are evaluated and thereby risk is reduced. However, since two identical production environments are active for a while, the cost of this option could double compared to the strategies we've discussed so far. This option also loses the advantage of SageMaker managing the routing logic.

In this strategy, while the model is evaluated in production, testing still involves synthetic traffic. Synthetic data can simulate the production volumes, but it is not trivial to reflect the live data patterns. What if you want to test the new model with live traffic? Canary deployment is the strategy that allows you to do this.

Canary deployment

In a Canary deployment, the setup is very similar to Blue/Green deployments, with two different production environments hosting the old and new models. However, instead of using synthetic test data with a new model, you use a portion of the live traffic. Initially, a small portion of the inference traffic from the model consumer will be served by the new model. The rest of the inference requests continue to use the previous version. During the testing phase, the designated set of users using the new model should remain the same, and this requires *stickiness*. When you are satisfied with the new model, gradually increase the percentage of requests that are sent to the new model, until all live traffic is served by the new model. Finally, the old model can be deleted.

Unlike the other strategies we've discussed so far, switching between the two different environments is not implemented by SageMaker. To make the switch between the environments completely transparent to the model consumer, a switching component must be used between the consumer and the endpoints. Examples of switching components include load balancers, DNS routers, and more.

The following diagram shows the steps involved in updating a deployed model using this strategy:

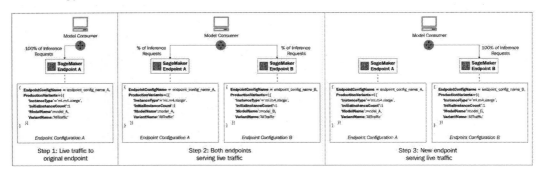

Figure 9.7 – Canary deployment with SageMaker Endpoint Production Variants

As with the Blue/Green deployments, the advantage of this approach is that risk to the model consumers is reduced as the new model is tested in the production environment. Additionally, the model is gradually exposed to live traffic instead of a sudden switch. But this strategy does require you to manage the logic of gradually increasing traffic for the new model. Additionally, since two identical production environments are active for a certain period, the cost of this option is also significantly higher.

Shadow deployment

In a Shadow deployment, the setup is, once again, very similar to a Canary deployment in that two different production environments are hosting the old and new models, and inference traffic is sent to both. However, only responses from the old model are sent back to the model consumer.

The traffic that's sent to the old model is collected and also sent to the new model, either immediately or after a delay. While the production traffic is sent to the new model as well as the old, the output from the new model is only captured and stored for analysis, not sent to model consumers. The new model should be tested against functional, business, and traffic load with the live traffic. The following diagram shows the steps involved in updating a model that's been deployed using this strategy:

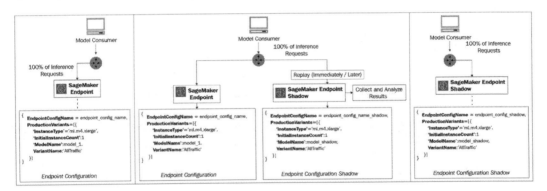

Figure 9.8 – Shadow deployment with SageMaker Endpoint Production Variants

As with the Canary deployments, the advantage of this approach is that all risks to the model consumers are reduced as the new model is tested in the production environment.

> **Note**
>
> An example notebook that demonstrates the end-to-end A/B deployment strategy is provided in the following GitHub repository. You can use this as a starting point for implementing other deployment strategies: https://gitlab.com/randydefauw/packt_book/-/blob/main/CH09/a_b_deployment_with_production_variants.ipynb.

Now that you know about the multiple deployment strategies you can use to update production models, in the next section, we will discuss how to select a strategy to meet your specific requirements.

Selecting an appropriate deployment strategy

As you have seen so far, the initial deployment of a machine model is only one step of making it available to consumers. New versions of models are built regularly. Before making the new models available to the consumers, the model quality and infrastructure that's needed to host the model should be evaluated carefully. There are multiple factors to consider when selecting the deployment strategy to initially deploy and continue to update models. For example, not all models can be tested in production due to budget and resource constraints. Similarly, some model consumers can tolerate the model being unavailable for certain periods.

This section will summarize the deployment strategies you can use to deploy and update real-time SageMaker Endpoints. You will get an idea of the pros and cons for each strategy, in addition to when should it be used.

Selecting a standard deployment

Model consumers are not business or revenue critical and are risk-tolerant. For example, a company's internal employee attrition prediction models are not time-critical and can be re-executed on errors:

Pros	Con
Easy to implement.	High risk to the model consumer with the possibility of incorrect predictions, since neither the model nor the hosting infrastructure configuration is evaluated in the production environment.
Cost-effective since only one endpoint and one production variant are active at any given time.	
Zero downtime since switching between old and new models is managed by SageMaker.	
Rollback is managed by SageMaker.	

Figure 9.9 – Pros and cons of a standard deployment

Selecting an A/B deployment

You should use A/B deployments to explore the effect different sets of hyperparameters have on model quality, new or different slices of the training dataset, and different feature engineering techniques:

Pros	Con
Well understood pattern and easy to implement.	Increased cost since multiple production variants are active simultaneously.
Zero downtime since switching between old and new models is managed by SageMaker.	
Rollback is managed by SageMaker.	
Reduced risk to model consumers since the new model is tested in production.	

Figure 9.10 – Pros and cons of A/B deployment

Selecting a Blue/Green deployment

You should use this deployment with mission-critical model consumers, such as e-commerce applications, that are sensitive to model downtime:

Pros	Cons
Reduced risk because of testing in production prior to serving live traffic.	Since the production environment is duplicated and two endpoints are simultaneously active, cost is increased.
Being able to easily switch between the environments managed by SageMaker makes for easy rollbacks.	Risk is minimized but not eliminated, since testing does not happen with live traffic.
	Switching inference traffic between old and new models is not gradual leading to possible wide-scale outages.

Figure 9.11 – Pros and cons of Blue/Green deployment

Selecting a Canary deployment

You should use this deployment with mission-critical model consumers, such as financial services models, that are not risk-tolerant:

Pro	Con
Reduced risk due to gradual shift of inference requests to new models.	Since the production environment is duplicated and two endpoints are simultaneously active, cost is increased.

Figure 9.12 – Pros and cons of a Canary deployment

Selecting a Shadow deployment

You should use this deployment with mission-critical model consumers, such as financial services models, that are not risk-tolerant:

Pro	Con
Reduced risk because the new model is analyzed and evaluated with live traffic before it is made available to model consumers.	Since the production environment is duplicated and two endpoints are simultaneously active, cost is increased.

Figure 9.13 – Pros and cons of Shadow deployment

You should choose an appropriate model strategy using the trade-offs discussed in the preceding subsections for ease of implementation, acceptable model downtime, the risk tolerance of the consumers, and the costs that must be taken into account for you to meet your needs.

Summary

In this chapter, we reviewed the reasons we should update production ML models. You learned how to use Production Variants to host multiple models using a single SageMaker Endpoint. You then learned about multiple deployment strategies that balance the cost and risk of model updates with ease of implementation and rollbacks. You also learned about the various steps involved and the configurations to use for Standard, A/B, Blue/Green, Canary, and Shadow deployments.

This chapter concluded with a comparison of the pros and cons and the applicability of each deployment strategy to specific use cases. Using this discussion as guidance, you can now choose an appropriate strategy to update your production models so that they meet your model availability and model quality requirements.

In the next chapter, we will continue our discussion of deploying models and learn about optimizing model hosting and infrastructure costs.

10
Optimizing Model Hosting and Inference Costs

The introduction of more powerful computers (notably with **graphical processing units**, or **GPUs**) and powerful **machine learning** (**ML**) frameworks such as TensorFlow has resulted in a generational leap in ML capabilities. As ML practitioners, our purview now includes optimizing the use of these new capabilities to maximize the value we get for the time and money we spend.

In this chapter, you'll learn how to use multiple deployment strategies to meet your training and inference requirements. You'll learn when to get and store inferences in advance versus getting them on demand, how to scale inference services to meet fluctuating demand, and how to use multiple models for model testing.

In this chapter, we will cover the following topics:

- Real-time inference versus batch inference
- Deploying multiple models behind a single inference endpoint
- Scaling inference endpoints to meet inference traffic demands

- Using Elastic Inference for deep learning models
- Optimizing models with SageMaker Neo

Technical requirements

You will need an AWS account to run the examples included in this chapter. If you have not set up the data science environment yet, please refer to *Chapter 2, Data Science Environments*, which walks you through the setup process.

The code examples included in the book are available on GitHub at `https://github.com/PacktPublishing/Amazon-SageMaker-Best-Practices/tree/main/Chapter10`. You will need to install a Git client to access them (`https://git-scm.com/`).

The code for this chapter is in the `CH10` folder of the GitHub repository.

Real-time inference versus batch inference

SageMaker provides two ways to obtain inferences:

- **Real-time inference** lets you get a single inference per request, or a small number of inferences, with very low latency from a live inference endpoint.
- **Batch inference** lets you get a large number of inferences from a batch processing job.

Batch inference is more efficient and more cost-effective. Use it whenever your inference requirements allow. We'll explore batch inference first, and then pivot to real-time inference.

Batch inference

In many cases, we can make inferences in advance and store them for later use. For example, if you want to generate product recommendations for users on an e-commerce site, those recommendations may be based on the users' prior purchases and which products you want to promote the next day. You can generate the recommendations nightly and store them for your e-commerce site to call up when the users browse the site.

There are several options for storing batch inferences. Amazon DynamoDB is a common choice for several reasons, such as the following:

- It is fast. You can look up single values within a few milliseconds.
- It is scalable. You can store millions of values at a low cost.

- The best access pattern for DynamoDB is looking up values by a high-cardinality primary key. This fits well with many inference usage patterns, for example, when we want to look up a stored recommendation for an individual user.

You can use other data stores, including DocumentDB and Aurora, depending on your access patterns.

In the CH10 folder of the GitHub repository, you'll find the optimize.ipynb notebook. The *Real-time and Batch Inference* section of this repository walks you through performing both batch and real-time inference using a simple XGBoost model. The following code lets you run a batch inference job:

```
batch_input = "s3://{}/{}/{}/".format(s3_bucket, s3_prefix,
'test')
batch_output = "s3://{}/{}/{}/".format(s3_bucket, "xgboost-
sample", 'xform')
transformer = estimator.transformer(instance_count=1,
instance_type='ml.m5.4xlarge', output_path=batch_output, max_
payload=3)
transformer.transform(data=batch_input, data_type='S3Prefix',
content_type=content_type, split_type='Line')
```

This job takes approximately 3 minutes to run.

Real-time inference

When you deploy a SageMaker model to a real-time inference endpoint, SageMaker deploys the model artifact and your inference code (packaged in a Docker image) to one or more inference instances. You now have a live API endpoint for inference, and you can invoke it from other software services on demand.

You pay for the inference endpoints (instances) as long as they are running. Use real-time inference in the following situations:

- The inferences are dependent on *context*. For example, if you want to recommend a video to watch, the inference may depend on the show your user just finished. If you have a large video catalog, you can't generate all the possible permutations of recommendations in advance.

- You may need to provide inferences for *new events*. For example, if you are trying to classify a credit card transaction as fraudulent or not, you need to wait until your user actually attempts a transaction.

The following code deploys an inference endpoint:

```
from sagemaker.deserializers import JSONDeserializer
from sagemaker.serializers import CSVSerializer
predictor = estimator.deploy(initial_instance_count=1,
                             instance_type='ml.m5.2xlarge',
                             serializer=CSVSerializer(),
                             deserializer=JSONDeserializer()
                             )
```

Once the endpoint is live, we can obtain inferences using the endpoint we just deployed:

```
result = predictor.predict(csv_payload)
print(result)
```

Using our simple XGBoost model, an inference takes approximately 30 milliseconds to complete.

Cost comparison

Consider a scenario where we want to predict the measurements for the next day for all of our weather stations and make them available for lookup on an interactive website. We have approximately 11,000 unique stations and 7 different parameters to predict for each station.

With a real-time endpoint using the `ml.m5.2xlarge` instance type, we pay $0.538 per hour, or approximately $387 per month. With batch inference, we pay $1.075 per hour for an `ml.m5.4xlarge` instance. The job takes 3 minutes to run per day, or 90 minutes per month. That's about $1.61.

The batch inference approach is typically much more cost-effective if you do not need context-sensitive real-time predictions. Serving predictions out of a NoSQL database is a better option.

Deploying multiple models behind a single inference endpoint

A SageMaker inference endpoint is a logical entity that actually holds a load balancer and one or more instances of your inference container. You can deploy either multiple versions of the same model or entirely different models behind a single endpoint. In this section, we'll look at these two use cases.

Multiple versions of the same model

A SageMaker endpoint lets you host multiple models that serve different percentages of traffic for incoming requests. That capability supports common **continuous integration (CI)/continuous delivery (CD)** practices such as canary and blue/green deployments. While these practices are similar, they have slightly different purposes, as explained here:

- A **canary deployment** means that you let the new version of a model host a small percentage of traffic that lets you test a new version of the model on a subset of traffic until you are satisfied that it is working well.

- A **blue/green deployment** means that you run two versions of the model at the same time, keeping an older version around for quick failover if a problem occurs in the new version.

In practice, these are variations on a theme. In SageMaker, you designate how much traffic each model variant handles. For canary deployments, you'd start with a small fraction (usually 1-5%) for the new model versions. For blue/green deployments, you'd use 100% for the new version but flip back to 0% if a problem occurs.

There are other ways to accomplish these deployment modes. For example, you can use two inference endpoints and handle traffic shaping using DNS (Route 53), a load balancer, or Global Accelerator. But managing the traffic through SageMaker simplifies your operational burden and reduces cost, as you don't have to have two endpoints running.

In the *A/B Testing* section of the notebook, we'll create another version of the model and create a new endpoint that uses both models:

1. We'll start by training another version of the model with a hyperparameter change (maximum tree depth of 10 instead of 5), as follows:

```
hyperparameters_v2 = {
        "max_depth":"10",
        "eta":"0.2",
        "gamma":"4",
        "min_child_weight":"6",
        "subsample":"0.7",
        "objective":"reg:squarederror",
        "num_round":"5"}

estimator_v2 = \ sagemaker.estimator.Estimator(image_
uri=xgboost_container,
                    hyperparameters=hyperparameters,
```

```
                    role=sagemaker.get_execution_role(),
                    instance_count=1,
                    instance_type='ml.m5.12xlarge',
                    volume_size=200, # 5 GB
                    output_path=output_path)

predictor_v2 = estimator_v2.deploy(initial_instance_
count=1,
                            instance_type='ml.m5.2xlarge',
                            serializer=CSVSerializer(),
                            deserializer=JSONDeserializer()
                            )
```

2. Next, we define endpoint variants for each model version. The most important
    parameter here is `initial_weight`, which specifies how much traffic should
    go to each model version. By setting both versions to `1`, the traffic will split evenly
    between them. For an A/B test, you might start with weights of `20` for the existing
    version and `1` for the new version:

```
model1 = predictor._model_names[0]
model2 = predictor_v2._model_names[0]
from sagemaker.session import production_variant

variant1 = production_variant(model_name=model1,
                            instance_type="ml.m5.xlarge",
                            initial_instance_count=1,
                            variant_name='Variant1',
                            initial_weight=1)
variant2 = production_variant(model_name=model2,
                            instance_type="ml.m5.xlarge",
                            initial_instance_count=1,
                            variant_name='Variant2',
                            initial_weight=1)
```

3. Now, we deploy a new model using the following two model variants:

```
from sagemaker.session import Session

smsession = Session()

smsession.endpoint_from_production_variants(
    name='mmendpoint',
    production_variants=[variant1, variant2]
)
```

4. Finally, we can test the new endpoint:

```
from sagemaker.deserializers import JSONDeserializer
from sagemaker.serializers import CSVSerializer
import boto3
from botocore.response import StreamingBody

smrt = boto3.Session().client("sagemaker-runtime")

for tl in t_lines[0:50]:
    result = smrt.invoke_
endpoint(EndpointName='mmendpoint',
        ContentType="text/csv", Body=tl.strip())
    rbody = StreamingBody( \
raw_stream=result['Body'], \
content_length= \
int(result['ResponseMetadata']['HTTPHeaders']['content-
length']))
    print(f"Result from
{result['InvokedProductionVariant']} = " + \
f"{rbody.read().decode('utf-8')}")
```

You'll see output that looks like this:

```
Result from Variant2 = 0.16384175419807434
Result from Variant1 = 0.16383948922157288
Result from Variant1 = 0.16383948922157288
Result from Variant2 = 0.16384175419807434
Result from Variant1 = 0.16384175419807434
```

```
Result from Variant2 = 0.16384661197662354
```

Notice that the traffic is flipping between the two versions of the model according to the weights we specified. In a production use case, you should automate the model endpoint update in your CI/CD or MLOps automation tools.

Multiple models

In other cases, you may need to run entirely different models. For example, perhaps you want one model to serve weather inferences for the United States and another model to serve weather inferences for Germany. You can build models that are sensitive to differences between these two countries. You can host both models behind the same endpoint and direct traffic to them based on the incoming request.

Or, for an A/B test, you might want to control which traffic goes to your new model version rather than letting a load balancer perform random weighted distribution. If you have an application server that identifies which consumers should use the new model version, you can direct that traffic to a specific model behind an inference endpoint.

In the *Multiple models in a single endpoint* notebook section, we'll walk through an example of creating models optimized for different air quality parameters. When we want a prediction, we specify which type of parameter we want, and the endpoint directs our request to the appropriate model. This use case is quite realistic; it may turn out that it's difficult to predict both particulate matter (PM25) and ozone (O3) using the same model:

1. First, we're going to prepare new datasets that only contain data for a single parameter by creating a Spark processing job:

```
spark_processor.run(
    submit_app="scripts/preprocess_param.py",
    submit_jars=["s3://crawler-public/json/serde/json-
serde.jar"],
    arguments=['--s3_input_bucket', s3_bucket,
                '--s3_input_key_prefix', s3_prefix_parquet,
                '--s3_output_bucket', s3_bucket,
                '--s3_output_key_prefix', f"{s3_output_
prefix}/o3",
                '--parameter', 'o3',],
    spark_event_logs_s3_uri="s3://{}/{}/spark_event_
logs".format(s3_bucket, 'sparklogs'),
    logs=True,
    configuration=configuration
```

```
)
```

We'll repeat the preceding step for PM25 and O3.

2. Now, we will train new XGBoost models against the single-parameter training sets, as follows:

```
estimator_o3 = sagemaker.estimator.Estimator(image_
uri=xgboost_container,
                         hyperparameters=hyperparameters,
                         role=sagemaker.get_execution_role(),
                         instance_count=1,
                         instance_type='ml.m5.12xlarge',
                         volume_size=200,
                         output_path=output_path)
```

```
content_type = "csv"
train_input = TrainingInput("s3://{}/{}/{}/{}/".
format(s3_bucket, s3_output_prefix, 'o3', 'train'),
content_type=content_type)
validation_input = TrainingInput("s3://{}/{}/{}/{}/".
format(s3_bucket, s3_output_prefix, 'o3', 'validation'),
content_type=content_type)
```

```
# execute the XGBoost training job
estimator_o3.fit({'train': train_input, 'validation':
validation_input})
```

3. Next, we define the multi-model class:

```
model = estimator_o3.create_model(role=sagemaker.get_
execution_role(), image_uri=xgboost_container)
```

```
from sagemaker.multidatamodel import MultiDataModel
model_data_prefix = f's3://{s3_bucket}/{m_prefix}/mma/'
```

```
model_name = 'xgboost-mma'
mme = MultiDataModel(name=model_name,
                     model_data_prefix=model_data_prefix,
                     model=model)
```

4. Next, we deploy the multi-model endpoint:

```
predictor = mme.deploy(initial_instance_count=1,
                       instance_type='ml.m5.2xlarge',
                       endpoint_name=model_name,
                       serializer=CSVSerializer(),
                       deserializer=JSONDeserializer())
```

5. At this point, the endpoint does not actually have any models behind it. We need to add them next:

```
for est in [estimator_o3, estimator_pm25]:
    artifact_path = \ est.latest_training_job.describe()
['ModelArtifacts']['S3ModelArtifacts']
    m_name = artifact_path.split('/')[4]+'.tar.gz'


    # This is copying over the model artifact to the S3
location for the MME.
    mme.add_model(model_data_source=artifact_path, model_
data_path=m_name)

list(mme.list_models())
```

6. We're ready to test the endpoint. Download two test files, one for each parameter:

```
s3.download_file(s3_bucket, f"{s3_output_prefix}/
pm25/test/part-00120-81a51ddd-c8b5-47d0-9431-
0a5da6158754-c000.csv", 'pm25.csv')
s3.download_file(s3_bucket, f"{s3_output_prefix}/o3/test/
part-00214-ae1a5b74-e187-4b62-ae4a-385afcbaa766-c000.
csv", 'o3.csv')
```

7. Read the files and get inferences, specifying which model we want to use:

```
with open('pm25.csv', 'r') as TF:
    pm_lines = TF.readlines()
with open('o3.csv', 'r') as TF:
    o_lines = TF.readlines()


for tl in pm_lines[0:5]:
    result = predictor.predict(data = tl.strip(), target_
```

```
model='pm25.tar.gz')
    print(result)


for tl in o_lines[0:5]:
    result = predictor.predict(data = tl.strip(), target_
model='o3.tar.gz')
    print(result)
```

Now that we've seen how to deploy multiple models for testing or other purposes, let's turn to handling fluctuating traffic demands.

Scaling inference endpoints to meet inference traffic demands

When we need a real-time inference endpoint, the processing power requirements may vary based on incoming traffic. For example, if we are providing air quality inferences for a mobile application, usage will likely fluctuate based on time of day. If we provision the inference endpoint for peak load, we will pay too much during off-peak times. If we provision the inference endpoint for a smaller load, we may hit performance bottlenecks during peak times. We can use inference endpoint auto-scaling to adjust capacity to demand.

There are two types of scaling, vertical and horizontal. **Vertical scaling** means that we adjust the size of an individual endpoint instance. **Horizontal scaling** means that we adjust the number of endpoint instances. We prefer horizontal scaling as it results in less disruption for end users; a load balancer can redistribute traffic without having an impact on end users.

There are four steps to configure autoscaling for a SageMaker inference endpoint:

- Set the minimum and maximum number of instances.
- Choose a scaling metric.
- Set the scaling policy.
- Set the cooldown period.

Although you can set up autoscaling automatically using the API, in this section, we'll go through the steps in the console. To begin, go to the **Endpoints** section of the SageMaker console, as shown in the following screenshot:

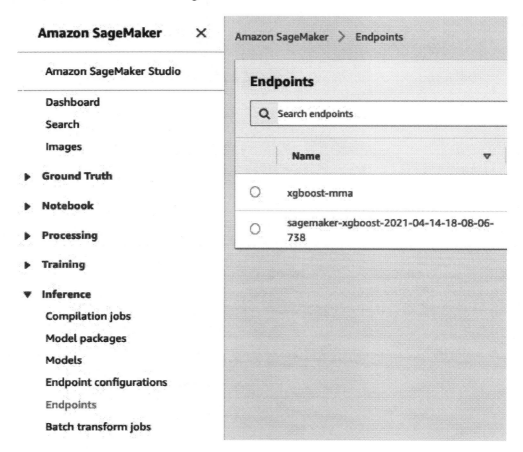

Figure 10.1 – Endpoints listed in the SageMaker console

Select one of your endpoints, and in the section called **Endpoint runtime settings**, choose **Configure auto scaling**:

Variant name ▲	Current weight ▽	Desired weight	Instance type ▽	Elastic Inference	Current instance count ▽	Desired instance count ▽	Instance min - max	Automatic scaling
● AllTraffic	1	1	ml.m5.2xlarge	-	1	1	-	No

Endpoint runtime settings — Update weights | Update instance count | Configure auto scaling

Figure 10.2 – Endpoint runtime settings

Now, let's walk through the more detailed inference endpoint settings.

Setting the minimum and maximum capacity

You can set boundaries on the minimum and maximum number of instances an endpoint can use. These boundaries let you protect against surges in demand that will result in unexpected costs. If you anticipate periodic spikes, build a circuit breaker into your application to shed load before it hits the inference endpoint. The following screenshot shows these settings in the console:

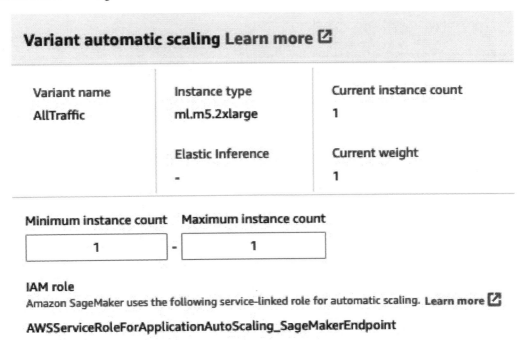

Figure 10.3 – Setting minimum and maximum capacity

If your load is highly variable, you can start with a small instance type and scale up aggressively. This prevents you from paying for a larger instance type that you don't always need.

Choosing a scaling metric

We need to decide when to trigger a scaling action. We do that by specifying a CloudWatch metric. By default, SageMaker provides two useful metrics:

- InvocationsPerInstance reports the number of inference requests sent to each endpoint instance over some time period.
- ModelLatency is the time in microseconds to respond to inference requests.

We recommend `ModelLatency` as a metric for autoscaling, as it reports on the end user experience. Setting the actual value for the metric will depend on your requirements and some observation of endpoint performance over time. For example, you may find that latency over 100 milliseconds results in a degraded user experience if the inference result passes through several other services that add their own latency before the result reaches the end user.

Setting the scaling policy

You can choose between **target tracking** and **step scaling**. Target tracking policies are more useful and try to adjust capacity to keep some target metric within a given boundary. Step scaling policies are more advanced and increase capacity in incremental steps.

Setting the cooldown period

The **cooldown period** is how long the endpoint will wait after one scaling action before starting another scaling action. If you let the endpoint respond instantaneously, you'd end up scaling too often. As a general rule, scale up aggressively and scale down conservatively.

The following screenshot shows how to configure the target metric value and cooldown period if you use the default scaling policy:

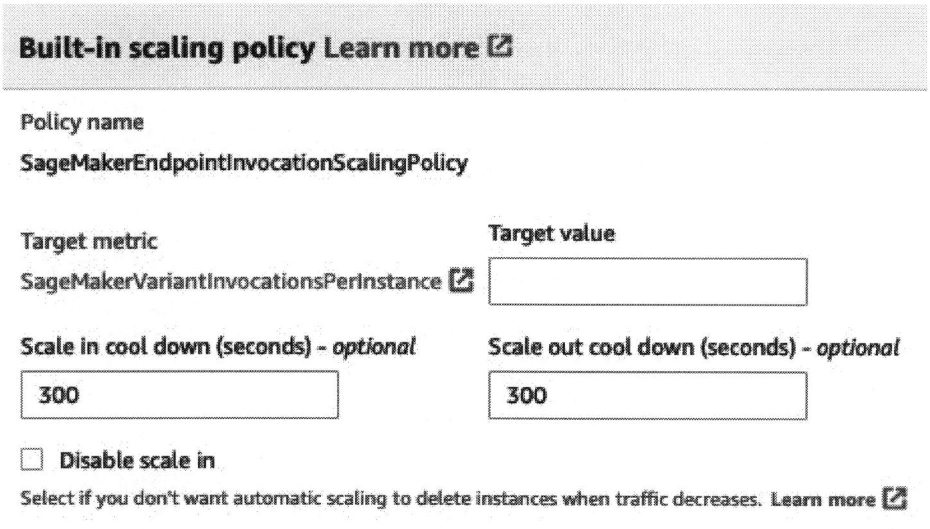

Figure 10.4 – Setting a target metric value and cooldown period

Next, let's look at another optimization technique for deep learning models.

Using Elastic Inference for deep learning models

If you examine the overall cost of ML, you may be surprised to see that the bulk of your monthly cost comes from real-time inference endpoints. Training jobs, while potentially resource-intensive, run for some time and then terminate. Managed notebook instances can be shut down during off hours. But inference endpoints run 24 hours a day, 7 days a week. If you are using a deep learning model, inference endpoint costs become more pronounced, as instances with dedicated GPU capacity are more expensive than other comparable instances.

When you obtain inferences from a deep learning model, you do not need as much GPU capacity as you need during training. **Elastic Inference** lets you attach fractional GPU capacity to regular EC2 instances or **Elastic Container Service** (**ECS**) containers. As a result, you can get deep learning inferences quickly at a reduced cost.

The *Elastic Inference* section in the notebook shows how to attach an Elastic Inference accelerator to an endpoint, as you can see in the following code block:

```
predictor_ei = predictor.deploy(initial_instance_count = 1,
instance_type = 'ml.m5.xlarge',
                    serializer=CSVSerializer(),
                    deserializer=JSONDeserializer(),
                    accelerator_type='ml.eia2.medium')
```

Consider a case where we need some GPU capacity for inference. Let's consider three options for the instance type and compare the cost. Assume that we run the endpoint for 720 hours per month. The next table compares the monthly cost for different inference options, using published prices at the time of writing:

Instance type	Cost per hour	Monthly cost	RAM (GB)	CPU	Network throughput	Trillions of operations per second
ml.p2.xlarge	$1.125	$810	61	4	High	8.74
ml.inf1.xlarge	$0.515	$370.80	8	4	Up to 25 Gigabits	Up to 64
ml.m5.xlarge with ml.eia2.medium accelerator	$0.269 + $0.168	$314.64	16	4	Up to 10 Gigabits	8

Figure 10.5 – Inference cost comparison

You'll need to look at your specific use case and figure out the best combination of RAM, CPU, network throughput, and GPU capacity that meets your performance requirements at the lowest cost. If your inferences are entirely GPU-bound, the Inferentia instance will probably give you the best price-performance balance. If you need more traditional compute resources with some GPU, the P2/P3 family will work well. If you need very little overall capacity, Elastic Inference provides the cheapest GPU option.

In the next section, we'll cover one more optimization technique for models deployed to specific hardware.

Optimizing models with SageMaker Neo

In the previous section, we saw how Elastic Inference can reduce inference costs for deep learning models. Similarly, SageMaker Neo lets you improve inference performance and reduce costs by compiling trained ML models for better performance on specific platforms. While that will help in general, it's particularly effective when you are trying to run inference on low-powered edge devices.

In order to use SageMaker Neo, you simply start a compilation job with a trained model in a supported framework. When the compilation job completes, you can deploy the artifact to a SageMaker endpoint or to an edge device using the *Greengrass* IoT platform.

The *Model optimization with SageMaker Neo* section in the notebook demonstrates how to compile our XGBoost model for use on a hosted endpoint:

1. First, we need to get the length (number of features) of an input record:

   ```
   ncols = len(t_lines[0].split(','))
   ```

2. Now, we'll compile one of our trained models. We need to specify the target platform, which in this case is just a standard ml_m5 family:

   ```
   import sagemaker
   from sagemaker.model import Model


   n_prefix = 'xgboost-sample-neo'
   n_output_path = 's3://{}/{}/{}/output'.format(s3_bucket,
   n_prefix, 'xgboost-neo')


   m1 = Model(xgboost_container,model_data=estimator\
   latest_training_job.describe()['ModelArtifacts']
   ['S3ModelArtifacts'],
             role=sagemaker.get_execution_role())
   ```

```
neo_model = ml.compile('ml_m5',
                {'data':[1, ncols]},
                n_output_path,
                sagemaker.get_execution_role(),
                framework='xgboost',
                framework_version='latest',
                job_name = 'neojob')
```

3. Once the compilation job finishes, we can deploy the compiled model as follows:

```
neo_predictor = neo_model.deploy(initial_instance_count =
1, instance_type = 'ml.m5.xlarge',
                        serializer=CSVSerializer(),
                        deserializer=JSONDeserializer(),
                        endpoint_name='neo_endpoint')
```

4. Let's test the endpoint to see whether we see a speed-up:

```
for tl in t_lines[0:5]:
    result = smrt.invoke_endpoint(EndpointName='neo_
endpoint',
                    ContentType="text/csv",
                    Body=tl.strip())
    rbody = \ StreamingBody(raw_
stream=result['Body'],content_
length=int(result['ResponseMetadata']['HTTPHeaders']
['content-length']))
    print(f"Result from
{result['InvokedProductionVariant']} = {rbody.read().
decode('utf-8')}")
```

After sending in a few invocation requests, let's check the CloudWatch metrics. Back in the console page for the compiled endpoint, click on **View invocation metrics** in the **Monitor** section, as shown in the following screenshot:

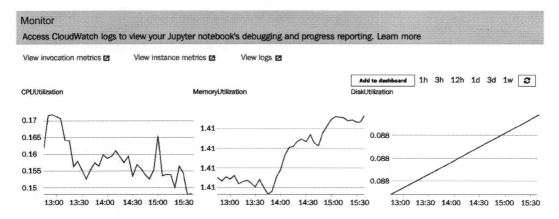

Figure 10.6 – The Monitor section of the endpoint console

You'll now see the CloudWatch metrics console, as seen in the following screenshot. Here, choose the **ModelLatency** and **OverheadLatency** metrics:

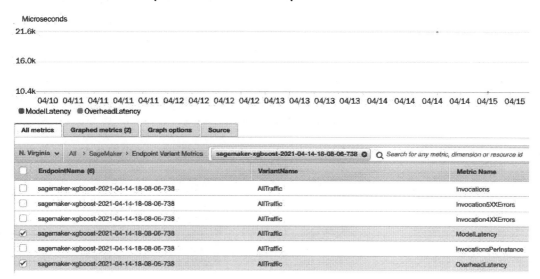

Figure 10.7 – CloudWatch metrics console

The model latency in my simple tests showed 10 milliseconds for a regular XGBoost endpoint and went down to 9 milliseconds after compiling with Neo. The impact of a compiled model will be much more significant if you are using a deep learning model on a lower-powered device.

Summary

In this chapter, we looked at several ways to improve inference performance and reduce inference cost. These methods include using batch inference where possible, deploying several models behind a single inference endpoint to reduce costs and help with advanced canary or blue/green deployments, scaling inference endpoints to meet demand, and using Elastic Inference and SageMaker Neo to provide better inference performance at a lower cost.

In the next chapter, we'll discuss monitoring and other important operational aspects of ML.

11

Monitoring Production Models with Amazon SageMaker Model Monitor and Clarify

Monitoring production **machine learning (ML)** models is a critical step to ensure that the models continue to meet business needs. Besides the infrastructure hosting the model, there are other important aspects of ML models that should be monitored regularly. As models age over a period of time, the real-world inference data distribution may change as compared to the data used for training the model. For example, consumer purchase patterns may change in the retail industry and economic conditions such as mortgage rates may change in the financial industry.

This gradual misalignment between the training and the live inference datasets can have a big impact on model predictions. Model quality metrics such as accuracy may degrade over time as well. Degraded model quality has a negative impact on business outcomes. Regulatory requirements, such as ensuring that ML models are unbiased and explainable, add another angle to model monitoring. Comprehensive monitoring of production models for these aspects allows you to proactively identify if and when a production model needs to be updated. Updating a production model needs both retraining and deployment resources. The costs involved in updating a production model should be weighed against the opportunity costs of effectively serving the model consumers.

This chapter addresses the challenge of monitoring production models using two managed services – **Amazon SageMaker Model Monitor** and **Amazon SageMaker Clarify**. These managed services eliminate the need to build custom tooling to monitor models and detect when corrective actions need to be taken. By the end of this chapter, you will be able to monitor production models for data drift, model quality, model bias, and model explainability. You will further learn how to automate remediation actions for the issues detected during monitoring.

In this chapter, we are going to cover the following main topics:

- Basic concepts of Amazon SageMaker Model Monitor and Amazon SageMaker Clarify
- End-to-end architectures for monitoring ML models
- Best practices for monitoring ML models

Technical requirements

You will need an AWS account to run the examples included in this chapter. If you have not set up the data science environment yet, please refer to *Chapter 2*, *Data Science Environments*, which walks you through the setup process.

The code examples included in the book are available on GitHub at `https://github.com/PacktPublishing/Amazon-SageMaker-Best-Practices/tree/main/Chapter11`. You will need to install a Git client to access them (`https://git-scm.com/`).

Basic concepts of Amazon SageMaker Model Monitor and Amazon SageMaker Clarify

In this section, let's review the capabilities provided by two SageMaker features: Model Monitor and Clarify.

Amazon SageMaker Model Monitor provides capabilities to monitor data drift and the model quality of models deployed as SageMaker real-time endpoints. Amazon SageMaker Clarify provides capabilities to monitor the deployed model for bias and feature attribution drift. Using a combination of these two features, you can monitor the following four different aspects of ML models deployed on SageMaker:

- **Data drift**: If the live inference traffic data served by the deployed model is statistically different from the training data the model was trained on, the model prediction accuracy will start to deteriorate. Using a combination of a training data baseline and periodic monitoring to compare the incoming inference requests with the baseline data, SageMaker Model Monitor detects data drift. Model Monitor further generates data drift metrics that are integrated with Amazon CloudWatch. Using these CloudWatch alerts, you can generate data drift detection alerts.

- **Model quality**: Monitoring model quality involves comparing labels predicted by a model to the actual labels, also called the ground truth inference labels. Model Monitor periodically merges data captured from real-time inferences with the ground truth labels to compare model quality drift against a baseline generated with training data. Similar to data drift metrics, model quality metrics are integrated with CloudWatch, so alerts can be generated if the model quality falls below a threshold.

- **Bias drift**: Statistically, significant drift between the live inference traffic data and the training data could also result in bias in the model over a period of time. This could happen even after detecting and addressing bias in the training data before training and deploying the model. SageMaker Clarify continuously monitors a deployed model for bias and generates bias metrics that are integrated with CloudWatch metrics.

- **Feature attribution drift**: Along with introducing bias in deployed models, drift in live inference data distribution can also cause drift in feature attribution values. Feature attribution ranks the individual features of a dataset according to their relative importance to a model trained using that dataset using an importance score. The feature importance score provides one way of explaining the model predictions by providing insight into which features played a role in making predictions. SageMaker Clarify compares the feature attribution or feature rankings in the training data to the feature attribution or feature rankings in live inference traffic data. Similar to other types of monitoring, feature attribution drift metrics are generated and integrated with CloudWatch.

Monitoring an ML model with SageMaker Model Monitor or SageMaker Clarify involves four high-level steps, as shown in the following diagram:

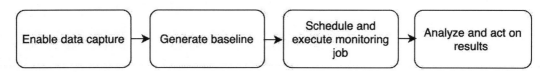

Figure 11.1 – High-level steps for model monitoring

Let's see what is involved in each of these steps in a bit more detail:

1. **Enable data capture**: The first step is to enable data capture on the real-time endpoint. On enabling data capture, input to and output from the SageMaker endpoint is captured and saved in Amazon **Simple Storage Service (S3)**. Input captured includes the live inference traffic requests and output captured includes predictions from the deployed model. This is a common step for all four types of monitoring: data drift, model quality, bias drift, and feature attribution drift monitoring.

2. **Generate baseline**: In this step, the training or validation data is analyzed to generate a baseline. The baseline generated will be further used in the next step to compare against the live inference traffic. The baseline generation process computes metrics about the data analyzed and suggests constraints for the metrics. The baseline generated is unique to the type of monitoring.

3. **Schedule and execute monitoring job**: To continuously monitor the real-time endpoint, the next step is to create a monitoring schedule to execute at a predefined interval. Once the monitoring schedule is in place, SageMaker Processing jobs are automatically kicked off to analyze the data captured from the endpoint in a specific interval. For each execution of the monitoring job, the processing job compares live traffic data captured with the baseline. If the metrics generated on the live traffic data captured in a period are outside the range of constraints suggested by the baseline, a violation is generated. The scheduled monitoring jobs also generate monitoring reports for each execution, which are saved in an S3 bucket. Additionally, CloudWatch metrics are also generated, the exact metrics being unique to the type of monitoring.

4. **Analyze and act on results**: Reports generated by the monitoring job can either be downloaded directly from S3 or visualized in a SageMaker Studio environment. In the Studio environment, you can also visualize the details of the monitoring jobs and create charts that compare the baseline metrics with the metrics calculated by the monitoring job.

To remediate issues discovered, you can use the CloudWatch metrics emitted from the monitoring job. The specific metrics depend on the type of the monitoring job. You can configure CloudWatch alerts for these metrics, based on the threshold values suggested by the baseline job. CloudWatch alerts allow you to automate responses to violations and metrics generated by monitoring jobs.

Now that you know what aspects of an ML model can be monitored, what the steps involved in monitoring are, and how you can respond to the issues discovered, you can build a monitoring solution that meets your business needs. In the next section, you will learn how to build end-to-end model monitoring architectures for the different types of monitoring.

End-to-end architectures for monitoring ML models

In this section, you will put together the four high-level steps of monitoring to build end-to-end architectures for **data drift**, **model quality**, **bias drift**, and **feature attribution drift monitoring**. Along with the architecture, you will dive into the unique aspects of the individual steps as applicable to each type of monitoring.

For all four types of monitoring, the first and last steps – enabling data capture and analyzing monitoring results – remain the same. We will discuss these two steps in detail for the first type of monitoring – data drift monitoring. For the other three types of monitoring, we will only briefly mention them.

Data drift monitoring

You monitor a production model for data drift to ensure that the distribution of the live inference traffic the deployed model is serving does not drift away from the distribution of the dataset used for training the model. The end-to-end architecture for the monitoring model for data drift is shown in the following diagram:

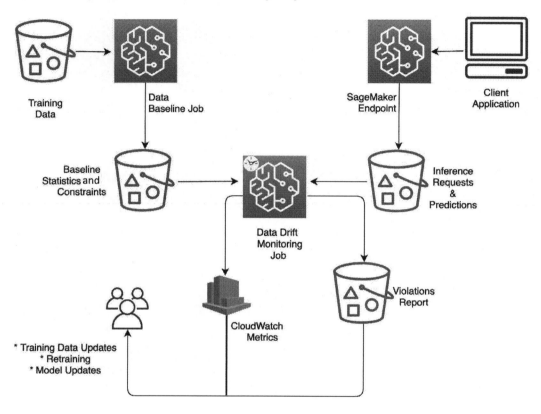

Figure 11.2 – Data drift monitoring: end-to-end architecture

Let's dive into the four high-level steps involved in this end-to-end architecture:

1. **Enable data capture for the deployed endpoint**: The first step is to deploy a SageMaker endpoint with data capture enabled. As you can see from the following sample code, configuring data capture includes specifying the percentage of inference traffic to capture and the S3 location to save the captured traffic:

```
from sagemaker.model_monitor import DataCaptureConfig
data_capture_config = DataCaptureConfig(
enable_capture=True,
```

```
sampling_percentage=100,   destination_s3_uri=s3_capture_
upload_path
)
```

To deploy the model, create the endpoint by passing in the data capture configuration as follows:

```
predictor = model.deploy(initial_instance_count=1,
                    instance_type='ml.m4.xlarge',
                    endpoint_name=endpoint_name,
                    data_capture_config = data_capture_config)
```

The following code shows a sample of the data captured. As you can see, both the request to and response from the endpoint along with event metadata are captured:

```
{
  "captureData": {
    "endpointInput": {
      "observedContentType": "text/csv",
      "mode": "INPUT",
      "data": "0,2020,12,4,31,0,19.0,0.0,6.0,0.0,0.0,0.0,0
.0,0.0,0.0,1.0\n",
      "encoding": "CSV"
    },
    "endpointOutput": {
      "observedContentType": "text/csv; charset=utf-8",
      "mode": "OUTPUT",
      "data": "-4.902510643005371",
      "encoding": "CSV"
    }
  },
  "eventMetadata": {
    "eventId": "e68592ca-948c-44dd-a764-608934e49534",
    "inferenceTime": "2021-06-28T18:41:16Z"
  },
  "eventVersion": "0"
}
```

2. **Generate baseline**: The second step is to configure and execute a data baseline job. This baseline job uses SageMaker Processing to analyze the training data at scale. For data drift monitoring, use `DefaultModelMonitor` to configure the infrastructure to execute the processing job on and the maximum runtime. Sample code is shown as follows:

```
from sagemaker.model_monitor import DefaultModelMonitor
from sagemaker.model_monitor.dataset_format import DatasetFormat
my_default_monitor = DefaultModelMonitor(
    role=role,
    instance_count=1,
    instance_type="ml.m5.xlarge",
    volume_size_in_gb=20,
    max_runtime_in_seconds=3600,
)
```

Use the `suggest_baseline` method on `DefaultModelMonitor` to configure and kick off the baseline job. To configure the baseline job, specify where the baseline data is and where you want the baseline results to be saved in S3, as follows:

```
my_default_monitor.suggest_baseline(
    baseline_dataset=baseline_data_uri + "/training-dataset-with-header.csv",
    dataset_format=DatasetFormat.csv(header=True),
    output_s3_uri=baseline_results_uri,
    wait=True
)
```

The baseline job results in two files – `statistics.json` and `constraints.json` – saved in the S3 location you specified. The `statistics.json` file includes metadata analysis of the training data – such as sum, mean, min, and max values for numerical features and distinct counts for text features.

> **Note**
>
> This baseline job uses a SageMaker-provided container called `sagemaker-model-monitor-analyzer` to analyze the training dataset. This Spark-based container uses the open source **Deequ** framework to analyze datasets at scale.

The following figure shows a sample of statistics for string features generated by the baseline job:

	name	inferred_type	string_statistics.common.num_present	string_statistics.common.num_missing	string_statistics.distinct_count
0	value	String	163163.0	0.0	16902.0

Figure 11.3 – Statistics for string features generated by the data drift baseline job

Similarly, the following figure shows a sample of statistics for numerical features generated by the baseline job:

	name	inferred_type	numerical_statistics.mean	numerical_statistics.sum	numerical_statistics.std_dev	numerical_statistics.min	numerical_statistics.max
1	ismobile	Integral	0.000000	0.0	0.000000	0.0	0.0
2	year	Integral	2020.276110	329634311.0	0.469578	2018.0	2021.0
3	month	Integral	8.838076	1442047.0	4.975293	1.0	12.0
4	quarter	Integral	3.138310	512056.0	1.357080	1.0	4.0
5	day	Integral	22.355307	3647559.0	13.546739	1.0	31.0
6	isBadAir	Integral	0.085516	13953.0	0.279648	0.0	1.0
7	location	Fractional	1698.446891	277123690.0	1639.521162	0.0	7069.0
8	city	Fractional	368.281914	60089982.0	402.585782	0.0	2279.0
9	sourcename	Fractional	7.080349	1155251.0	10.258794	0.0	80.0
10	sourcetype	Fractional	0.000000	0.0	0.000000	0.0	0.0
11	no2	Fractional	0.239294	39044.0	0.426653	0.0	1.0
12	o3	Fractional	0.207192	33806.0	0.405294	0.0	1.0
13	pm10	Fractional	0.166747	27207.0	0.372750	0.0	1.0
14	pm25	Fractional	0.140988	23004.0	0.348009	0.0	1.0
15	so2	Fractional	0.138690	22629.0	0.345622	0.0	1.0
16	co	Fractional	0.106642	17400.0	0.308657	0.0	1.0

Figure 11.4 – Statistics for numerical features generated by the data drift baseline job

The constraints.json file captures the thresholds for the statistics for monitoring purposes. The constraints also include conditions such as whether a particular feature should be considered a string, not an integer or whether a specific field should be not-null. The following screenshot shows a sample of constraints generated by the baseline job, which indicates that the value feature should always be treated as a string:

	name	inferred_type	completeness	num_constraints.is_non_negative
0	value	String	1.0	NaN
1	ismobile	Integral	1.0	True
2	year	Integral	1.0	True
3	month	Integral	1.0	True
4	quarter	Integral	1.0	True
5	day	Integral	1.0	True
6	isBadAir	Integral	1.0	True
7	location	Fractional	1.0	True
8	city	Fractional	1.0	True
9	sourcename	Fractional	1.0	True

Figure 11.5 – Constraints generated by the data drift baseline job

The generated constraints also suggest completeness for each feature, which represents the percentage of values that can be non-null in the inference traffic. In this example, since completeness for all features is at 1.0, there cannot be any null values of these features in the inference traffic. Additionally, as suggested by num_constraints.is_non_negative, none of the integral and fractional features can be null.

The constraints generated are suggestions provided by the baseline job after analyzing the training data. You can choose to override the constraint file based on the domain knowledge you have about your specific use case. You can override the suggested constraint at the individual field level or override the entire file. In the constraints.json file, you will also see an emit_metrics : Enabled entry. This suggests that CloudWatch metrics will be emitted during monitoring.

3. **Schedule and execute a data drift monitoring job**: The third step is to configure and schedule a data drift monitoring job. To configure the data drift monitoring job, specify the endpoint to monitor, the location to store the monitoring results, the baseline statistics and constraints, and the schedule to execute the job on. The following sample code configures a monitoring job to be executed every hour:

```
my_default_monitor.create_monitoring_schedule(
    monitor_schedule_name=mon_schedule_name,
    endpoint_input=predictor.endpoint,
    output_s3_uri=s3_report_path,
    statistics=my_default_monitor.baseline_statistics(),
    constraints=my_default_monitor.suggested_
constraints(),
    schedule_cron_expression=CronExpressionGenerator.
hourly(),
    enable_cloudwatch_metrics=True
)
```

SageMaker executes the data drift monitoring job using SageMaker Processing periodically according to the schedule you specify. The monitoring job compares the captured inference requests to the baseline. For each execution of the monitoring job, generated results include a violations report and a statistics report saved in S3 and metrics emitted to CloudWatch.

The following table shows possible violations the monitoring job can generate:

data_type_check	This violation occurs when the observed data type of a feature in inference traffic analyzed during the current execution does not match the data type of the same feature inferred during baseline generation.
completeness_check	During the baseline step, the generated constraints suggest completeness (% of non-null items) for each feature. For any feature, if the completeness observed by the monitoring job execution is above the suggestion, a violation is flagged.
missing_column_check	This violation is generated if there are fewer features in inference traffic than the ones specified in the baseline.
extra_column_check	This violation is generated if there are a greater number of features than the ones specified in the baseline.
categorical_values_check	If there are unknown values for a categorical feature in the inference traffic as compared to the baseline this violation is flagged.

Figure 11.6 – Data drift monitoring violations

The monitoring job emits CloudWatch metrics for all features included in the training data. Common metrics generated for all features are `Completeness` and `BaselineDrift`. The `Completeness` metric indicates the percentage of values that can be null for a given feature in a specific interval. The `BaselineDrift` metric indicates how much a feature has drifted in a specific interval from the baseline. Additionally, for numerical features, a few other metrics emitted are `Max`, `Min`, `Sum`, `SampleCount`, and `AverageCount`, as observed during the interval.

For any of these metrics, you can configure a CloudWatch alert to be triggered based on threshold values suggested in the constraints file. If the feature values in the inference traffic observed during a given interval violate the threshold values, an alert is raised.

4. **Analyze and act on results**: The final step is to analyze and act on the monitoring results. As mentioned in the high-level monitoring steps discussion earlier, you can download the monitoring reports from S3 and analyze them in your notebook environment or use Studio to view the monitoring details. For example, downloading the violation report to a notebook environment and viewing the report contents shows results similar to the following screenshot:

	feature_name	constraint_check_type	description
0	value	data_type_check	Data type match requirement is not met. Expected data type: String, Expected match: 100.0%. Observed: Only 0.0% of data is String.
1	location	baseline_drift_check	Baseline drift distance: 0.3368768906168317 exceeds threshold: 0.1

Figure 11.7 – Violations generated by the data drift monitoring job

You can decide what actions you want to take on these alerts according to your business and operational requirements. You can automate actions such as updating the model, updating your training data, and retraining and updating the model as a response to the CloudWatch alert triggered.

> **Important note**
> An example notebook that provides a complete walk-through of using SageMaker Model Monitor for data drift monitoring is provided in the GitHub repo `https://gitlab.com/randydefauw/packt_book/-/blob/main/CH10/data_drift_monitoring/WeatherPredictionDataDriftModelMonitoring.ipynb`.

Model quality drift monitoring

You monitor the quality of a production model to ensure that the performance of the production model continues to meet your requirements. Model quality is measured by different metrics depending on the type of the underlying ML problem. For example, for classification problems, accuracy or recall are good metrics and **root mean square error (RMSE)** is a metric to use with regression problems.

The end-to-end architecture for monitoring a model for model quality drift is shown in the following diagram:

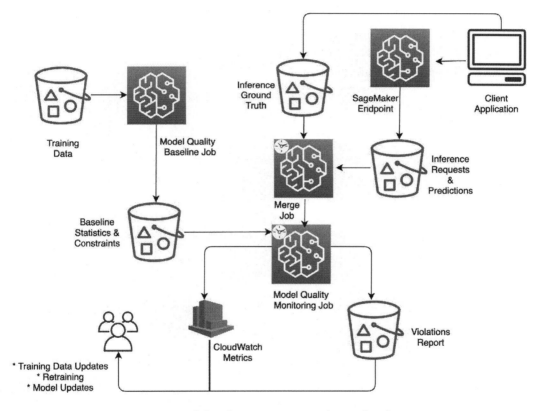

Figure 11.8 – Model quality monitoring: end-to-end architecture

The architecture is very similar to data drift monitoring with an additional step for merging the actual inference ground truth labels in an S3 bucket with the model predictions. Let's dive into the four high-level steps involved in this end-to-end architecture:

1. **Enable data capture for the deployed endpoint**: The first step is to deploy a SageMaker endpoint with data capture enabled and capture predictions made by the model in an S3 bucket.

2. **Generate baseline**: The second step is baseline generation. While the baseline job for data drift directly analyzes the training dataset for data distribution statistics, the model quality baseline job compares the labels in a baseline dataset with the predictions made by the model. So, instead of using the training data directly, you have to first generate a baseline dataset consisting of labels by running predictions against the model. You use the validation dataset to run predictions against the model and use the results as input to the baseline generation job.

The following sample code shows this process for a regression problem. Here, the baseline dataset is generated by running predictions against the model using the validation dataset. This baseline dataset has three different columns – probability, prediction, and label. While probability is the values returned by the model, prediction is inferred from the probability based on a threshold value. label represents the ground truth label from the validation set:

```
with open(f"test_data/{validate_dataset}", "w") as
baseline_file:

    baseline_file.
write("probability,prediction,label\n")  # Header of the
file

    for tl in t_lines[1:300]:

        #Remove the first column since it is the label

        test_list = tl.split(",")

        label = test_list.pop(0)

        test_string = ','.join([str(elem) for elem in
test_list])


        result = smrt.invoke_
endpoint(EndpointName=endpoint_name,

            ContentType="text/csv", Body=test_string)

        rbody = StreamingBody(raw_
stream=result['Body'],content_
length=int(result['ResponseMetadata']['HTTPHeaders']
['content-length']))

        prediction = rbody.read().decode('utf-8')

        baseline_file.
write(f"{prediction},{prediction},{label}\n")
```

```
        #print(f"label {label} ; prediction {prediction}
")
        print(".", end="", flush=True)
        sleep(0.5)
```

For model quality monitoring, you use `ModelQualityMonitor` to configure the infrastructure to execute the processing jobs and the maximum runtime, as shown in the following code:

```
# Create the model quality monitoring object
model_quality_monitor = ModelQualityMonitor(
    role=role,
    instance_count=1,
    instance_type="ml.m5.xlarge",
    volume_size_in_gb=20,
    max_runtime_in_seconds=1800,
    sagemaker_session=session,
)
```

Use the `suggest_baseline` method to configure and kick off the baseline job. To configure the baseline job, specify where the baseline data is and where you want the baseline results to be saved in S3, as follows:

```
cut the baseline suggestion job.
# You will specify problem type, in this case Binary
Classification, and provide other requirtributes.
job = model_quality_monitor.suggest_baseline(
    job_name=baseline_job_name,
    baseline_dataset=baseline_dataset_uri,
    dataset_format=DatasetFormat.csv(header=True),
    output_s3_uri=baseline_results_uri,
    problem_type="Regression",
    inference_attribute="prediction",
    probability_attribute="probability",
    ground_truth_attribute="label",
)
job.wait(logs=False)
```

The baseline job results in two files – `statistics.json` and `constraints.json` – saved in the S3 location you specified.

The following figure shows the statistics generated by the baseline job:

	0
mae.value	2.932787
mae.standard_deviation	0.065766
mse.value	14.988094
mse.standard_deviation	0.492384
rmse.value	3.871446
rmse.standard_deviation	0.064035
r2.value	-0.144170
r2.standard_deviation	0.051040

Figure 11.9 – Statistics generated by the model quality baseline job

Similarly, the following figure also shows the statistics generated by the baseline job:

	threshold	comparison_operator
mae	2.93279	GreaterThanThreshold
mse	14.9881	GreaterThanThreshold
rmse	3.87145	GreaterThanThreshold
r2	-0.14417	LessThanThreshold

Figure 11.10 – Constraints generated by the model quality baseline job

As you can see in *Figure 11.10*, one of the constraints generated is for the rmse model. It suggests that if the rmse value of the production model is greater than 3.87145 in any interval, it is an indication that the model quality is degrading. If any of the constraints suggested by the baseline job are either too restrictive or too lenient for your requirements, you can modify the constraints file.

3. **Schedule and execute the model quality monitoring job**: The third step is to schedule the model quality monitoring job. To monitor model quality, predictions of the model are first merged with the ground truth inference labels and then compared to the baseline to detect degraded accuracy. Predictions made by the model are already in S3 since data capture is enabled on the endpoint. But how about the ground truth inference labels?

The ground truth inference labels would depend on what the model is predicting and what the business use case is. For example, let's say you have a movie recommendation model that you are monitoring. A possible ground truth inference label in this case is whether the user actually watched the recommended movie or not. Maybe the user just clicked on the video but didn't watch it. So, your model-consuming application should have logic to create the ground truth inference labels and upload to an S3 bucket periodically.

With the predictions captured and the ground truth inferences provided by your model-consuming application, SageMaker executes a merge job, which is again a periodic job. While scheduling the merge job, take into consideration that the ground truth labels are only available after a certain delay. Once you have the merged data, it's time to monitor the model quality.

Here, you create a model quality monitoring job, a job that is executed periodically by SageMaker at a schedule you specify. The code is similar to the scheduling of the data monitoring job, so it is not repeated here. The monitoring job generates statistics and violations and emits CloudWatch metrics. The metrics generated are based on the type of the ML model. Example metrics for regression models include **mean absolute error**, **mean square error**, and **RMSE**. Similarly, for classification models, the metrics generated include `confusion_matrix`, `recall`, and `precision`.

> **Note**
> For a complete list of metrics generated, please review the SageMaker documentation at `https://docs.aws.amazon.com/sagemaker/latest/dg/model-monitor-model-quality-metrics.html`.

For any of these metrics, you can configure a CloudWatch alert to be triggered based on threshold values suggested in the constraints file. If model predictions for the inference traffic observed during a given interval violate the threshold values, a CloudWatch alert is raised.

4. **Analyze and act on results**: Finally, to analyze and act on the monitoring results, similar to the draft drift monitoring results, you can access the monitoring reports directly from S3, visualize them in your notebook or Studio environment, and finally, automate responses to the CloudWatch alerts raised.

Important note

An example notebook that provides a complete walk-through of using SageMaker Model Monitor for quality model monitoring is provided in the GitHub repo `https://gitlab.com/randydefauw/packt_book/-/blob/master/CH10/model_quality_monitoring/WeatherPredictionModelQualityMonitoring.ipynb`.

Bias drift monitoring

The concept of bias relates to the individual features of a dataset. Bias is typically measured for sensitive features called facets to identify whether any particular feature or a set of feature values are disproportionately represented in the dataset. Amazon Clarify provides capabilities to detect and monitor bias in a pre-training dataset and deployed models. The end-to-end architecture to monitor deployed models for bias drift is shown in the following diagram:

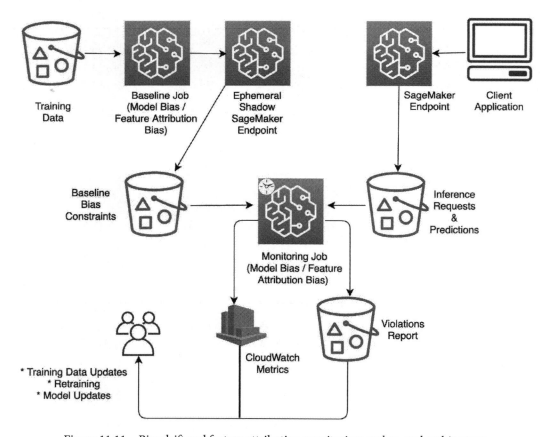

Figure 11.11 – Bias drift and feature attribution monitoring: end-to-end architecture

Let's dive into the four high-level steps involved in this end-to-end architecture:

1. **Enable data capture for the deployed endpoint**: The first step for bias drift monitoring remains the same as other types of monitoring – enabling data capture while deploying a SageMaker endpoint.

2. **Generate baseline**: The second step is creating a baseline to measure the bias metrics of the training data. A bias drift baseline job needs multiple inputs – the data to use for baselining, the sensitive features, or facets to check for bias, a model to give predictions, and finally, a threshold value to indicate when a model prediction is biased. Let's look at the various configuration objects that capture these details.

   Details of the data, such as the location of the validation dataset in the S3 bucket, the type of the dataset (CSV or JSON), and the headers and label of the data, along with the output location of the baseline job results, are captured using `DataConfig`. Sample code is as follows:

```
model_bias_data_config = DataConfig(
    s3_data_input_path=validation_dataset,
    s3_output_path=model_bias_baselining_job_result_uri,
    label=label_header,
    headers=all_headers,
    dataset_type='CSV'
)
```

   Details of sensitive features along with threshold values considered as bias are captured by `BiasConfig`. In the following code, we are monitoring for bias drift in the `"City"` feature:

```
model_bias_config = BiasConfig(
    label_values_or_threshold=[1],
    facet_name="City",
    facet_values_or_threshold=[100],
)
```

   To calculate the bias metrics, a deployed model to execute inferences is necessary. `ModelConfig` captures this model's related information as follows:

```
model_config = ModelConfig(
    model_name=model_name,
    instance_count=endpoint_instance_count,
    instance_type=endpoint_instance_type,
```

```
        content_type=dataset_type,
        accept_type=dataset_type,
)
```

Finally, `ModelPredictedLabelConfig` indicates how to extract a predicted label from the model output. For example, the following sample code indicates a prediction of `1` if the probability returned by the model is above `0.8`:

```
model_predicted_label_config = ModelPredictedLabelConfig(
        probability_threshold=0.8,
)
```

With `DataConfig`, `BiasConfig`, `ModelConfig`, and `ModelPredictedLabelConfig` in hand, you are ready to create and kick off a baseline job. Sample code is as follows:

```
model_bias_monitor = ModelBiasMonitor(
        role=role,
        sagemaker_session=sagemaker_session,
        max_runtime_in_seconds=1800,
)

model_bias_monitor.suggest_baseline(
        model_config=model_config,
        data_config=model_bias_data_config,
        bias_config=model_bias_config,
        model_predicted_label_config=model_predicted_label_
config,
)
```

During the baseline job execution, SageMaker creates a temporary endpoint called a **shadow endpoint**. A baselining job runs predictions on the validation dataset, calculates bias metrics, and suggests constraints on these metrics. Once the bias metrics are computed, the shadow endpoint is deleted.

Baseline job execution results in a constraints file that shows the bias metric values computed along with the suggested thresholds. A sample of the constraints generated is shown here:

```
{
        "version": "1.0",
        "post_training_bias_metrics": {
```

```
        "label": "value",
        "facets": {
          "city": [
            {
              "value_or_threshold": "(100.0, 2278.0]",
              "metrics": [
                {
                  "name": "AD",
                  "description": "Accuracy Difference (AD)",
                  "value": 0.008775168751768203
                },
                ...
              ]
            },
          "label_value_or_threshold": "(1.0,
130.24536736711912]"
        }
```

3. **Schedule and execute a model quality monitoring job**: The next step is to schedule a bias drift monitoring job. In this step, the monitored bias of the model will be compared against the baseline generated in the previous step. SageMaker executes the bias drift monitoring job using SageMaker Processing periodically according to the schedule you specify. The bias drift monitoring job generates a monitoring report and constraint violations along with CloudWatch metrics.

4. **Analyze and act on results**: Finally, analyzing the monitoring results and taking remedial actions is similar to the previous monitoring types.

Implementation of the end-to-end flow of this architecture is provided in the notebook. Review the notebook and the results of the execution to view the bias metrics generated.

> **Important note**
>
> An example notebook that provides a complete walk-through of using SageMaker Model Monitor for quality model monitoring is provided in the GitHub repo https://gitlab.com/randydefauw/packt_book/-/blob/master/CH10/bias_drift_monitoring/WeatherPredictionBiasDriftMonitoring.ipynb.

Feature attribution drift monitoring

Feature attribution ranks the individual features of a dataset according to their relative importance to a model trained using that dataset using an importance score. The feature importance score provides one way of explaining the model predictions by providing insight into which features played a role in making predictions. With continuous monitoring of the model, you can identify when the feature attribution of the live inference traffic starts to drift away from the feature attribution of the training dataset.

The end-to-end flow for monitoring feature attribution drift is the same as the flow for bias drift monitoring as previously shown in *Figure 11.11*. Let's dive into the four high-level steps involved in this end-to-end architecture:

1. **Enable data capture for the deployed endpoint**: The first step for feature attribution drift monitoring remains the same as other types of monitoring – enabling data capture while deploying a SageMaker endpoint.

2. **Generate baseline**: The second step is baseline generation. To generate a baseline for feature attribution drift monitoring, you rely on the SageMaker Clarify capability of providing local and global explanations. Clarify provides these explanations using a scalable implementation of **SHAP (SHapley Additive exPlanations)**, an open source framework.

    A baseline job needs multiple inputs – the data to use for baselining, a model to give predictions, and a configuration to specify how to calculate feature attribution ranks. These details are captured by different config objects. `DataConfig` and `ModelConfig`, which capture the data and model details, are the same as for bias drift monitoring.

    However, instead of using `BiasConfig` to capture sensitive features, you will need to configure `SHAPConfig`, which captures a baseline dataset to use, a number of samples to use in the Kernel SHAP algorithm, and a method for determining global SHAP values. Sample code is as follows:

```
# Here use the mean value of test dataset as SHAP
baseline
test_dataframe = pd.read_csv(test_dataset, header=None)
shap_baseline = [list(test_dataframe.mean())]


shap_config = SHAPConfig(
    baseline=shap_baseline,
    num_samples=100,
```

```
    agg_method="mean_abs",
    save_local_shap_values=False,
)
```

For feature attribution drift monitoring, you use
`ModelExplainabilityMonitor` to configure the infrastructure to execute
the processing jobs and the maximum runtime, as shown in the following code.
`ModelExplainabilityMonitor` explains model predictions using the feature
importance score and detects feature attribution drift:

```
model_explainability_monitor = ModelExplainabilityMonitor(
    role=role,
    sagemaker_session=sagemaker_session,
    max_runtime_in_seconds=1800,
)
```

With the different config objects in hand, you can now kick off the baseline job
as follows:

```
model_explainability_monitor.suggest_baseline(
    data_config=model_explainability_data_config,
    model_config=model_config,
    explainability_config=shap_config,
```

Baseline job execution results in a constraints file that shows the feature importance
values computed along with the suggested thresholds. A sample of the constraints
generated is shown here:

```
{
    "version": "1.0",
    "explanations": {
        "kernel_shap": {
            "label0": {
                "global_shap_values": {
                    "ismobile": 0.00404293281766823,
                    "year": 0.006527703849451637,
                    ...
                    "co": 0.03389338421306029
                },
                "expected_value": 0.1167794704437256
```

```
            }
        }
      }
    }
```

3. **Schedule and execute the model quality monitoring job**: The next step to schedule a feature attribution monitoring job is similar to scheduling the bias drift monitoring job.

4. **Analyze and act on results**: The final step of analyzing the monitoring results and taking remedial actions is similar to the previous monitoring types.

> **Important note**
>
> An example notebook that provides a complete walk-through of using SageMaker Model Monitor for quality model monitoring is provided in the GitHub repo `https://gitlab.com/randydefauw/packt_book/-/blob/master/CH10/bias_drift_monitoring/WeatherPredictionFeatureAttributionDriftMonitoring.ipynb`.

Let's now summarize the details of the four different monitoring types. The following table shows a summary of the monitoring types discussed so far and brings focus to the unique aspects of each monitoring type:

	Data drift	Model quality drift	Bias drift	Feature attribution drift
SageMaker feature to use	Model monitor	Model monitor	Clarify	Clarify
Class to use from SageMaker SDK	`DefaultModelMonitor`	`ModelQualityMonitor`	`ModelBiasMonitor`	`ModelExplainabilityMonitor`
Dataset used for baseline generation	Training	Model predictions generated using the validation dataset	Validation	Validation
Shadow/temporary model created for baseline generation	No	No	Yes	Yes
Baseline results	`Statistics.json` `Constraints.json`	`Statistics.json` `Constraints.json`	`Constraints.json`	`Constraints.json`
Monitoring results	Violations against thresholds	Violations against thresholds	Bias drift report	Feature attribution drift reports

Figure 11.12 – Summary of model monitoring

Now that you can put together end-to-end architecture for monitoring different aspects of deployed models using SageMaker Clarify and Model Monitor, in the next section, you will learn the best practices of using these capabilities along with some limitations.

Best practices for monitoring ML models

This section discusses best practices for monitoring models using SageMaker Model Monitor and SageMaker Clarify, taking into consideration the under-the-hood operation of these features and a few limitations as they stand at the time of publication of this book:

- **Choosing the correct data format**: Model Monitor and Clarify can only monitor for drift in tabular data. Therefore, ensure that your training data is in tabular format. For other data formats, you will have to build custom monitoring containers.

- **Choosing real-time endpoints as the mode of model deployment**: Model Monitor and Clarify support monitoring for a single-model real-time endpoint. Monitoring a model used with batch transform or multi-model endpoints is not supported. So, ensure that the model you want to monitor is deployed as a single-model real-time endpoint. Additionally, if the model is part of an inference pipeline, the entire pipeline is monitored, not the individual models that make up the pipeline.

- **Choosing sampling data capture – sampling percentage**: When you enable data capture on a real-time endpoint, a configuration parameter to pay attention to is **sampling percentage**, which indicates what percentage of the live traffic is captured. Choosing the values for this metric depends on your use case. It is a trade-off between the amount of inference traffic saved and the effectiveness of the model monitoring. If the value of this parameter is close to 100, you have more information stored, leading to more storage costs, and more data for the monitoring job to analyze, leading to a long execution time. On the other hand, a higher sampling percentage leads to capturing more inference traffic patterns to compare against the baseline.

  If your production model is operating in dynamic environments such as retail or financial services, where the consumer behavior or environment factors often change, impacting the model predictions, the best practice is to use a sampling percentage of 100.

- **Choosing a dataset for baseline generation**: For generating the baseline, the training dataset is typically a good dataset to use. For baseline generation, keep in mind that the first column in the training dataset is considered to be the label. Besides the label, ensure that the number and order of the features in the inference traffic match the training dataset.

Additionally, for bias drift and feature attribution drift, the baseline generation process stands up a shadow endpoint to collect predictions from. So, consider the limit of the number of active endpoints in your AWS account when executing a baseline job.

- **Choosing the monitoring schedule execution frequency**: Monitoring jobs, as you have seen so far, are executed on a periodic basis where the minimum interval length is 1 hour. This minimum interval is necessary because enough inference traffic needs to be collected to be compared against the baseline. When determining the monitoring execution frequency, you should select this interval based on the inference traffic your model is serving. For example, a model deployed as part of a busy e-commerce website may serve higher traffic volumes, so running a monitoring job every few hours will give you the chance to detect data and model quality issues quickly. However, every time a monitoring job is executed, it adds to your model monitoring costs. The monitoring job schedule should therefore consider the trade-off between the ability to robustly detect model issues and monitoring costs.

> **Note**
> There could be a delay of 0-20 minutes between the scheduled time and execution of the monitoring job.

- **Scheduling merge and monitoring jobs for model quality monitoring**: Model quality monitoring is unique among the four types of monitoring we have discussed in this chapter, in that the model-consuming application should provide ground truth inference labels to be used as part of monitoring. Due to this, you have to consider an additional fact that the model-consuming application may upload the ground truth inference labels using its own schedule. Without the ground truth inference labels in the S3 bucket, the merge job will fail.

To address this issue, use the `StartOffset` and `EndOffset` fields of the `ModelQualityJobInput` parameter. `StartOffset` specifies the time subtracted from the start time and `EndOffset` specifies the time subtracted from the end time of the monitoring job. Offsets are in the format of `-P#D`, `-P#M`, or `-P#H`, where D, M, and H represent days, minutes, and hours, respectively, and # is the number. For example, a `-P7H` value of `StartOffset` will cause the monitoring job to start 7 hours after the scheduled time.

Additionally, ensure that the monitoring schedule cadence is such that any given execution should be completed before the subsequent execution starts, allowing both the ground truth merge job and the monitoring job to complete for each interval.

- **Automating remediation actions**: While a monitoring solution proactively detects the data and model issues, without a proper plan to act on the issues, you cannot ensure the model's continued ability to meet your business needs. To reap the benefits of the model monitoring alerts generated, as much as possible, automate actions that you need to perform as a result. For example, automate notifications sent to operations and data science teams about possible data and model issues. Similarly, automate collecting or importing new training data and triggering re-training and testing of the models in non-production environments such as dev/QA and staging.

- **Choosing built-in versus custom monitoring**: SageMaker provides a built-in container called `sagemaker-model-monitor-analyzer` that provides the capabilities we have reviewed in this chapter so far. This Spark-based container built on the open source Deequ framework provides a range of capabilities, such as generating statistics, suggesting constraints, validating constraints against a baseline, and emitting CloudWatch metrics.

  Whenever possible, choose to use this built-in container since SageMaker takes on the burden of securing, managing, and updating this container with new capabilities. You can extend the capabilities of this container by providing your own preprocessing and postprocessing scripts. For example, you can use a custom preprocessing script to make small changes to data, such as converting from an array to flattened JSON as required by the baseline job. Similarly, you can perform postprocessing to make changes to monitoring results.

  In addition to using the SageMaker-provided container, you can also use your own containers for custom monitoring. Custom containers allow you to build your own monitoring schedules as well as your own logic for generating custom statistics, constraints, and violations, along with custom CloudWatch metrics. When creating a custom container, you should follow the input and output contracts published by SageMaker. Additionally, you will be responsible for registering, managing, and updating this custom container.

- **Including human reviews in the monitoring workflow**: For some critical ML applications, say, for example, a financial loan approval application, it will often be necessary to include human reviewers in the monitoring loop. Especially when the ML model returns predictions with low confidence, human experts need to ensure that the predictions are valid. Amazon A2I allows you to configure custom monitoring workflows to include human experts to review predictions from SageMaker models. Please see the *References* section for a link to a detailed blog on configuring custom human-in-the-loop workflows using SageMaker and Amazon A2I.

Use the best practices discussed in this section to create model monitoring configurations that best meet your business and organizational requirements.

Summary

In this chapter, you learned the importance of monitoring ML models deployed in production and the different aspects of models to monitor. You dove deep into multiple end-to-end architectures to build continuous monitoring, automate responses to detected data, and model issues using SageMaker Model Monitor and SageMaker Clarify. You learned how to use the various metrics and reports generated to gain insight into your data and model.

Finally, we concluded with a discussion on the best practices for configuring model monitoring. Using the concepts discussed in this chapter, you can build a comprehensive monitoring solution to meet your performance and regulatory requirements, without having to use various different third-party tools for monitoring various aspects of your model.

In the next chapter, we will introduce end-to-end ML workflows that stitch all the individual steps involved in the ML process together.

References

For additional reading material, please review the following reference:

- Automated monitoring of your ML models with Amazon SageMaker Model Monitor and sending predictions to human review workflows using Amazon A2I:

  ```
  https://aws.amazon.com/blogs/machine-learning/automated-
  monitoring-of-your-machine-learning-models-with-amazon-
  sagemaker-model-monitor-and-sending-predictions-to-human-
  review-workflows-using-amazon-a2i
  ```

Section 4: Automate and Operationalize Machine Learning

In this section, we will build automated workflows and MLOps pipelines for end-to-end ML solutions following best practices for security, reliability, performance, and cost optimization.

This section comprises the following chapters:

- *Chapter 12, Machine Learning Automated Workflows*
- *Chapter 13, Well-Architected Machine Learning with Amazon SageMaker*
- *Chapter 14, Managing SageMaker Features across Accounts*

12
Machine Learning Automated Workflows

For **machine learning (ML)** models that are deployed to production environments, it's important to establish a consistent and repeatable process to retrain, deploy, and operate these models. This becomes increasingly important as you scale the number of ML models running in production. The **machine learning development lifecycle (ML Lifecycle)** brings with it some unique challenges in operationalizing ML workflows. This will be discussed in this chapter. We will also discuss common patterns to not only automate your ML workflows, but also implement **continuous integration (CI)** and **continuous delivery/deployment (CD)** practices for your ML pipelines.

Although we will cover various options for automating your ML workflows and building CI/CD pipelines for ML in this chapter, we will focus particularly on detailed implementation patterns using Amazon SageMaker Pipelines and Amazon SageMaker projects. SageMaker Pipelines is purpose-built for activities that include the automation of the steps needed to build a model, such as **data preparation**, **model training**, and **model evaluation** tasks. SageMaker projects build on SageMaker Pipelines by incorporating CI/CD practices into your ML pipelines. SageMaker projects utilize SageMaker Pipelines in combination with the SageMaker model registry to build out end-to-end ML pipelines that also incorporate CI/CD practices such as source control, version management, and automated deployments.

In this chapter, we'll cover the following topics:

- Considerations for automating your SageMaker ML workflows
- Building ML workflows with Amazon SageMaker Pipelines
- Creating CI/CD ML pipelines using Amazon SageMaker projects

Considerations for automating your SageMaker ML workflows

In this section, we'll review a typical ML workflow that includes the basic steps for model building and deploy activities. Understanding the key SageMaker inputs and artifacts for each step is important in building automated workflows, regardless of the automation or workflow tooling you choose to employ.

This information was covered in *Chapter 8, Manage Models at Scale Using a Model Registry*. Therefore, if you have not yet read that chapter it's recommended to do so prior to continuing with this chapter. We'll build on that information and cover high-level considerations and guidance for building out automated workflows and CI/CD pipelines for SageMaker workflows. We'll also briefly cover the common AWS native service options when building automated workflows and CI/CD ML pipelines.

Typical ML workflows

An ML workflow contains all the steps required to build an ML model for an ML use case, followed by the steps needed to deploy and operate the model in production. *Figure 12.1* shows a typical ML workflow that includes model build and model deploy steps. Each step within the workflow often has a number of associated tasks. As an example, data preparation can include multiple tasks needed to transform data into a format that is consistent with your ML algorithm.

When we look at automating the end-to-end ML workflow, we look to automate the tasks included within a step, as well as how to orchestrate the sequence and timing of steps into an end-to-end pipeline. As a result, knowing the key inputs for each step, as well as the expected output or artifact of a step, is key in building end-to-end pipelines.

Additionally, model development is an iterative process. It may therefore take many experiments until you're able to find a candidate model that meets your model performance criteria. As a result, it's common to continue to experiment in a data science sandbox environment until you find a candidate model to register into a model registry. This would indicate that the model is ready to deploy to one or more target environments for additional testing, followed by deployment to a production environment.

Refer to the following figure for an example of a typical workflow:

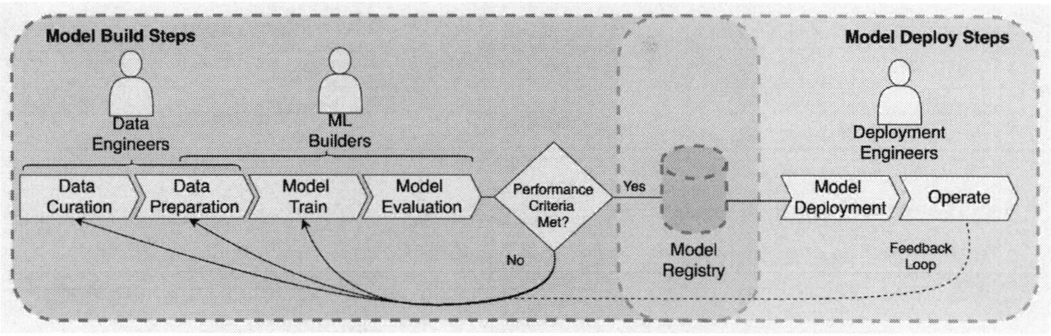

Figure 12.1 – Typical ML workflow

After the model is deployed, there may also be additional tasks required to integrate the model with existing client applications. There may also be tasks required to create a more complex inference workflow that includes multiple models and tasks required for inference. Finally, there would still be tasks required to operate that model. Although the *Operate* step comes at the end, the activities that need to be performed for the ongoing operation of that model need to be considered early on in the process. This is in order to include all necessary tasks within your automated workflow, as well as ensure key metrics are captured, and available for key personas. In addition, this allows you to set up alerts as needed. This includes activities such as the following:

- **Model monitoring**: This includes the tasks required to ensure your model performance does not degrade over time. This topic is covered in detail in *Chapter 11, Monitoring Production Models with Amazon SageMaker Model Monitor and Clarify*. However, when building your automated deployment workflows, it's important to consider the additional tasks that may need to be included and automated within your pipeline. As an example, SageMaker Model Monitor for data drift requires tasks such as baselining of your training data, enabling data capture on your endpoints, and scheduling a SageMaker monitoring job. All of these tasks should be automated and included in your automated workflow. You can also utilize *Human in the Loop* reviews with **Amazon Augmented AI (Amazon A2I)** to check low-confidence predictions that can be implemented along with, or complementary to, SageMaker Model Monitor.

- **System monitoring**: System monitoring includes capturing and alerting on metrics that are key to the resources hosting your model, as well as the other resources supporting the deployed ML solution. As an example, Amazon SageMaker will automatically capture key metrics about an endpoint, such as CPU/GPU utilization or the number of invocations. Setting thresholds and creating alerts in Amazon CloudWatch helps ensure the overall health of resources hosting models, as well as other solution components.

- **Model retraining**: To set up automatic model retraining, the tasks that are performed across your model build steps should be captured as code that can be executed as part of a model build pipeline. This pipeline would include automation of all of the tasks within each step, as well as orchestration of those steps.

- **Pipeline monitoring**: If you have automated pipelines set up for your model build and model deploy activities, it's key to also have monitoring in place on your pipeline to ensure you are notified in the event of a step failure in your pipeline.

We have covered the general steps in an ML workflow. However, each automated workflow and CI/CD pipeline can vary due to a number of factors. In the next section, we'll cover some of the considerations that are common across ML use cases.

Considerations and guidance for building SageMaker workflows and CI/CD pipelines

The steps and tasks performed as part of an ML workflow can vary depending on the use case; however, the following high-level practices are recommended when building an automated workflow for your ML use case:

- **Implement a model registry**: A **model registry** helps bridge the steps between the phases of model building experimentation and deploying your models to higher-level environments. A model registry captures key metadata, such as **model metrics**. It also ensures you're able to track key inputs and artifacts for traceability, as well as manage multiple model versions across environments.

- **Version inputs and artifacts**: The ability to roll back or recreate a specific model version or deployable artifact is dependent on knowing the specific versions of inputs and artifacts used to create that resource. As an example, to recreate a SageMaker endpoint, you need to know key version information, such as the model artifact and the inference container image. These inputs and artifacts should be protected from inadvertent deletion. They should also be tracked through an end-to-end pipeline to be able to confidently recreate resources as part of an automated workflow.

AWS-native options for automated workflow and CI/CD pipelines

In this chapter, we focus primarily on the SageMaker-native options for creating automated workflows, as well as layering on CI/CD practices in end-to-end pipelines. However, there are other options that can also be used for creating automated workflows that contain SageMaker tasks for model building and model deployment. There are also third-party options that contain operators or integrations with SageMaker. However, they are not covered in this book.

First, we'll cover a few of the AWS services and features that can be used to build automated workflows that include SageMaker tasks:

- **AWS Step Functions**: AWS Step Functions (`https://aws.amazon.com/step-functions/?step-functions.sort-by=item.additionalFields.postDateTime&step-functions.sort-order=desc`) allows you to create automated serverless workflows that include integration with a number of AWS services, as well as giving you the capability to integrate third-party tasks into your workflows. AWS Step Functions also has native support for SageMaker tasks, such as SageMaker processing jobs, SageMaker training jobs, and SageMaker hosting options.

  In addition, ML builders can choose to take advantage of the AWS Step Functions Data Science SDK (`https://docs.aws.amazon.com/step-functions/latest/dg/concepts-python-sdk.html`) to create ML workflows using Python instead of through Amazon States Language. Amazon States Language is the native pipeline syntax for AWS Step Functions. AWS Step Functions offers extensibility across AWS services with native integrations for the AWS services most commonly used in ML workflows, such as AWS Lambda, Amazon EMR, or AWS Glue.

- **Amazon Managed Workflows for Apache Airflow**: Amazon Managed Workflows for Apache Airflow (`https://aws.amazon.com/managed-workflows-for-apache-airflow/`) allows you to create automated ML workflows by using native integration with SageMaker among other AWS services that are commonly used. Many organizations and teams already use or have invested in Airflow, so this service provides a way to take advantage of those existing investments using a managed service that includes native integrations with SageMaker for model building and deployment steps.

- **Amazon SageMaker Operators for Kubernetes**: SageMaker Operators for Kubernetes (`https://docs.aws.amazon.com/sagemaker/latest/dg/amazon-sagemaker-operators-for-kubernetes.html`) allows teams to create SageMaker tasks natively using the Kubernetes API and command-line Kubernetes tools, such as **kubectl**.

- **Amazon SageMaker Components for Kubeflow Pipelines**: SageMaker Components for Kubeflow Pipelines allows teams to still utilize Kubeflow for workflow orchestration, while providing integrations with SageMaker so that you can create and run SageMaker jobs in managed environments without running them directly on your Kubernetes clusters. This is useful for taking advantage of end-to-end managed SageMaker features, but also for cases where you do not want to perform those tasks directly on your cluster.

Next, we'll cover a few of the AWS services and features that can be used to incorporate CI/CD practices into your ML pipelines. These services are not unique to ML and can also be substituted for third-party tools offering similar capabilities:

- **AWS CodeCommit**: AWS CodeCommit (`https://aws.amazon.com/codecommit/`) is a private Git-based source code repository. For ML pipelines, AWS CodeCommit can store any related source code, such as **infrastructure as code (IaC)/configuration as code (CaC)**, data processing code, training code, model evaluation code, pipeline code, and model deployment code. The structure of your repositories may vary, but in general, it's recommended to at least separate your model build and model deploy code.

- **AWS CodeBuild**: AWS CodeBuild (`https://aws.amazon.com/codebuild/`) is a fully managed build service that can be used for multiple purposes. These include compiling source code, running tests, and running custom scripts as part of a pipeline. For ML pipelines, AWS CodeBuild can be used for tasks such as testing through custom scripts and packaging AWS CloudFormation templates.

- **AWS CodePipeline**: AWS CodePipeline (`https://aws.amazon.com/codepipeline/`) is a fully managed CD service that can be used to orchestrate the steps of your ML pipeline. AWS CodePipeline can be used to orchestrate the steps for model build tasks, as well as model deploy tasks.

The preceding list of AWS services can be used to incorporate CI/CD practices for your ML pipelines. You can also optionally substitute the services above for third-party options, such as GitHub, BitBucket, or Jenkins.

In this section, we covered a high-level ML workflow in the context of automating the tasks within key steps, as well as providing overall orchestration to automate those steps. We also discussed some of the key considerations when building your ML workflows. We reviewed the AWS-native options for creating automated ML workflows. We then looked at the AWS services that can be used to incorporate CI/CD practices.

All of these, as well as many third-party options, are valid options when selecting the right tooling for automating your SageMaker workflows. The decision to custom build workflows using the services mentioned in the preceding list, or the decision to substitute the services above with third-party options, typically comes from either personal preference or having organizational standards or requirements to utilize existing tooling.

For the remainder of this chapter, we'll focus on the SageMaker-native capabilities for automating your ML workflows and incorporating CI/CD practices.

Building ML workflows with Amazon SageMaker Pipelines

Model build workflows cover all of the steps performed when developing your model, including data preparation, model training, model tuning, and model deployment. In this case, model deployment can include the tasks necessary to evaluate your model, as well as batch use cases that do not need to be deployed to higher environments. SageMaker Pipelines is a fully managed service that allows you to create automated model build workflows using the SageMaker Python SDK.

SageMaker Pipelines includes built-in step types (`https://docs.aws.amazon.com/sagemaker/latest/dg/build-and-manage-steps.html`) for executing SageMaker tasks, such as SageMaker Processing for data pre-processing, and SageMaker Training for model training. Pipelines also include steps for controlling how your pipeline works. For example, the pipeline could include conditional steps that could be used to evaluate the output of a previous step to determine whether to proceed to the next step in the pipeline.

To include steps that perform tasks using other AWS services or non-AWS tasks, you must use the **callback step**. This is useful if you are using another AWS service for a task in your pipeline. One example could be if you are using AWS Glue for data preprocessing. *Figure 12.2* builds on the previous workflow illustration to indicate where SageMaker Pipelines fits into the end-to-end workflow, as well as providing examples of the supported SageMaker features for each model build workflow step:

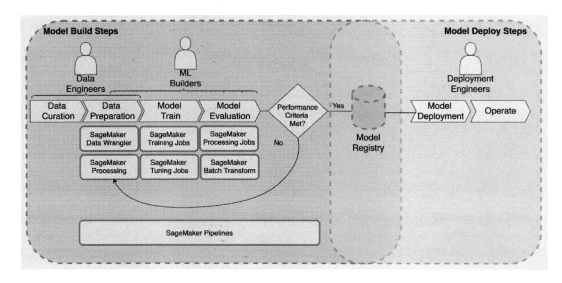

Figure 12.2 – SageMaker Pipelines model building workflows

In this section, you'll build out a SageMaker pipeline for your ML use case. The pipeline will include all of the steps necessary for data preparation, model training, and model evaluation. Because we don't need every SageMaker feature to build our pipeline, you'll only be using the features noted in the following diagram:

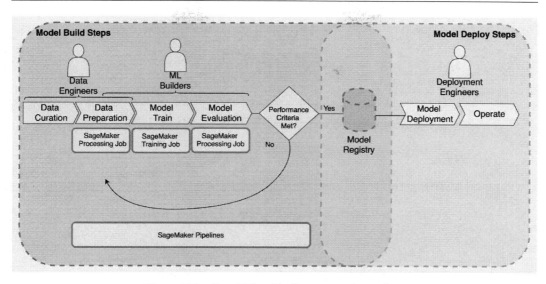

Figure 12.3 – SageMaker Pipelines example pipeline

For each step in your SageMaker pipeline, you first need to configure the task that you will execute (for example, a training job) and then configure the SageMaker Pipelines step for that task. After all, steps have been configured, you chain the steps together and then execute the pipeline. The following sections will walk you through the steps in building your SageMaker pipeline for your example use case.

Building your SageMaker pipeline

In this section, we'll walk through the steps needed to configure each step in your SageMaker pipeline, as well as how to chain those steps together and finally execute your model build pipeline. For each step in your pipeline, there are two steps to follow:

1. Configure the SageMaker job.
2. Configure the SageMaker Pipelines step.

Figure 12.4 illustrates the steps that we will use to build the pipeline:

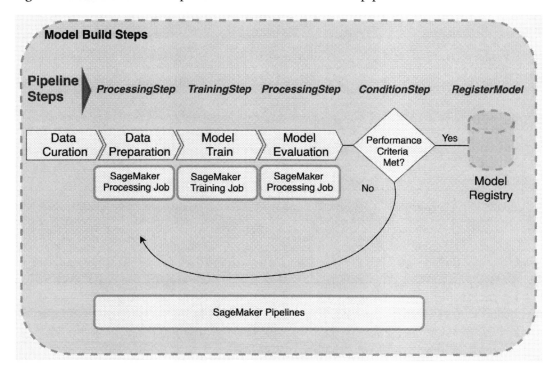

Figure 12.4 – Pipeline use case with SageMaker steps

We'll start with the data preparation step, where we'll use SageMaker Processing to transform our raw data into the format expected by the algorithm.

Data preparation step

In this step, you'll configure the SageMaker processing job that will be used to transform your data into a format expected by the algorithm. For this, we'll use the same configuration from *Chapter 4, Data Preparation at Scale Using Amazon SageMaker Data Wrangler and Processing*:

1. First, we'll configure the SageMaker processing job, as follows:

```
from sagemaker.spark.processing import PySparkProcessor


spark_processor = PySparkProcessor(
    base_job_name="spark-preprocessor",
    framework_version="3.0",
    role=role,
```

```
        instance_count=15,
        instance_type="ml.m5.4xlarge",
        max_runtime_in_seconds=7200, )


configuration = [
    {
        "Classification": "spark-defaults",
        "Properties": {"spark.executor.memory": "18g",
                "spark.yarn.executor.memoryOverhead": "3g",
                    "spark.driver.memory": "18g",
                "spark.yarn.driver.memoryOverhead": "3g",
                    "spark.executor.cores": "5",
                    "spark.driver.cores": "5",
                "spark.executor.instances": "44",
                "spark.default.parallelism": "440",
                "spark.dynamicAllocation.enabled": "false"
                    },
        },
    {
        "Classification": "yarn-site",
        "Properties": {"yarn.nodemanager.vmem-check-
enabled": "false",
        "yarn.nodemanager.mmem-check-enabled": "false"},
        }
]
```

2. Next, we'll configure the SageMaker Pipelines step that will be used to execute your data preparation tasks. For this, we'll use the built-in processing step (`https://docs.aws.amazon.com/sagemaker/latest/dg/build-and-manage-steps.html#step-type-processing`) that tells Pipelines this step will be a SageMaker processing job. *Figure 12.5* shows the high-level inputs and outputs/artifacts that `ProcessingStep` used for data preprocessing will expect:

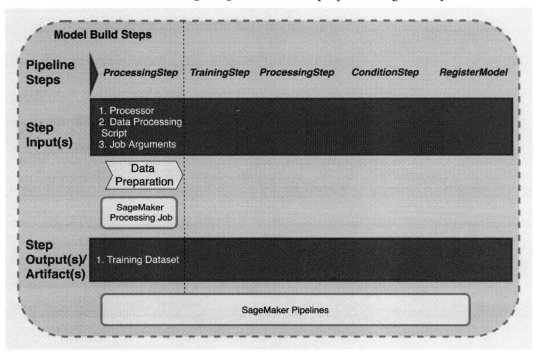

Figure 12.5 – Data preparation pipeline step

We previously configured the processor, so we will now use that processor (combined with the other inputs shown in *Figure 12.4*) to set up our Pipelines step, as follows:

1. First, we'll enable **step caching**. Step caching tells SageMaker to check for a previous execution of a step that was called with the same arguments. This is so that it can use the previous step values of a successful run instead of re-executing a step with the exact same arguments. You should consider using step caching to avoid unnecessary tasks and costs. As an example, if the second step (model training) in your pipeline fails, you can start the pipeline again without re-executing the data preparation step if that step has not changed, as follows:

```
from sagemaker.workflow.steps import CacheConfig
cache_config = CacheConfig(enable_caching=True, expire_
after="T360m")
```

2. Next, we'll define the runtime arguments using the get_run_args method. In this case, we are passing the Spark processor that was previously configured, in combination with the parameters identifying the inputs (raw weather data), the outputs (train, test, and validation datasets), and additional arguments the data processing script accepts as input. The data processing script, preprocess. py, is a slightly modified version of the processing script used in *Chapter 4, Data Preparation at Scale Using Amazon SageMaker Data Wrangler and Processing*. Refer to the following script:

```
from sagemaker.processing import ProcessingInput,
ProcessingOutput

run_args = pyspark_processor.get_run_args(
    "preprocess.py",
    submit_jars=["s3://crawler-public/json/serde/json-
serde.jar"],
    spark_event_logs_s3_uri=spark_event_logs_s3_uri,
    configuration=configuration,
    outputs=[ \
        ProcessingOutput(output_name="validation",
destination=validation_data_out, source="/opt/ml/
processing/validation"),
        ProcessingOutput(output_name="train",
destination=train_data_out, source="/opt/ml/processing/
train"),
        ProcessingOutput(output_name="test",
destination=test_data_out, source="/opt/ml/processing/
test"),
    ],
    arguments=[
        '--s3_input_bucket', s3_bucket,
        '--s3_input_key_prefix', s3_prefix_parquet,
        '--s3_output_bucket', s3_bucket,
        '--s3_output_key_prefix', s3_output_prefix+'/
prepared-data/'+timestamp
    ]
)
```

3. Next, we'll use the runtime parameters to configure the actual SageMaker Pipelines step for our data preprocessing tasks. You'll notice we're using all of the parameters we configured previously to build the step that will execute as part of the pipeline:

```
from sagemaker.workflow.steps import ProcessingStep


step_process = ProcessingStep(
    name="DataPreparation",
    processor=pyspark_processor,
    inputs=run_args.inputs,
    outputs=run_args.outputs,
    job_arguments=run_args.arguments,
    code="modelbuild/pipelines/preprocess.py",
)
```

Model build step

In this step, you'll configure the SageMaker training job that will be used to train your model. You'll use the training data produced from the data preparation step, in combination with your training code and configuration parameters.

> **Important note**
>
> Although we do not cover it in this chapter specifically, it is important to note that SageMaker Pipelines now integrates with SageMaker Experiments, allowing you to capture extra metrics, as well as view corresponding plots in SageMaker Pipelines.

For this, we'll use the same configuration from *Chapter 6, Training and Tuning at Scale*. Refer to the following steps:

1. First, we'll configure the SageMaker training job, as follows:

```
# initialize hyperparameters
hyperparameters = {
        "max_depth":"5",
        "eta":"0.2",
        "gamma":"4",
        "min_child_weight":"6",
```

```python
        "subsample":"0.7",
        "objective":"reg:squarederror",
        "num_round":"5"}


# set an output path where the trained model will be
saved
m_prefix = 'pipeline/model'
output_path = 's3://{}/{}/{}/output'.format(s3_bucket, m_
prefix, 'xgboost')


# this line automatically looks for the XGBoost image URI
and builds an XGBoost container.
# specify the repo_version depending on your preference.
image_uri = sagemaker.image_uris.retrieve("xgboost",
region, "1.2-1")


# construct a SageMaker estimator that calls the xgboost-
container
xgb_estimator = sagemaker.estimator.Estimator(image_
uri=image_uri,
                        hyperparameters=hyperparameters,
                      role=sagemaker.get_execution_role(),
                        instance_count=1,
                        instance_type='ml.m5.12xlarge',
                        volume_size=200, # 5 GB
                        output_path=output_path)
```

2. Next, we'll configure the SageMaker Pipelines step that will be used to execute your model training task. For this, we'll use the built-in `training step` (https://docs.aws.amazon.com/sagemaker/latest/dg/build-and-manage-steps.html#step-type-training). This tells Pipelines this step will be a SageMaker training job. *Figure 12.6* shows the high-level inputs and outputs/artifacts that a **Training step** will expect:

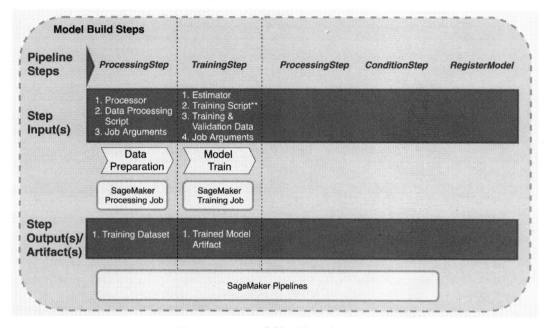

Figure 12.6 – Model build pipeline step

We previously configured the estimator, so we will now use that estimator combined with the other inputs shown in *Figure 12.6* to set up our Pipelines step:

```python
from sagemaker.inputs import TrainingInput
from sagemaker.workflow.steps import TrainingStep


step_train = TrainingStep(
    name="ModelTrain",
    estimator=xgb_estimator,
    cache_config=cache_config,
    inputs={
        "train": TrainingInput(
```

```
        s3_data=step_process.properties.
ProcessingOutputConfig.Outputs["train"].S3Output.S3Uri,
            content_type="text/csv",
        ),
        "validation": TrainingInput(
            s3_data=step_process.properties.
ProcessingOutputConfig.Outputs["validation"].S3Output.S3Uri,
            content_type="text/csv",
        ),
    },
)
```

Model evaluation step

In this step, you'll configure a SageMaker processing job that will be used to evaluate your trained model using the model artifact produced from the training step in combination with your processing code and configuration:

1. First, we'll configure the SageMaker processing job starting with ScriptProcessor. We will use this to execute a simple evaluation script, as follows:

```
from sagemaker.processing import ScriptProcessor


script_eval = ScriptProcessor(
    image_uri=image_uri,
    command=["python3"],
    instance_type=processing_instance_type,
    instance_count=1,
    base_job_name="script-weather-eval",
    role=role,
)
```

2. Next, we'll configure the SageMaker Pipelines step that will be used to execute your model evaluation tasks. For this, we'll use the built-in Processing step (`https://docs.aws.amazon.com/sagemaker/latest/dg/build-and-manage-steps.html#step-type-processing`). This tells Pipelines this step will be a SageMaker processing job. *Figure 12.7* shows the high-level inputs and outputs/artifacts that a Processing step used for model evaluation will expect:

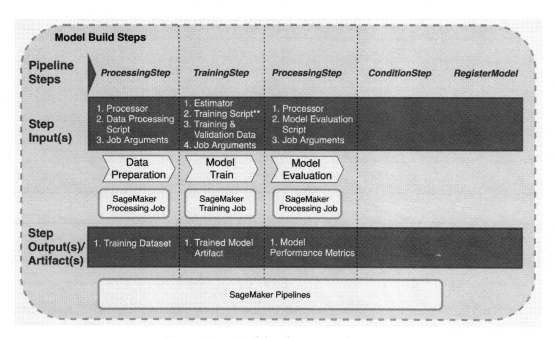

Figure 12.7 – Model evaluation pipeline step

We previously configured the processor, so we will now use that processor combined with the other inputs shown in *Figure 12.7* to set up our Pipelines step. To do this, we'll first set up the property file that will be used to store the output, in this case, model evaluation metrics, of our processing job. Then, we'll configure the `ProcessingStep` definition as follows:

```python
from sagemaker.workflow.properties import PropertyFile


evaluation_report = PropertyFile(
    name="EvaluationReport", output_name="evaluation",
path="evaluation.json"
)
step_eval = ProcessingStep(
    name="WeatherEval",
    processor=script_eval,
    cache_config = cache_config,
    inputs=[
        ProcessingInput(
            source=step_train.properties.ModelArtifacts.
S3ModelArtifacts,
            destination="/opt/ml/processing/model",
        ),
        ProcessingInput(
            source=step_process.properties.
ProcessingOutputConfig.Outputs["test"].S3Output.
S3Uri,   destination="/opt/ml/processing/test",
        ),
    ],
    outputs=[
        ProcessingOutput(output_name="evaluation", source="/
opt/ml/processing/evaluation"),
    ],
    code="modelbuild/pipelines/evaluation.py",
    property_files=[evaluation_report],
)
```

Conditional step

In this step, you'll configure a built-in conditional step that will determine whether to proceed to the next step in the pipeline based on the results of your previous model evaluation step. Setting up a conditional step requires a list of conditions or items that must be true. This is in combination with instructions on the list of steps to execute based on that condition. *Figure 12.8* illustrates the inputs and outputs required for a conditional step:

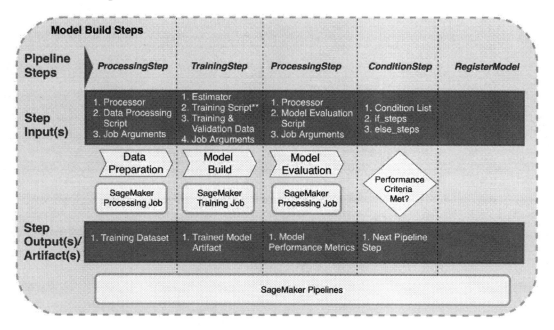

Figure 12.8 – Conditional pipeline step

In this case, we're going to set up a condition using the **mean squared error** (MSE) metric. If the metric is less than or equal to *nn*, then we will indicate the steps to proceed with using the `if_steps` parameter. In this case, the next steps if the condition were true would be to register the model and then create the model that packages your model for deployment. You can optionally specify `else_steps` to indicate the next steps to perform if the condition is not true. In this case, we will simply terminate the pipeline if the condition is not true:

```python
from sagemaker.workflow.conditions import
ConditionLessThanOrEqualTo
from sagemaker.workflow.condition_step import (
    ConditionStep,
    JsonGet
)

cond_lte = ConditionLessThanOrEqualTo(
    left=JsonGet(
        step=step_eval,
        property_file=evaluation_report,
        json_path="regression_metrics.mse.value"
    ),
    right=6.0
)

step_cond = ConditionStep(
    name="MSECondition",
    conditions=[cond_lte],
    if_steps=[step_register, step_create_model],
    else_steps=[]
)
```

Register model step(s)

In this final step, you'll package the model and configure a built-in register model (`https://docs.aws.amazon.com/sagemaker/latest/dg/build-and-manage-steps.html#step-type-register-model`) step that will register your model to a model package group in SageMaker model registry. As seen in *Figure 12.9*, the inputs we'll use to register the model contain information about the packaged model, such as the model version, estimator, and S3 location of the model artifact. This information, when combined with additional information such as model metrics and inference specifications, is used to register the model version:

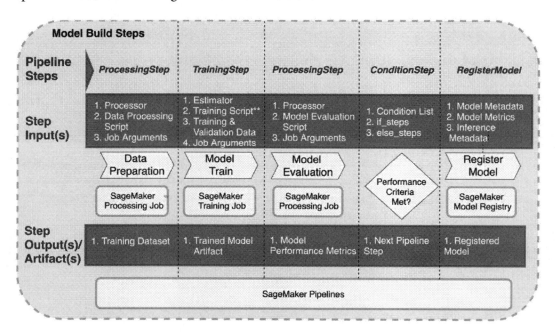

Figure 12.9 – Conditional pipeline step

This step will use data from the prior steps in the pipeline to register the model and centrally store key metadata about this specific model version. In addition, you'll see an `approval_status parameter`. This parameter can be used to trigger downstream deployment processes (these will be discussed in more detail under SageMaker Projects):

```
from sagemaker.model_metrics import MetricsSource, ModelMetrics
from sagemaker.workflow.step_collections import RegisterModel


model_metrics = ModelMetrics(
    model_statistics=MetricsSource(
```

```
            s3_uri="{}/evaluation.json".format(
step_eval.arguments["ProcessingOutputConfig"]["Outputs"][0]
["S3Output"]["S3Uri"]
        ),
        content_type="application/json",
    )
)
step_register = RegisterModel(
    name="RegisterModel",
    estimator=xgb_train,
    model_data=step_train.properties.ModelArtifacts.
S3ModelArtifacts,
    content_types=["text/csv"],
    response_types=["text/csv"],
    inference_instances=["ml.t2.medium", "ml.m5.xlarge"],
    transform_instances=["ml.m5.xlarge"],
    model_package_group_name=model_package_group_name,
    approval_status=model_approval_status,
    model_metrics=model_metrics,
)
```

Creating the pipeline

In the preceding steps, we configured the tasks and steps that will be used as part of the model build pipeline. We now need to chain those steps together to create the SageMaker Pipeline.

When configuring pipeline steps and creating a SageMaker pipeline, it is important to identify the parameters that could vary per pipeline execution and may be more dynamic. For example, the instance type for processing or training may be something you want to be able to change with each execution of your pipeline without directly modifying your pipeline code. This is where parameters become important in being able to dynamically pass in parameters at execution time. This allows you to change configurations (such as changing the instance type parameters) with each execution of your pipeline, based on different environments or as your data grows.

The following code shows the chaining together of our previously configured pipeline steps, as well as identifying the parameters we want to be able to pass in on each execution:

```
from sagemaker.workflow.pipeline import Pipeline


pipeline_name = f"WeatherPipeline"
pipeline = Pipeline(
    name=pipeline_name,
    parameters=[
        processing_instance_type,
        processing_instance_count,
        training_instance_type,
        model_approval_status,
        input_data
    ],
    steps=[step_process, step_train, step_eval, step_cond],
)
```

Executing the pipeline

Now that we've defined and configured our steps and the pipeline itself, we want to be able to execute the pipeline. To do this, you'll need to perform a few steps. These steps need to be performed for each pipeline execution. A pipeline can be started in multiple ways:

- Programmatically within a notebook (as shown in the example notebook for this chapter)
- Under Pipelines in the SageMaker Studio UI
- Programmatically via another resource
- Through an EventBridge source triggered by an event or schedule

In this section, we'll focus on the steps required to execute your pipeline from your example notebook. First, you need to submit the pipeline definition to the SageMaker Pipelines service. This is done through an `upsert` that passes in the IAM role as an argument. Keep in mind that an `upsert` will create a pipeline definition if it doesn't exist or update the pipeline if it does. Also, the role that is passed is used by SageMaker Pipelines to create and launch all of the tasks defined in the steps. Therefore, you need to ensure that the role is scoped to the API permissions you need for your pipeline. It's a best practice to only include the API permissions that are actually needed so as to avoid overly permissive roles.

In the following code, you need to load the pipeline definition and then submit that definition through `upsert`:

```
import json

json.loads(pipeline.definition())

pipeline.upsert(role_arn=role)
```

Once your pipeline definition is submitted, you're ready to start the pipeline using the following code:

```
execution = pipeline.start()
```

There are multiple ways to check the status and progress of your pipeline steps. You can view your pipeline in the Studio console and click on each step to get metadata about each step, including the step logs. In addition, you can programmatically check the status of your pipeline execution. To do this, you can run `execution.describe()` to view the pipeline execution status, or `execution.list_steps()` to view the execution status and each step.

Running your pipelines ad hoc from a notebook is often acceptable during your model-building activities. However, when you're ready to move your models to production, it's common at that stage to find the most consistent and repeatable ways to trigger or schedule your model-building pipelines for model retraining.

To do this, you can utilize the integration between SageMaker Pipelines and Amazon EventBridge (https://docs.aws.amazon.com/sagemaker/latest/dg/pipeline-eventbridge.html). This integration allows you to trigger the execution of your SageMaker pipeline through event rules. These rules can be based on an event, such as the completion of an AWS Glue job, or they can be scheduled.

Pipeline recommended practices

In this section, we covered how to set up a SageMaker pipeline using your example weather use case. As you build your own pipelines, they will likely vary in terms of the configuration required and the steps that should be included. However, the following general recommendations apply across use cases (unique considerations are highlighted where applicable):

1. SageMaker Pipelines has built-in steps supporting a variety of SageMaker jobs and the ability to utilize callback for custom steps. The built-in integrations with SageMaker steps simplify building and managing the pipeline. It is therefore recommended to **utilize SageMaker-native steps for the tasks in your pipeline** when possible.

2. **Utilize runtime parameters** for job arguments that are more likely to change between executions or environments, such as the size or number of ML instances running your training or processing jobs. This allows you to pass values in when you start the execution of the pipeline, as opposed to modifying your pipeline code every time.

3. **Enable step caching** to take advantage of eliminating unnecessary execution of steps in your pipeline. This will reduce costs, as well as reducing pipeline time when a previous pipeline step has already been successfully executed with the same parameters.

In this section, we covered automating your model build ML workflows using SageMaker Pipelines. In the next section, we'll cover creating an end-to-end ML pipeline that goes beyond automation and incorporates CI/CD practices.

Creating CI/CD pipelines using Amazon SageMaker Projects

In this section, we'll discuss using Amazon SageMaker Projects to incorporate CI/CD practices into your ML pipelines. SageMaker Projects is a service that uses SageMaker Pipelines and the SageMaker model registry, in combination with CI/CD tools, to automatically provision and configure CI/CD pipelines for ML. *Figure 12.10* illustrates the core components of SageMaker Projects. With Projects, you have the advantage of a CD pipeline, source code versioning, and automatic triggers for pipeline execution:

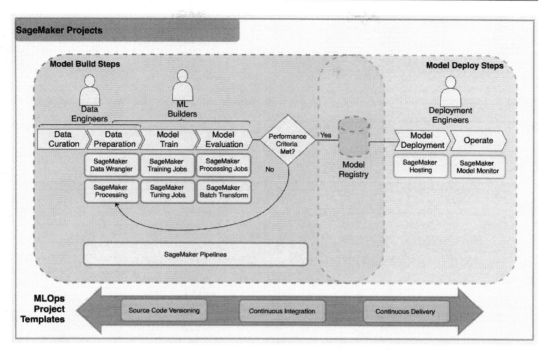

Figure 12.10 – SageMaker Projects

Projects are made available through built-in SageMaker MLOps project templates or by creating your own organization's MLOps templates. The underlying templates are offered through AWS Service Catalog, via SageMaker Studio, and contain CloudFormation templates that preconfigure CI/CD pipelines for the selected template. Because projects rely on CloudFormation to provision pipelines, this ensures the practice of IaC/CaC to be able to consistently and reliably create CI/CD ML pipelines.

There are three core types of built-in SageMaker MLOps project templates. *Figure 12.11* shows the three primary types: 1. **Build and Train Pipeline**, 2. **Deploy Pipeline**, 3. **Build, Train, and Deploy Pipeline**.

Refer to the following figure:

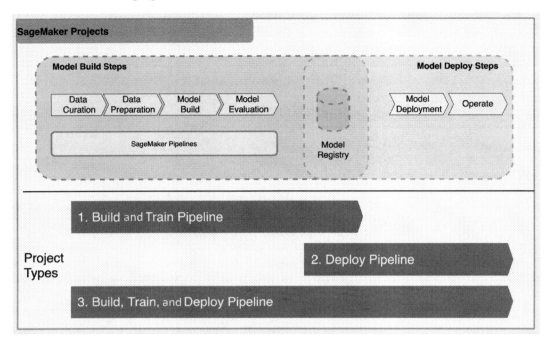

Figure 12.11 – SageMaker Projects

First, there is a build and train template. This covers the tasks required in data preparation, feature engineering, model training, and evaluation. This template is useful when you are performing model build activities on SageMaker but deploying your model somewhere else. It is also useful if you have batch-only use cases. In this case, Projects will automatically provision and seed a source code repository for a model build pipeline, set up pipeline triggers for changes to that code repository, and create a model group in the model registry. You are then responsible for going in and modifying that pipeline code to match your use case.

Second, there is a model deployment template. This template is useful when you are looking to standardize SageMaker for hosting. In this case, Projects will automatically provision and seed a source code repository for a model deploy pipeline that deploys to a SageMaker endpoint based on triggers and information pulled from the model registry.

Finally, there are end-to-end templates that cover all phases, including build, train, and deploy. These templates cover AWS Developer Services (AWS CodePipeline, AWS CodeCommit, AWS CodeBuild), or allow the option to utilize third-party source code repositories (GitHub, GitHub Enterprise, BitBucket, or Jenkins) for orchestration. In this case, Projects will automatically provision and seed source code for both model build and model deploy activities. Projects will also set up the triggers for both model build, and model deploy activities. Again, you are then responsible for going in and modifying seed code to meet your use case.

In this section, we examined SageMaker projects. We concluded that it is a service that can be used to incorporate CI/CD practices into your ML pipelines. We'll now cover some of the recommended practices when using SageMaker projects.

SageMaker projects recommended practices

In the preceding section, we covered SageMaker projects as a way to incorporate CI/CD practices into your ML pipelines by using a managed AWS service that will automatically provision and configure the integrations that are required. We'll now cover some of the general recommended practices when using SageMaker projects.

As you use SageMaker projects, the customizations for your use case can vary between customizing the code within the built-in MLOps project templates or creating your own fully custom MLOps project templates. As a result, there can be a lot of variance between pipelines in order to meet the requirements of your organization and use case. However, there are some general recommendations that apply across use cases, as follows:

- Utilize built-in MLOps project templates when they meet your requirements.

- When you have unique requirements, such as additional deployment quality gates, create custom MLOps project templates.

- When creating custom MLOps project templates, it is often easier to use the AWS CloudFormation templates used for the built-in MLOps project templates as a starting point and then modify accordingly. All of the built-in MLOps project templates are available and visible in AWS Service Catalog.

In this section, we covered adding CI/CD practices to your automated workflows using SageMaker projects. We also discussed the MLOps project template options that are available. Finally, we discussed additional considerations and best practices when using SageMaker projects.

Summary

In this chapter, we first covered general considerations for automating your SageMaker workflows. We then discussed automating your SageMaker model build workflows, specifically through using SageMaker Pipelines. The steps required to build out a pipeline for your weather use case were highlighted in order to illustrate SageMaker Pipeline usage. Finally, we discussed how you can enhance that automated model build workflow by using SageMaker projects to incorporate CI/CD practices, in addition to the automation offered by SageMaker Pipelines.

In the next chapter, we'll discuss the AWS Well-Architected Framework, specifically looking at how best practices across each Well-Architected pillar map to SageMaker workloads.

13

Well-Architected Machine Learning with Amazon SageMaker

When running workloads in the cloud, you want to make sure that the workload is architected correctly to take advantage of all that the cloud can offer. AWS Well-Architected Framework helps you with this, by providing a formal approach for learning best practices across five critical pillars applicable to any workload deployed to AWS. The pillars are operational excellence, security, reliability, performance efficiency, and cost optimization.

The framework provides guidance on how to improve your architecture and make trade-offs between the pillars both during the initial development and continued updates of the workload. While you can use Well-Architected Framework to evaluate your workload from a general technology perspective, while building **machine learning (ML)** applications, it would be great to have focused guidance across the five pillars specific to ML. AWS Machine Learning Lens provides this focused guidance, which you can use to compare and measure your ML workload on AWS against best practices.

> **Important Note**
>
> For an in-depth review of the Well-Architected Framework and Machine Learning Lens, please review these two white papers from AWS: `https://docs.aws.amazon.com/wellarchitected/latest/framework/wellarchitected-framework.pdf` and `https://docs.aws.amazon.com/wellarchitected/latest/machine-learning-lens/wellarchitected-machine-learning-lens.pdf`.

So far in this book, we have discussed how to use different Amazon SageMaker capabilities across all phases of ML workloads. In this chapter, we will learn how to combine guidance from both the generic Well-Architected Framework and Machine Learning Lens and apply it to the end-to-end ML workloads built on SageMaker.

Please note that this chapter does not introduce any new SageMaker features, but rather dives into how you can apply the capabilities you already know to build a well-architected ML workload. You will learn how SageMaker's specific capabilities are combined with other AWS services across the five pillars, with some of the capabilities playing a key role in multiple pillars.

In this chapter, we are going to cover the following main topics:

- Best practices for operationalizing ML workloads
- Best practices for securing ML workloads
- Best practices for building reliable ML workloads
- Best practices for building performant ML workloads
- Best practices for building cost-optimized ML workloads

Best practices for operationalizing ML workloads

Many organizations start their ML journey with a few experiments of building models to solve one or more business problems. Cloud platforms, in general, and ML platforms such as SageMaker make this experimentation easy by providing seamless access to elastic compute infrastructure and built-in support for various ML frameworks and algorithms. Once these experiments have proven successful, the next natural step is to move the models into production. Typically, at this time, organizations want to move out of the research-and-development phase and into operationalizing ML.

The idea of MLOps is gaining popularity these days. MLOps, at a very high level, involves bringing together people, processes, and technology to integrate ML workloads into release management, CI/CD, and operations. Without diving into all the details of MLOps, in this section, we will discuss best practices for operationalizing ML workloads using technology. We will also discuss which SageMaker features play a role in various aspects of operationalizing ML workloads.

Let's now look at best practices for operationalizing ML workloads on AWS in the following sections.

Ensuring reproducibility

To successfully operationalize the end-to-end ML system, you must first ensure its reproducibility through versioned data, code, and artifacts. Best practice is to version all inputs used to create models, including training data, data preparation code, algorithm implementation code, parameters, and hyperparameters, in addition to all trained model artifacts. A versioning strategy is also about helping in the model-update phase and allowing for easy rollback to a specific known working version if a model update fails or if the updated model does not meet your requirements.

Tracking ML artifacts

Iterative development of ML models using different algorithms and hyperparameters for each algorithm results in many training experiments and multiple model versions. Keeping track of these experiments and resulting models along with each model's lineage is important to meet auditing and compliance requirements. Model lineage also helps with root-cause analysis in case of degrading model performance.

While you can certainly build a custom tracking solution, best practice is to use a managed service such as SageMaker Experiments. Experiments allows you to track, organize, visualize, and compare ML models across all phases of the ML lifecycle including feature engineering, model training, model tuning, and model deployment. With SageMaker Experiments, you can easily choose to deploy or update the model with a specific version. Experiments also provides you with the model lineage capability. For a detailed discussion of SageMaker Experiments' capabilities, please refer to the *Amazon SageMaker Experiments* section of *Chapter 6, Training and Tuning at Scale*.

Additionally, you can also use the Amazon SageMaker ML Lineage Tracking capability, which keeps track of information about the individual steps of an ML workflow from data preparation to model deployment. With the information tracked, you can reproduce the workflow steps, track model and dataset lineage, and establish model governance and audit standards.

Automating deployment pipelines

Automated pipelines minimize human intervention in moving a trained ML model from lower-level environments such as development and staging into a production environment. The aim is to have a codified deployment pipeline created with Infrastructure-as-Code and Configuration-as-Code, with manual and automated quality gates incorporated into the pipeline. Manual quality gates can ensure that models are promoted to the production environment only after ensuring that there are no operational concerns such as security exposure. Automated quality gates, on the other hand, can be used to evaluate model metrics such as precision, recall, or accuracy. Pipelines result in consistent deployment as well as providing the ability to reliably recreate ML-related resources across multiple environments with minimal human intervention.

Using Amazon SageMaker Pipelines, you can build automated model workflows. You can build every step of the ML lifecycle as a pipeline step to develop and deploy models and monitor the pipelines. You can further manage dependencies between each step, build the correct sequence, and execute the steps automatically. A service that brings in CI/CD practices to ML workloads is SageMaker Projects. This service helps you move models from concept to production. Additionally, you can easily meet governance and audit standards using a combination of SageMaker Projects and SageMaker Pipelines, by automatically tracking code, datasets, and model versions through each step of the ML lifecycle. This enables you to go back and replay model-generation steps, troubleshoot problems, and reliably track the lineage of models at scale. For a detailed discussion of automated workflows and MLOps, please refer to *Chapter 12, Machine Learning Automated Workflows*.

Monitoring production models

Continued monitoring of deployed models is a critical step in operationalizing ML workloads, since a model's performance and effectiveness may degrade over time. Ensuring that the model continues to meet your business needs starts with the identification of the metrics that measure both model-related metrics and business metrics. Ensure that all metrics critical to model evaluation against your business KPIs are defined early on and collected during monitoring.

Once the metrics are identified, to ensure the continued high quality of the deployed model, use the Amazon SageMaker Model Monitor capabilities and its integration with CloudWatch to proactively detect issues, raise alerts, and automate remediation actions. In addition to detecting model-quality degradation, you can monitor data drift, bias drift, and feature attribution drift to meet your reliability, regulatory, and model explainability requirements.

CloudWatch alerts that have been triggered because of model monitoring can be used to automate activities such as invalidating the current model, reverting to an older model version, or retraining a new model based on new ground truth data. Updates to production models should consider trade-offs between the risk of introducing changes, the cost of retraining, and the potential value of having a newer model in production. For a detailed discussion of model monitoring, please refer to *Chapter 11, Monitoring Production Models with Amazon SageMaker Model Monitor and Clarify.*

> **Important note**
>
> While this section has focused on SageMaker-native approaches for operationalizing ML workloads, please note that similar automated pipelines can be built using a combination of SageMaker APIs and other AWS services such as CodePipeline, Step Functions, Lambda, and SageMaker Data Science SDK. Multiple MLOps architectures are documented along with sample code at `https://github.com/aws-samples/mlops-amazon-sagemaker-devops-with-ml`.

The following table summarizes the various AWS services and features applicable to operationalizing ML workloads:

AWS service/feature	How you should use it for operationalizing ML
SageMaker Experiments	Track experiments related to an ML project including multiple training and hyperparameter tuning jobs.
SageMaker ML Lineage Tracking	Track model lineage to connect a trained model back to its origins of the data, algorithm, and parameters used.
SageMaker Pipelines	Build automated workflows to include all phases of ML for automated, repeatable, and reproducible workflows.
SageMaker Projects	Bring CI/CD practices to ML workloads.
SageMaker Model Monitor	Implement continued monitoring of deployed models for data drift, model quality, bias drift, and feature-attribution drift. Ensure that model meets business and regulatory requirements.
CodePipeline, Lambda, SageMaker Data Science SDK	Build automated workflows calling SageMaker APIs.

Figure 13.1 – AWS Services used for operationalizing ML workloads

In the next section, you will learn how SageMaker integrates with other AWS services to enable secure ML workloads.

Best practices for securing ML workloads

When securing an ML workload, you should take into consideration infrastructure and network security, authentication and authorization, encrypting data and model artifacts, logging and auditing, and meeting regulatory requirements. In this section, we will discuss best practices for security ML workloads using a combination of SageMaker and related AWS services.

Let's now look at best practices for securing ML workloads on AWS in the following sections.

Isolating the ML environment

To build secure ML workloads, you need an isolated compute and network environment. To achieve this for ML on SageMaker, deploy all resources such as notebooks, studio domain, training jobs, processing jobs, and endpoints within a **Virtual Private Cloud (VPC)**. A VPC provides an isolated environment where all traffic between various SageMaker components flows within the network. You can add another layer of isolation by using security groups that include rules for both inbound and outbound traffic allowed by subnets within the VPC, thereby isolating your ML resources further.

Even if you use SageMaker without a VPC, all resources run in an environment managed by AWS on single-tenancy EC2 instances, which ensures that your ML environments are isolated from other customers. However, deploying ML resources, such as training containers, in a VPC allows you to monitor all network traffic in and out of these resources using VPC Flow Logs. Additionally, you can use VPC endpoints and AWS PrivateLink to enable communication between SageMaker and other AWS services such as S3 or CloudWatch. This keeps all traffic flowing between the various services within the AWS network without exposing the traffic to the public internet.

Disabling internet and root access

By default, SageMaker notebook instances are internet-enabled to allow you to download external libraries and customize your working environment. Additionally, root access is enabled on these notebooks, giving you the flexibility to leverage external libraries.

Only use these default settings in a lower-level sandbox and development environments to figure out the optimal working notebook environment. In all other non-production and production environments, launch SageMaker resources in your own VPC and turn off root access to prevent downloading and installing unauthorized software. Import all necessary libraries into a private repository such as AWS CodeArtifact before you isolate your environment. This allows you to seamlessly download specific versions of libraries without having to reach out to the internet.

Additionally, use codified lifecycle configurations to automate setting up the notebook environment. Similarly, training and deployed inference containers managed by SageMaker are internet-enabled by default. When launching training and inference resources, use `VPCConfig` and `EnableNetworkIsolation` flags to protect these resources from external network traffic. In this case, all downloads and uploads of data and model artifacts are routed through your VPC. At the same time, the training and inference containers remain isolated from the network and do not have access to any resource within your VPC or on the internet.

Enforcing authentication and authorization

Implement a strong mechanism to determine who can access the ML resources (authentication) and what resources authenticated users can access (authorization). SageMaker is natively integrated with AWS IAM, a service used to manage access to all AWS services and resources. IAM allows you to define fine-grained access controls using IAM users, groups, roles, and policies. You can implement least-privilege access using a combination of identity-based policies to specify what an IAM user, role, or group can do and resource-based policies to specify who has access to the resource and what actions they can perform on it.

When designing these IAM policies, it is tempting to start with wide-open IAM policies with good intentions of tightening them as you go. However, best practice is to start with tight policies that grant minimal required access and add additional permissions when required. Periodically review and refine policies to ensure that no unnecessary permissions are granted. The IAM service provides the Access Advisor capability, which shows you when various AWS services are last accessed by different entities such as IAM groups, users, roles, and policies. Use this information to refine the policies. All the service API calls are also logged by CloudTrail, and you can use the CloudTrail history to determine which permissions can be removed based on the usage patterns.

Securing data and model artifacts

IAM policies can also be used for access-control of data and models in S3. Additionally, you can use a security service called Amazon Macie to protect and classify data in S3. Macie internally uses ML to automatically discover, classify, and protect sensitive data. It automatically recognizes sensitive data such as **personally identifiable information (PII)** or **intellectual property (IP)**, providing visibility into data access and movement patterns. Macie continuously monitors for anomalies in data-access patterns and proactively generates alerts on unauthorized access and data leaks.

The next important aspects to secure are data and model artifacts of an ML system, both at rest and in transit. To secure data in transit within a VPC, use **Transport Layer Security (TLS)**. To secure data at rest, best practice is to use encryption to block malicious actors from reading your data and model artifacts. You can use either client-side or server-side encryption. SageMaker comes with built-in encryption capabilities to protect training data and model artifacts both at rest and in transit. For example, when launching a training job, you can specify the encryption key to be used. You have the flexibility of using SageMaker-managed keys, AWS-managed keys, or your own customer-managed keys.

Logging, monitoring, and auditing

SageMaker is natively integrated with CloudWatch and CloudTrail. You can capture logs from SageMaker training, processing, and inference in CloudWatch, which can further be used for troubleshooting. All SageMaker (and other AWS services) API calls are logged by CloudTrail, allowing you to track down which IAM user, AWS account, or source IP address made the API call along with when the call occurred.

Meeting regulatory requirements

For many organizations, ML solutions need to comply with regulatory standards and pass compliance certifications that vary significantly across countries and industries. Amazon SageMaker complies with a wide range of compliance programs, including PCI, HIPAA, SOC 1/2/3, FedRAMP, and ISO 9001/27001/27017/27018.

The following table summarizes the various AWS services applicable to securing ML workloads:

AWS service/feature	How you should use it for securing ML
IAM	By implementing authentication, authorization, and access control through IAM users, groups, roles, and policies.
IAM access advisor/ CloudWatch Event history	By identifying opportunities to refine IAM policies.
CloudWatch/ CloudTrail	By collecting logs, implementing monitoring, and auditing.
VPC	By providing infrastructure and network isolation.
VPC endpoints	By routing traffic through the AWS network and avoiding exposure to the public internet.
Private links	By routing traffic through the AWS network and avoiding exposure to the public internet.

Figure 13.2 – AWS services used for securing ML workloads

In the next section, you will learn how SageMaker integrates with other AWS services to build reliable ML workloads.

Best practices for reliable ML workloads

For a reliable system, there are two considerations at the core:

- First, the ability to recover from planned and unplanned disruptions
- Second, the ability to meet unpredictable increases in traffic demands

Ideally, the system should achieve both without affecting downstream applications and end consumers. In this section, we will discuss best practices for building reliable ML workloads using a combination of SageMaker and related AWS services.

Let's now look at some best practices for securing ML workloads on AWS in the following sections.

Recovering from failure

For an ML workload, the ability to recover gracefully should be part of all the steps that make up the iterative ML process. A failure can occur with data storage, data processing, model training, or model hosting, which may result from a variety of events ranging from system failure to human error.

For ML on SageMaker, all data (and model artifacts) is typically saved in S3. This ensures decoupling between ML data and the computation processing. To prevent an inadvertent loss of data, best practice is to use a combination of IAM and S3 policies to ensure least privilege-based access to data. Additionally, use S3 versioning and object tagging to enable versioning and traceability of data (and model artifacts) for easy recovery or recreation in the event of failure.

Next, consider the reliability of ML training, which is often a long, time-consuming process. It is not uncommon to see training jobs that run over multiple hours and even multiple days. If these long-running training jobs are disrupted due to a power outage, OS fault, or other unexpected error, having the ability to reliably resume from where the job stopped is critical. ML checkpointing should be used in this situation. On SageMaker, a few built-in algorithms and all supported deep learning frameworks provide the capability of turning on checkpointing when a training job is launched. When you enable checkpointing, SageMaker automatically saves snapshots of the model state during training. This enables you to reliably restart a training job from the last saved checkpoint.

Tracking model origin

Let's say your training goes off without a hitch and you have a trained model artifact saved in an S3 bucket. What happens if you lose this model artifact due to human error, such as someone in your team deleting it by mistake? In a reliable ML system, you need to be able to recreate this model using the same data, version of the code, and parameters as the original model. Hence, it is important to keep track of all these aspects during training. Using SageMaker Experiments, you can keep track of all the steps and artifacts that went into creating a model so you can easily recreate the model as necessary. Another benefit of tracking with SageMaker Experiments is the ability to troubleshoot issues in production for reliable operation.

In addition to relying on Experiments to be able to recreate a specific version of a model artifact, use a combination of IAM and S3 policies to ensure least privilege-based access to minimize the risk of accidental model-artifact deletion. Implement measures such as requiring MFA for model artifact deletion and storing a secondary copy of the artifact as required by your organization's disaster recovery strategy.

Automating deployment pipelines

To ensure that all steps leading up to model deployment are executed consistently, use a CI/CD pipeline with access controls to enforce least privilege-based access. Deployment automation combined with manual and automated quality gates ensures that all changes can be effectively validated with dependent systems prior to deployment. Amazon SageMaker Pipelines has the capability to bring CI/CD practices to ML workloads for improved reliability. Codifying the CI/CD pipelines using SageMaker Pipelines provides you with an additional capability of dealing with the model endpoint itself being deleted inadvertently. Using the Infrastructure-as-Code approach, the endpoint can be recreated. This requires a well-defined versioning strategy in place for your data, code, algorithms, hyperparameters, model artifacts, container images, and more. Version everything and document your versioning strategy. For a detailed discussion of SageMaker Pipelines capabilities, please refer to the *Amazon SageMaker Pipelines* section of *Chapter 12, Machine Learning Automated Workflows*.

Additionally, follow the *train once and deploy everywhere* strategy. Because of the decoupled nature of the training process and results, you can share the trained model artifact across multiple environments. This prevents retraining in multiple environments and introducing unexpected changes to the model.

Handling unexpected traffic patterns

Once the model is deployed, you must ensure the reliability of the deployed model in serving the inference requests. The model should be able to handle spikes in inference traffic and continue to operate at the quality necessary to meet the business requirements.

To handle traffic spikes, deploy the model with the Autoscaling-enabled SageMaker real-time endpoint. With Autoscaling enabled, SageMaker automatically increases (and decreases) the computation capacity behind the hosted model in response to the dynamic shifts in the inference traffic. Autoscaling provided by SageMaker is horizontal scaling, meaning it adds new instances or removes existing instances to handle the inference traffic variations.

Continuous monitoring of deployed model

To ensure the continued high quality of the deployed model, use the Amazon SageMaker Model Monitor capabilities and its integration with CloudWatch to proactively detect issues, raise alerts, and automate remediation actions when a production model is not performing as expected. In addition to model quality, you can monitor data drift, bias drift, and feature-attribution drift to meet your reliability, regulatory, and model explainability requirements. Ensure that all metrics critical to model evaluation against your business KPIs are defined and monitored. For a detailed discussion of model monitoring, please refer to *Chapter 11, Monitoring Production Models with Amazon SageMaker Model Monitor and Clarify*.

Updating model with new versions

Finally, you must consider how to update a production model reliably. SageMaker endpoint production variants can be used to implement multiple deployment strategies such as A/B, Blue/Green, Canary, and Shadow deployments. The advanced deployment strategies along with detailed implementation are discussed in *Chapter 9, Updating Production Models Using Amazon SageMaker Endpoint Production Variants*. Depending on the model consumer's tolerance for risk and downtime, choose an appropriate deployment strategy.

The following table summarizes the various AWS services applicable to building reliable ML workloads:

AWS service/feature	How you should use it for securing ML
IAM	By implementing least privilege-based access to data and model artifacts
SageMaker Experiments	By tracking a trained model back to its origins of the data, algorithm, and parameters used for easy recreation of the model
SageMaker Autoscaling	By adaptively updating inference hosting capacity to satisfy dynamic inference traffic demands
SageMaker Pipelines	By implementing codified CI/CD pipelines for repeatable, reproducible workflows
SageMaker Model Monitor	By continuously monitoring deployed models for data drift, model quality, bias drift, and feature-attribution drift

Figure 13.3 – AWS service capabilities used for reliable ML workloads

In the next section, you will learn how SageMaker integrates with other AWS services to build reliable, performance-efficient workloads.

Best practices for building performant ML workloads

Given the compute- and time-intensive nature of ML workloads, it is important to choose the most performant resources appropriate for each individual phase of the workload. Computation, memory, and network bandwidth requirements are unique to each phase of the ML process. Besides the performance of the infrastructure, the performance of the model as measured by metrics such as accuracy is also important. In this section, we will discuss best practices to apply in selecting the most performant resources for building ML workloads on SageMaker.

Let's now look at best practices for building performant ML workloads on AWS in the following sections.

Rightsizing ML resources

SageMaker supports a variety of ML instance types with a varying combination of CPU, GPU, FPGA, memory, storage, and networking capacity. Each instance type, in turn, supports multiple instance sizes. So, you have a range of choices to choose from to suit your specific workload. The best practice is to choose different compute resource configurations for data processing, building, training, and hosting your ML model. This is made possible by the decoupled nature of SageMaker, which allows you to choose different instance types and sizes for different APIs. For example, you can choose `ml.c5.medium` for a notebook instance as your working environment, use a cluster of four `ml.p3.large` GPU instances for training, and finally host the trained model on two `ml.m5.4xlarge` instances with Elastic Inference attached. Additionally, in the SageMaker Studio environment, you can change the notebook instance type seamlessly without any interruption to your work.

While you have the flexibility of choosing different compute options for different ML phases, how do you choose the specific instance types and sizes to use? This comes down to understanding your workload and experimentation. For example, if you know that the training framework and algorithm of your choice will need GPU support, choose a GPU cluster to train on. While it may be tempting to use GPUs for all training, traditional algorithms may not work well on GPUs due to the communication overheads involved. Some built-in algorithms, such as XGBoost, implement an open source algorithm that has been optimized for CPU computations. SageMaker also provides optimized versions of frameworks, such as TensorFlow and PyTorch, which include optimizations for high-performance training across Amazon EC2 instance families.

Monitoring resource utilization

Once you make your initial choice of instances and kick off training, SageMaker training jobs emit CloudWatch metrics for resource utilization that you can use to improve your training runs the next time. Additionally, when you enable Debugger with your training jobs, SageMaker Debugger provides visibility into training jobs and the infrastructure a training job is executing on. Debugger also monitors and reports on the system resources such as CPU, GPU, and memory, providing you with insights into resource underutilization and bottlenecks. If you use TensorFlow or PyTorch for your deep learning training jobs, Debugger provides you with a view into framework metrics that can be used to speed up your training jobs. For a detailed discussion of Debugger's capabilities, please refer to *Chapter 7, Profile Training Jobs with Amazon SageMaker Debugger.*

Rightsizing hosting infrastructure

Once the model is trained and ready to be deployed to choose instances for real-time endpoints, consider what your target performance is. Target performance is a combination of how many requests to serve in each period and the desired latency for each request, for example, 10,000 requests per minute with a maximum of a 1 millisecond response time. Once you have the target performance in mind, perform load testing in a non-production environment to figure out the instance type, instance size, and number of instances to host the model on. Recommended best practice is to deploy the endpoint with at least two instances across two availability zones for high availability.

Once you decide on the instance type to use, start with the minimum number of instances necessary to meet your steady-state traffic and take advantage of the Autoscaling capability of SageMaker hosting. Using Autoscaling, SageMaker can automatically scale the inference capacity depending on the utilization and request traffic thresholds you configure. Capacity adjustments to meet your performance requirements are done by updating the endpoint configuration without any downtime.

Additionally, you can scale up the hosting infrastructure for deep learning models using Amazon **Elastic Inference** (**EI**). While training a deep learning model may need a full-fledged GPU, hosting a training deep learning model may need only a slice of GPU to function. EI allows you to accelerate deep learning inferences using SageMaker ML instances. Alternatively, if you have a large-scale ML inference application, you can run inferences on `Inf1` instances, which are best suited to applications such as search, recommendation engines, and computer vision, at a low cost.

While real-time endpoints provide access to models deployed on SageMaker, some workloads may warrant inference at the edge due to latency requirements, for example, models used to determine defective product parts in a manufacturing plant. In such cases, the model needs to be deployed on cameras within the manufacturing plant. For such use cases, use SageMaker Neo and SageMaker Edge Manager to optimize, deploy, and manage models at the edge.

> **Important note**
>
> While real-time endpoints and models deployed at the edge provide synchronous predictions, batch transform is used for asynchronous inferences with more tolerance for longer response times. Use experimentation to determine the right instance type, size, and number of instances to be used for batch transform with job completion time in mind.

Continuous monitoring of deployed model

Once the model is actively serving inference traffic, use SageMaker Model Monitor to continuously monitor ML models for data drift, model-quality performance, feature-importance drift, and bias drift. Behind the scenes, Model Monitor uses distributed processing jobs. As with batch processing, use experimentation and load testing to determine the processing job resources necessary to complete each scheduled monitoring job execution. For a detailed discussion of Model Monitor, please refer to *Chapter 11, Monitoring Production Models with Amazon SageMaker Model Monitor and Clarify.*

The following table summarizes the various SageMaker features and how they are applicable for building performant ML workloads:

AWS service/feature	How it is applicable to the performance of ML workloads
SageMaker Debugger	Analyzes resource utilization during training and applies recommendations for performance improvements
SageMaker Autoscaling	Adaptively updates inference hosting capacity to satisfy dynamic inference traffic demands
SageMaker Model Monitor	Continued monitoring of deployed models against defined model and business metrics
SageMaker Neo and Edge Manager	Optimizes, deploys, and manages models at the edge
Elastic Inference	Accelerates GPU-based deep learning inferences by attaching a slice of GPU to CPU instances
Inf1 instances	Provides high-performance ML inference at a low cost

Figure 13.4 – AWS service capabilities for building performant ML workloads.

In the next section, you will learn how SageMaker integrates with other AWS services to build cost-optimized workloads.

Best practices for cost-optimized ML workloads

For many organizations, the lost opportunity cost of not embracing disruptive technologies such as ML outweighs the ML costs. By implementing a few best practices, these organizations can get the best possible returns on their ML investment. In this section, we will discuss best practices to apply for cost-optimized ML workloads on SageMaker.

Let's now look at best practices for building cost-optimized ML workloads on AWS in the following sections.

Optimizing data labeling costs

Labeling of data used for ML training, typically done at the very beginning of the ML process, can be tedious, error-prone, and time-consuming. Labeling at scale consumes many working hours, making this an expensive task, too. To optimize cost for data labeling, use SageMaker Ground Truth. Ground Truth provides capabilities for data labeling at scale using a combination of human workforce and active learning. When active learning is enabled, a labeling task is routed to humans only if a model cannot confidently finish the task. The human-labeled data is then used to train the model to improve accuracy. Therefore, as the labeling job progresses, less and less data needs to be labeled by humans. This results in faster completion of the job at reduced costs. For a detailed discussion of Ground Truth capabilities, please refer to *Chapter 3, Data Labeling with Amazon SageMaker Ground Truth*.

Reducing experimentation costs with models from AWS Marketplace

ML is inherently iterative and experimental. Having to run multiple algorithms with different sets of hyperparameters each time leads to several training jobs before you can determine a model that meets your needs. All this training adds up in terms of time and costs.

A big part of experimentation is the research and reuse of readily available pre-trained models that may suit your needs. AWS Marketplace for ML gives you a catalog of datasets and models made available by vendors vetted by AWS. You can subscribe to models that meet your needs and potentially save the time and costs involved in developing your own models. If you do, however, end up developing your own models, you can use the marketplace to monetize your models by making them available to others.

Using AutoML to reduce experimentation time

If the marketplace models don't meet your needs or if your organization has the **build rather than buy** policy, first check whether your dataset and use case are suitable for AutoPilot. At the time of writing this book, AutoPilot supports tabular data and classification and regression problems. AutoPilot automatically analyzes datasets and builds multiple models with different combinations of algorithms and hyperparameters and finally selects the best algorithm for the list. This saves both time and cost. Additionally, the service provides transparency through two notebooks – a data preparation notebook and a model candidate selection notebook, which details all the behind-the-scenes steps performed by AutoPilot. So, even if you don't end up using the model built and recommended by AutoPilot, you can use these notebooks as a starting point for your own experimentation and modify them using your business domain knowledge.

However, at the time of publication of this book, AutoPilot only supports regression and classification using tabular data. For other data types and problems, you will have to build and train your model.

Iterating locally with small datasets

During ML experimentation, iterate with a smaller dataset in the SageMaker notebook's local environment first. Once you iron out details such as code bugs and data issues, you can scale up with the full dataset and distributed training clusters managed by SageMaker. This phased approach will let you iterate faster at lower costs. SageMaker SDK makes this easy by supporting `instance-type = "local"` for the training API so that you can reuse the same code in the local environment or on the distributed cluster. Note that at the time of publication, local mode only works in SageMaker notebook instances, not in the Studio environment.

Rightsizing training infrastructure

When you are ready to launch a distributed training cluster, it is important to choose the right number and type of instances in the cluster. For built-in or custom algorithms that do not support distributed training, your cluster will always have a single instance. For algorithms and frameworks that do support distributed training, take advantage of data parallelism and model parallelism as discussed in *Chapter 6, Training and Tuning at Scale,* to complete training faster, thereby reducing the overall training costs.

While there are various instance types with different capacity configurations available, it is important to rightsize the training instances based on the ML algorithm used. For example, simple algorithms may not train faster on the larger instance types since they cannot take advantage of hardware parallelism. Even worse, they may even train slower due to high GPU communication overhead. Best practice for cost optimization is to start with a smaller instance, scale out first by adding more instances to the training cluster, and then scale up to more powerful instances. However, if you are using a deep learning framework and distributed training, best practice would be to scale up to more GPUs/CPUs on a single instance before scaling out because the network I/O involved may negatively impact the training performance.

In addition to selecting the right infrastructure, you can also use optimized versions of ML frameworks that result in faster training. SageMaker provides optimized versions of multiple open source ML frameworks including TensorFlow, Chainer, Keras, and Theano. SageMaker versions of these popular frameworks are optimized for high performance on all SageMaker ML instances.

Optimizing hyperparameter-tuning costs

Hyperparameter tuning is also an expensive task, using sophisticated search and algorithms. Best practice is to rely on the automated model tuning capability provided by managed SageMaker Automatic Model Tuning, also known as **hyperparameter tuning (HPT)**. Automatic model tuning finds the best version of a model by running multiple training jobs using the algorithm and hyperparameter ranges specified by you. HPT then chooses the hyperparameter values that result in the best model as measured by the objective metric you specify. Behind the scenes, HPT uses ML techniques that can determine optimal hyperparameters with a limited number of training jobs.

You can further speed up the HPT jobs using warm start mode. With warm start, you no longer must start an HPT job from scratch; instead, you can create a new HPT job based on one or more parent jobs. This allows you to reuse the training jobs conducted in the parent jobs as prior knowledge. Warm start allows you to reduce the time and cost associated with model tuning.

Saving training costs with Managed Spot Training

SageMaker Managed Spot Training applies the cost-saving construct of Spot Instances and applies it to hyperparameter tuning and training. The Managed Spot Training capability takes advantage of checkpointing, to resume training jobs easily. Since you don't have to run the training from the start again, this reduces your overall training costs.

Using insights and recommendations from Debugger

When it comes to deep learning on SageMaker, training with GPU is very powerful, but training costs can add up quickly. SageMaker Debugger provides insight into deep learning training both into the ML framework in use and the underlying compute resources. The deep profiler capability provides you with recommendations that you can implement to improve training performance and reduce resource wastage. For a detailed discussion of Debugger's capabilities, please refer to *Chapter 7, Profile Training Jobs with Amazon SageMaker Debugger*.

Saving ML infrastructure costs with SavingsPlan

Once you enable SavingsPlan in your AWS account, it analyzes your ML resource usage within a time of your choice – the past 7, 30, or up to 60 days. The service then recommends the right plan to use to optimize costs. You can also select a pre-payment option from three different options: no upfront costs, partial upfront (50% or more), or all upfront. Once you configure these options, SavingsPlan provides you with details of how your monthly spend can be optimized. Additionally, it also suggests an hourly usage commitment that maximizes your savings. The plans cover all ML instance families, notebook instances, Studio instances, training instances, batch transform instances, real-time endpoint instances, Data Wrangler instances, and SageMaker Processing instances, thereby helping to optimize costs across various phases of ML workloads.

While Managed Spot Training and SavingsPlan are both cost-saving approaches, they are not meant to be combined. With SavingsPlan, you are billed every hour of the commitment regardless of whether it is fully used. Best practice is to use SavingsPlan and Managed Spot Training usages separately. For example, use SavingsPlan for predictable steady-state recurring training workloads and Managed Spot Training for new training workloads and prototyping where you do not have a clear idea of monthly costs yet.

Optimizing inference costs

Inference costs typically make up most ML costs. Inference costs are discussed in detail in *Chapter 10, Optimizing Model Hosting and Inference Costs*, which details several ways to improve inference performance while reducing inference costs. These methods include using batch inference where possible, deploying several models behind a single inference endpoint to reduce cost and help with advanced canary or blue/green deployments, scaling inference endpoints to meet demand, and using EI and SageMaker Neo to provide better inference performance at a lower cost.

Stopping or terminating resources

Ensure that you terminate or at least stop the ML resources once you are done. While the instances for training, hyperparameter tuning, batch inferences, and processing jobs will be managed and automatically deleted by SageMaker, you are responsible for notebook instances, endpoint, and monitoring schedules. Stop or delete these resources to avoid unnecessary costs using automation with scripts that stop resources based on idle time or a schedule.

The following table summarizes the various SageMaker features and how they are applicable for building cost-optimized ML workloads:

AWS service/feature	How it is applicable to the performance of ML workloads
AWS Marketplace	Subscribes to and reuses existing models from vetted sources Monetizes models you develop
SageMaker Debugger	Analyzes resource utilization during training and applies recommendations for cost optimizations
SageMaker Autoscaling	Adaptively updates inference hosting capacity to satisfy dynamic inference traffic demands
Managed Spot Training	Uses EC2 spot instances to run training instead of on-demand instances.
AutoPilot	Automatically trains regression and classification models on tabular data
SavingsPlan	Applies recommendations from usage-based pricing model by committing to consistent usage for 1 or 3 years
EI	Accelerates GPU-based deep learning inferences by attaching a slice of GPU to CPU instances
`Infl` instances	Provide high-performance ML inference at a low cost

Figure 13.5 – AWS service capabilities for cost-optimized ML workloads

This section concludes the discussion on applying best practices to build well-architected ML workloads on AWS.

Summary

In this chapter, you reviewed the five pillars – operational excellence, security, reliability, performance, and cost optimization – that make up the Well-Architected Framework. You then dove into the best practices for each of these pillars, with an eye to applying these best practices to ML workloads. You learned how to use the SageMaker capabilities with related AWS services to build well-architected ML workloads on AWS.

As you architect your ML applications, you typically must make trade-offs between the pillars depending on your organization's priorities. For example, when getting started with ML, cost-optimization may not be at the top of your mind but establishing operational standards may be important. However, as the number of ML workloads scale, cost-optimization could become an important consideration. By applying the best practices you learned in this chapter, you can architect and implement ML applications that meet your organization's needs and periodically evaluate your applications against the best practices.

In the next chapter, you will apply all these best practices and see how to operate in multiple AWS environments that reflect the real world.

14
Managing SageMaker Features across Accounts

AWS publishes best practices around the management and governance of workloads. These practices touch on many areas, such as cost optimization, security, compliance, and ensuring the operational efficiency of workloads scaled on AWS. Multi-account patterns are one common architectural consideration when building, deploying, and operating workloads that utilize the features of Amazon SageMaker.

In this section, we won't cover the well-established recommendations and considerations around the governance of AWS workloads across AWS accounts. Rather, we will specifically focus on some of the considerations around the usage of AWS features across AWS accounts. For more information about general recommendations for choosing the right account strategy, please refer to **AWS Management and Governance services** (https://aws.amazon.com/products/management-and-governance/) and the **AWS Multi-Account Landing Zone strategy – AWS Control Tower** (https://docs.aws.amazon.com/controltower/latest/userguide/aws-multi-account-landing-zone.html).

The concept of a multi-account strategy is built on the **AWS Well-Architected Framework**, where having multiple AWS accounts allows you to better govern and manage machine learning activities on **Amazon SageMaker** across the **Machine Learning Development Lifecycle (ML Lifecycle)**. The benefits of using multiple AWS accounts are documented for general workloads.

In this chapter, we'll discuss the following topics as they relate to managing SageMaker features across multiple AWS accounts:

- Examining an overview of the AWS multi-account environment
- Understanding the benefits of using multiple AWS accounts with Amazon SageMaker
- Examining multi-account considerations with Amazon SageMaker

Examining an overview of the AWS multi-account environment

There are many variations of multi-account strategies that are valid. Multi-account implementations can vary based on the organizational and technical needs of a customer. For the purposes of this chapter, we will focus on a basic multi-account strategy, focusing on only the accounts that are most relevant to a machine learning workload using Amazon SageMaker. We don't explicitly call out accounts (such as security or logging) because they are already well defined in the context of AWS governance practices. *Figure 14.1* illustrates the general, high-level accounts we will use to discuss the concepts in this chapter.

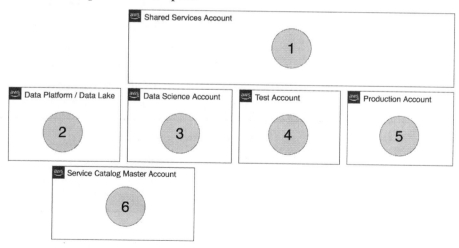

Figure 14.1 – Example of AWS accounts and SageMaker features

Using *Figure 14.1* as an example, the following AWS accounts may be used as part of an end-to-end ML Lifecycle. Please keep in mind that account naming and resource placement may vary considerably across implementations. Each account is described at a high level, in order to focus more on the account purpose versus the naming standard itself:

1. **Shared Services account**: This account can be named many things, and is also referred to as a **DevOps** or application management account. For the purposes of this chapter, we refer to this account as the one that can often include the services and tooling used for the management of end-to-end pipelines and the ongoing management of workloads.

2. **Data platform/data lake**: This account acts as the central repository for datasets, both raw and curated, used for model-building activities.

3. **Data science account**: This account (or accounts) represents the environments where model development activities are performed.

4. **Test account**: This account represents the environment where a model will be tested. This account typically includes integration and performance testing.

5. **Production account**: This account represents the environment hosting models supporting live applications and workloads. This account typically has the highest levels of controls and restrictions.

6. **Service Catalog master account**: The purpose of this account is to maintain a central hub of products that can be offered through the **AWS Service Catalog** and used to consistently provision resources in spoke accounts, such as the **data science account**. A spoke account is an AWS account that has been given access to portfolios managed from the master account.

Again, these accounts are high-level representations of a potential account structure and are not inclusive of every variation that is valid given the requirements of your own environments. In the next section, we'll discuss the benefits of using multiple AWS accounts specifically as they relate to using Amazon SageMaker across the ML Lifecycle

Understanding the benefits of using multiple AWS accounts with Amazon SageMaker

In this section, we'll cover the general, high-level benefits of using multiple AWS accounts. We'll also discuss the considerations that are specific to using Amazon SageMaker across the ML Lifecycle:

- **Benefit #1**: Implementing specific security controls

  Using multiple AWS accounts allows customers to implement security controls that are specific to the workload, environment, or data. As an example, some workloads may have unique security requirements (such as PCI compliance) and require additional controls. Using multiple accounts allows you to maintain fine-grained controls that are isolated and auditable at the AWS account level.

  For the model-building activities included in the ML Lifecycle, using multiple AWS accounts allows you to create and manage data science environments that include the controls that are specific to machine learning, as well as to your security requirements. With machine learning, data scientists need access to live production data. Typically, that data should be scrubbed of any sensitive data before a data scientist gains access. However, there are use cases where a data scientist may need access to that sensitive data. By separating data science environments that have access to sensitive data and those that do not have access to sensitive data, you're able to implement controls at the account level, as well as to audit at the account level.

  For model deployment activities included in the ML Lifecycle, you will want to ensure your models serving live traffic or providing critical inference data are managed and controlled. This would be the case with any other production application. You wish to ensure availability. Just as you would not implement a live web application in the same account where developers have broad access, the same is true for machine learning workloads serving live production workloads.

As an example, a **SageMaker endpoint** serving a production application should be hosted in an AWS account that has all of the controls and restricted access in place (you would want this to be the case as with any other production workload). This ensures the endpoint isn't inadvertently deleted in a lower-level account that may have fewer controls and broader access permissions granted.

- **Benefit #2**: Supporting the needs of multiple teams

  Large organizations and enterprises are often looking for scalable mechanisms to support the resource needs and responsibilities of different teams. Across lines of business, it's common to have separate AWS accounts. The same is true for machine learning workloads. An example here includes **data science environments** (as discussed in *Chapter 2, Data Science Environments*), where each team may have different requirements for an environment in which to build machine learning models. In this case, it's common to have multiple data science environments supporting multiple teams, as well as supporting the requirements across and within teams.

Examining multi-account considerations with Amazon SageMaker

In this section, we'll cover multi-account considerations with Amazon SageMaker. We'll first look at a general reference architecture, then discuss some of the considerations for specific SageMaker features across the ML Lifecycle.

Figure 14.2 shows an example of a multi-account structure mapping key SageMaker features and other common AWS services to the accounts they are typically used in. This is not a one-size-fits-all view, as there may be other AWS services or third-party tools that are performing one or more of the functions performed by the AWS services shown. As an example, your model registry may be the **SageMaker model registry**, or it could alternatively be **Amazon DynamoDB** or a tool such as **MLflow**:

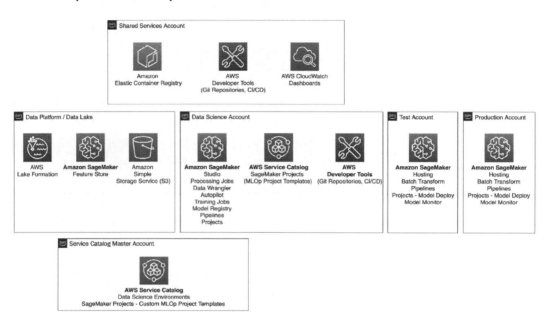

Figure 14.2 – Example of service use across AWS accounts

The placement of the AWS, or equivalent, supporting the ML Lifecycle map to the phase, model build, or model deploy. This is in combination with the benefits addressed earlier in being able to implement security controls by accounts, as well as to support the requirements of the different roles and personas that operate within each account. The naming and structure of accounts may vary across multi-account implementations. Therefore, in the following list, we describe the purpose of each account, knowing these may vary across implementations:

- A Shared Services account, or DevOps account, is often used to centralize the tooling that is used to manage workloads across multiple accounts and environments. In this case, you see a few common services, such as the **Amazon Elastic Container Registry** for managing SageMaker compatible images for training and inference. You also often find developer tools that enable **continuous integration (CI)/ continuous delivery or deployment (CD)** practices.

- There are the tools that are needed to automate and orchestrate the steps of the machine learning workflow across accounts. These can include native **AWS Developer Tools** or third-party tooling such as **GitHub** or **Jenkins**. The tools and services used in this account require cross-account **identity and access management (IAM)** permission policies. Finally, you need to create centralized dashboards for monitoring the health of your machine learning workloads. These shared dashboards are often placed in the Shared Services account, an **infrastructure account**, or one of the environment- or workload-specific accounts, such as production.

- The **data platform**, or **data lake account**, contains a data lake using a native service, such as **AWS Lake Formation** or a custom data lake. This account is also a common option for placing the centralized feature store that is used to store features for use across teams.

- The data science account is primarily used for model building activities so this includes all of the activities required to perform data understanding, feature engineering, model training across experiments, and model evaluation. This account requires access to SageMaker features needed for those model-building activities including features such as **Amazon SageMaker Studio, SageMaker training jobs, SageMaker Pocessing jobs**, and **SageMaker Data Wrangler**.

- In addition to the common features needed for model building, there are additional AWS services that get provisioned in this account when you are using **SageMaker projects**. By default, SageMaker projects automatically provision and configure AWS Developer Tools and the AWS Service Catalog products for built-in MLOps project templates in the account you are using for your model-building activities.

- Workload or environment-specific accounts, such as test and production, are used to host live models. These accounts also commonly host the broader solution where your model is used. From a SageMaker perspective, the features used in these accounts typically focus on model deploy and operate activities.

- Finally, you may also have an **AWS Service Catalog master** or infrastructure account that contains the portfolios of products that can be shared across multiple teams. This is known as the hub account. This can be used to create and manage a central catalog of products for data science environments or for custom MLOps project templates with SageMaker projects.

Some AWS features are very specific to the persona and phase in the ML Lifecycle where they are needed. As an example, SageMaker training jobs are typically needed by data scientists for model-building activities or are needed as part of an automated model retraining workflow. However, there are several AWS services that span phases of the ML Lifecycle that require some unique considerations. These will be explored further in the next section.

Considerations for SageMaker features

There are several SageMaker features that require additional considerations when attempting to implement them in a multi-account strategy, specifically because these features are used across the ML Lifecycle. Considerations for features, such as SageMaker Processing, SageMaker training jobs, and SageMaker hosting, are generally specific to a phase in the lifecycle. Therefore, their placement across accounts is covered in *Figure 14.3*. In this section, we'll cover a few of the SageMaker features that span the ML Lifecycle and require additional consideration as part of your multi-account strategy.

Amazon SageMaker Pipelines

SageMaker Pipelines allows you to code your machine learning pipelines using the Amazon SageMaker Python SDK. Pipelines includes SageMaker native steps focused on data preparation (via SageMaker Processing), model training (via SageMaker training jobs), and model deployment (via SageMaker batch transform). **Pipelines** also includes `CallbackStep` to integrate with other AWS services or third-party tasks. Finally, Pipelines has built-in steps for pipeline functionality, such as a conditional step. All of the current capabilities within SageMaker Pipelines focus on model building and model deployment for batch inference. As a result, we'll look at two common patterns that have cross-account considerations when using SageMaker Pipelines.

In the first pattern, we'll discuss an end-to-end pipeline scenario where you are deploying a model for real-time inference using SageMaker hosting. In this case, you can use SageMaker Pipelines in your data science account to create a pipeline that can be used to automate the model-building activities. These activities include data preparation, model training, model evaluation, and a conditional step for model registration. Once a model passes evaluation and is registered, it can be used as a trigger for downstream deployment to your accounts (such as testing or production) that will host and integrate deployed endpoints. This same pipeline can be used for your retraining workflows.

In this case, model deployment to higher environments can be done using a cross-account resource policy, as shown in *Figure 14.3*. The cross-account resource policy is created for the **model group** in the **SageMaker model registry**. That model group contains the model versions, the Amazon ECR repository for the inference image, and the S3 location of the model artifacts. A cross-account resource policy can be created with all three of these resources that then allows you to deploy a model that was created in your data science environment into your application or workload environments (such as testing or production).

Refer to the following figure:

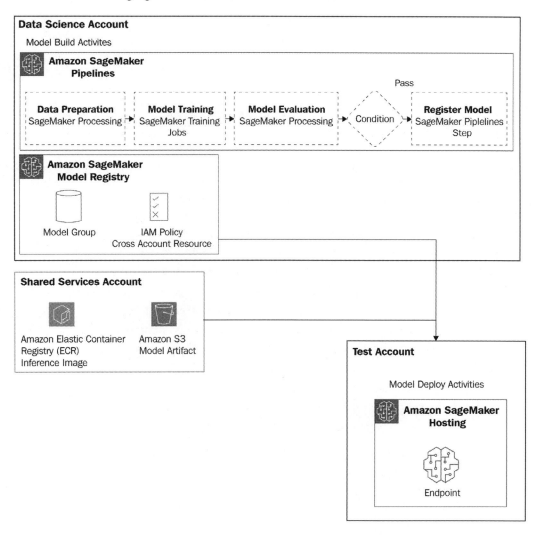

Figure 14.3 – Cross-account resource policy to deploy a model trained in a data science account

In the second pattern, we'll discuss an end-to-end pipeline scenario where you are deploying a model for batch inference using SageMaker hosting. In this case, you can use SageMaker Pipelines in your data science account to create a pipeline that can be used to automate the model-building activities. These include data preparation, model training, model evaluation, a conditional step for model registration, and a batch transform step. In this case, there are two options depending on your use case and requirements:

- **Run your end-to-end pipeline in your data science account**: This option is valid if you are using batch transform to validate your models or you're running batch jobs that don't have production-level availability requirements.

- **Run your end-to-end pipeline in workload accounts**: This option is valid if you are using batch transform to deploy models that have production-level availability requirements and/or require integration with systems in higher-level environments.

Amazon SageMaker projects

Amazon SageMaker projects build on SageMaker Pipelines by incorporating CI/CD practices (such as source and version control) combined with automated deployment pipelines into one or more target environments. When considering integrating SageMaker projects with multiple AWS accounts, the following are key points to understand:

- When you enable project templates for your Studio domain or domain users, the account where projects are enabled is the one that will be used for the built-in MLOps project templates offered through AWS Service Catalog. If you build custom MLOps project templates, you can still use the hub-and-spoke model to manage your portfolio and products in a Service Catalog master account.

- All built-in MLOps project templates will provision and configure the following resources in the same account where projects are enabled: **AWS CodePipeline**, **AWS CodeBuild**, **AWS CodeCommit**, and **Amazon EventBridge**. This is important as some organizations assume or require these services to be centrally configured and managed through a shared services account (or equivalent).

- The built-in MLOps project templates will deploy your SageMaker endpoints to the same account where projects are enabled. This behavior can be modified. However, the model registry still exists in the data science account.

Amazon SageMaker Feature Store

Amazon SageMaker Feature Store allows creating and sharing features, both for model-building activities and model inference. Because a feature store can be used for both model-building activities as well as a dependency for model inference, it's important to ensure features remain consistent across teams and are consistently available when needed.

When you create a feature store, it gets instantiated in the account that you created it in. However, that may not be the optimal choice when centralizing features for sharing across teams, or when using the feature store for real-time inference. If you create the feature store in your data science account, that account may have fewer controls and more access permissions in place for a broader set of roles. This creates risk when supporting production applications.

There are two common cross-account patterns related to Feature Store that facilitate feature sharing and consistency across teams, as well as allowing the flexibility for team- or organization-specific feature stores when needed.

In the first pattern, shown in *Figure 14.4*, a central feature store is created in a separate AWS account that is accessible via an IAM cross-account role for both the population and consumption of features. For the population of features, this is typically done through a feature pipeline that is automated and collecting data at regular frequencies. However, it can also be done from the data science environment for more static features. Features can then be consumed for both inference as well as for model-building activities. Model-building activities often consume features from the offline feature store using cross-account permissions:

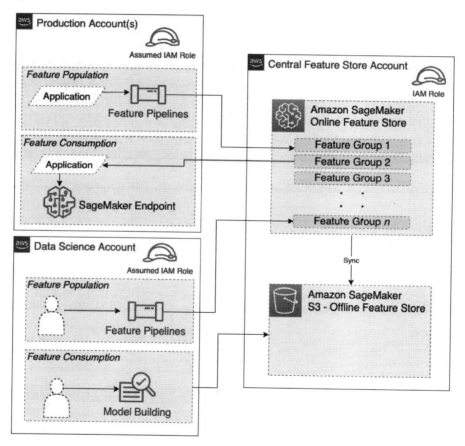

Figure 14.4 – Central Feature Store pattern

In the second pattern, similar to *Figure 14.4*, there is a central feature store that is used for sharing features that may be common or useful across teams, but there is also the flexibility for individual teams to create their own feature stores in separate AWS accounts. This pattern is useful to facilitate the ability to share common features in a central store, while also allowing workload- or application-specific features to be secured in an account that only requires access by the specific teams or applications that need those features.

Amazon SageMaker Data Wrangler

Amazon SageMaker Data Wrangler allows data scientists to explore and prepare data for machine learning during the model build phases of the ML Lifecycle. Because Data Wrangler is purpose-built for feature engineering and data preparation, the most common persona that will work with Data Wrangler are **ML builders**. Most model-building activities are going to happen inside one or more data science accounts; however, you typically need a way to securely access data from a data platform or data lake account for those model-building activities.

Figure 14.5 illustrates a common pattern for enabling cross-account access from a data science account, where Data Wrangler is being used, to a data platform/data lake account, where the data typically resides. In this case, we are using AWS Lake Formation for our secure data lake. The same concepts apply when utilizing other technologies for your data lake; however, the implementation may differ:

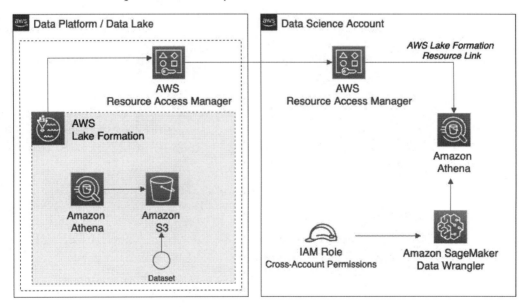

Figure 14.5 – Cross-account access for SageMaker Data Wrangler

With Data Wrangler, you're able to enable cross-account permissions using AWS IAM. To do this, you need to set up cross-account permissions for Data Wrangler in the data science account that allows access to the data tables stored in your data platform/data lake account. This is accomplished through Lake Formation permissions. This setup allows you to still provide access to datasets for your data scientists, but also allows you to take advantage of the security controls that Lake Formation offers.

For example, you can choose to share only specific tables or even to share only specific columns of tables stored in your data lake. Tables are shared using AWS Resource Access Manager. This provides a way to share Lake Formation tables across AWS accounts. This allows users to access shared tables in secondary accounts. These shared tables are accessible directly in Lake Formation, but they are also available as a data source, via Amazon Athena, in your Data Wrangler UI.

Summary

In this chapter, we discussed the benefits of using multiple accounts to manage and operate machine learning workloads that use Amazon SageMaker across the ML Lifecycle. We also looked at common patterns for account isolation across the ML Lifecycle. Finally, we focused specifically on the SageMaker features that are most often used across accounts, and the considerations you should be aware of when architecting and building end-to-end machine learning solutions.

This chapter wraps up the book where we covered best practices for SageMaker across features spanning the machine learning lifecycle of data preparation, model training, and operations. In this book, we discussed best practices, as well as considerations, that you can draw on when creating your own projects. We used an example use case, using open weather data to demonstrate the concepts throughout the chapters of the book. This was done so you can get hands-on with the concepts and practices discussed. We hope you're able to apply these practices to your own projects while benefiting from the overall capabilities and features offered by Amazon SageMaker.

References

Please see the following references for general AWS best practices on governance and multi-account strategies, as well as information specific to SageMaker features:

- Establishing best practices in your AWS environment: `https://aws.amazon.com/organizations/getting-started/best-practices/`
- AWS Control Tower – AWS services to establish and manage multiple AWS accounts: `https://aws.amazon.com/controltower/`
- SageMaker – Deploying a model to a different AWS account: `https://aws.amazon.com/premiumsupport/knowledge-center/sagemaker-cross-account-model/`

- SageMaker Data Wrangler – Enable cross-account access: `https://aws.amazon.com/blogs/machine-learning/enable-cross-account-access-for-amazon-sagemaker-data-wrangler-using-aws-lake-formation/`

- SageMaker Pipelines – Multi-account deployments: `https://aws.amazon.com/blogs/machine-learning/multi-account-model-deployment-with-amazon-sagemaker-pipelines/`

- SageMaker Feature Store: `https://aws.amazon.com/blogs/machine-learning/enable-feature-reuse-across-accounts-and-teams-using-amazon-sagemaker-feature-store/`

Packt>

Packt.com

Subscribe to our online digital library for full access to over 7,000 books and videos, as well as industry leading tools to help you plan your personal development and advance your career. For more information, please visit our website.

Why subscribe?

- Spend less time learning and more time coding with practical eBooks and Videos from over 4,000 industry professionals

- Improve your learning with Skill Plans built especially for you

- Get a free eBook or video every month

- Fully searchable for easy access to vital information

- Copy and paste, print, and bookmark content

Did you know that Packt offers eBook versions of every book published, with PDF and ePub files available? You can upgrade to the eBook version at packt.com and as a print book customer, you are entitled to a discount on the eBook copy. Get in touch with us at customercare@packtpub.com for more details.

At www.packt.com, you can also read a collection of free technical articles, sign up for a range of free newsletters, and receive exclusive discounts and offers on Packt books and eBooks.

Other Books You May Enjoy

If you enjoyed this book, you may be interested in these other books by Packt:

Learn Amazon SageMaker

Julien Simon

ISBN: 978-1-80020-891-9

- Create and automate end-to-end machine learning workflows on Amazon Web Services (AWS)
- Become well-versed with data annotation and preparation techniques
- Use AutoML features to build and train machine learning models with AutoPilot
- Create models using built-in algorithms and frameworks and your own code
- Train computer vision and NLP models using real-world examples
- Cover training techniques for scaling, model optimization, model debugging, and cost optimization

Packt is searching for authors like you

If you're interested in becoming an author for Packt, please visit authors. packtpub.com and apply today. We have worked with thousands of developers and tech professionals, just like you, to help them share their insight with the global tech community. You can make a general application, apply for a specific hot topic that we are recruiting an author for, or submit your own idea.

Share your thoughts

Now you've finished *Amazon SageMaker Best Practices*, we'd love to hear your thoughts! Scan the QR code below to go straight to the Amazon review page for this book and share your feedback or leave a review on the site that you purchased it from.

https://packt.link/r/1-801-07052-0

Your review is important to us and the tech community and will help us make sure we're delivering excellent quality content.

Index

N

Made in the USA
Las Vegas, NV
25 September 2021